The Twilight of the Middle Class

The Twilight of the Middle Class

POST–WORLD WAR II AMERICAN FICTION
AND WHITE-COLLAR WORK

Andrew Hoberek

PRINCETON UNIVERSITY PRESS
PRINCETON AND OXFORD

Library of Congress Cataloging-in-Publication Data

Hoberek, Andrew, 1967–
The twilight of the middle class: post–World War II American Fiction
and white-collar work/Andrew Hoberek.
  p.   cm.
Includes bibliographical references (p.) and index.
ISBN-13: 978-0-691-12145-1 (cloth: alk. paper)—ISBN-13: 978-0-691-12146-8
(pbk.: alk. paper)
ISBN-10: 0-691-12145-1 (cloth: alk. paper)—ISBN-10: 0-691-12146-X
(pbk.: alk. paper)
1. American fiction—20th century—History and criticism. 2. Middle class
in literature. 3. Literature and society—United States—History—20th century.
4. World War, 1939–1945—United States—Literature and the war.
5. White collar workers in literature. I. Title
PS374.M494H63 2005
813′.54093552—dc22   2004062441

British Library Cataloging-in-Publication Data is available.

This book has been composed in Garamond

Printed on acid-free paper. ∞

pup.princeton.edu

Printed in the United States of America

10 9 8 7 6 5 4 3 2 1

*For Audrey, who taught me to love books and history,
and Natch, who taught me to think about work*

Contents

Acknowledgments

THIS BOOK—appropriately for one concerned with critiquing individualizing models of mental labor—would have been very different without the work put into it by other people. In its earliest stages, I presented portions of this project to the American Studies and Mass Culture workshops at the University of Chicago. More recently, chapters have benefited from the thoughtful attention of the members of the Missouri Americanist Group: Richard Callahan, John Evelev, Mark Gallagher, Mo Lee, Richard Lester, Catherine Rymph, Kristin Schwain, Jeffrey R. Williams, Paul Young, and especially Frances Dickey. Others who have read and commented on chapters include Jennifer Burns, John Burt, Tracy Floreani, Maria Farland, Amy Hungerford, Cathy Jurca, Michael Kreyling, Stacey Margolis, Lee Medovoi, Tim Melley, Chris Newfield, Stacey Olster, Susan Radomsky, Bruce Robbins, Peter Sattler, Michael Szalay, Michael Trask, Ken Warren, Fred Whiting, and Christopher Wilson. Rachel Adams, Sean McCann, and Walter Benn Michaels read the whole manuscript and offered trenchant advice. Much of what is worthwhile in this book is due to these people, while its faults are chargeable only to me.

This project benefited in its infancy from the thoughtful guidance of Bill Brown and Chris Looby. It would have been impossible without the contributions of Gerald Graff, who was not only my dissertation advisor but also my boss in the University of Chicago's Master of Arts Program in the Humanities and who, I'm happy to say, remains my friend. Under Jerry's tutelage I learned to write for an audience, to not take myself too seriously, and to be kind. The academy would be a better place if there were more people like Jerry in it.

Among my many excellent colleagues at the University of Puget Sound and the University of Missouri, Tim Materer merits special mention: I couldn't imagine a better senior colleague. Students at MU who've taught me as much as I've taught them include Andy Heisel, Lania Knight, Michael Piafsky, Jeremy Reed, and Ramsay Wise. Jason Arthur belongs in this category, as well, although he gets his own sentence for his invaluable assistance with the manuscript. Joe Scott helped out with the research. I'm grateful to the University of Missouri Research Board for a fellowship that enabled me to spend a year working on this project.

In what have been difficult times for young academics trying to publish first books, I was lucky to have Mary Murrell—an editor whose work I already admired—take an interest in this project. My sadness at Mary's departure from Princeton University Press before this book's completion has been offset by the pleasure of working with Hanne Winarsky, Carmel Lyons, and my excellent copyeditor, Jonathan Munk. Patrick O'Donnell and Marshall Brown gave me boosts early in my career by publishing my first articles. An earlier version of my chapter on Ralph Ellison appeared under the same title in *Modern Language Quarterly* 59.1 (March 1998); I am grateful for permission to include the revised version here.

Shoshannah Cohen, Brad Prager, and Dave Stewart have been friends in good times and bad, at work and play, nearby and at (too great) a distance. Natch Hoberek, Audrey Hoberek, Dawn Hoberek, Jody Hoberek-Atkins, Tom Atkins, Barbara Chu, Sandi Chu, and Derek Lustig have been . . . well, family.

Pride of place in these acknowledgments goes to Pat Chu. For fifteen years Pat has been my partner in every sense of the word. I'm not entirely sure how I ended up with someone so smart, beautiful, and willing to indulge my goofy side, but I'm not asking any questions.

The Twilight of the Middle Class

The Twilight of the Middle Class

> " . . . privileged and deprived, an American sort of thing."
> —Don DeLillo, *Underworld* (1997)

MORRIS DICKSTEIN POSES his recent study of post–World War II American fiction *Leopards in the Temple* (2002) as a corrective to the by now standard tendency to emphasize the cold war in accounts of this period.[1] But while Dickstein takes the critics of cold war culture to task for what he sees as their oversimplification of both art and politics, he concurs with them on at least one major point. "If social suffering, poverty, and exploitation topped the agenda of the arts in the 1930s," Dickstein writes "neurosis, poverty, and alienation played the same role in the forties and fifties when economic fears were largely put to rest."[2] The idea that postwar culture abandoned the economic for the psychological has likewise been central to studies of cold war culture, where it underwrites the argument that postwar culture was characterized by a (deeply political) rejection of the more overtly political concerns of the thirties. Thus Thomas Hill Schaub argues in *American Fiction in the Cold War* (1991) that postwar authors, participating in "the anti-Stalinist discourse of the new liberalism," prioritized "psychological terms of social analysis . . . over economics and class consciousness as the dominant discourse of change."[3] While they differ on how to interpret the shift from economics to psychology—from capitalism and class struggle to "psychological nuance and linguistic complexity" (Dickstein 20)—Dickstein and critics like Schaub agree that this shift is the defining characteristic of postwar fiction.

It is perhaps for this reason that critics of cold war culture themselves downplay the very questions of "economics and class consciousness" for whose omission they take postwar writers to task. We might expect these critics to see Dickstein's more neutral, and at times even celebratory, account of this shift as continuous with cold war triumphalism—a latter day version of Richard Nixon's economic boosterism in his 1959 "kitchen debate" with Nikita Kruschev.[4] Yet when they mention the postwar economy, it is often in similar terms. In his account of the postwar vogue of wide-screen movies like Cecil B. DeMille's 1956 *The Ten Commandments*, for instance, Alan Nadel reads these films as visual analogues of "the expansive economic and technological growth of America in the 1950s."[5] Nadel's brief mention of the economy is rare, moreover. Often critics of cold war culture simply bracket the economy, restricting their analyses to the political and cultural realms. Even the Marxist critic Barbara Foley succumbs to this tendency, arguing that Ralph Ellison's *Invisible Man* (1952) engages in the red-baiting endemic to postwar anticommunism but nowhere addressing the economic framework within which—we might expect a Marxist to believe—the novel's politics are embedded.[6] "If Ellison's own experiences with the left during the years represented in the Harlem section of *Invisible Man* was not one of unremitting bitterness and betrayal," she asks, "what then might have been the source of the novel's overwhelmingly negative portrayal of the Brotherhood?" (541). Foley's answer is political bad faith and careerism. While Ellison's successive revisions of the draft certainly support this contention,[7] Foley does not consider that Ellison might also be responding (as I will argue in my own chapter on *Invisible Man*) to economic issues relevant to the world of the fifties rather than the thirties. Her essay on Herman Melville's "Bartleby the Scrivener," by contrast, exhaustively describes the economic and class issues that rove New York City during the period of the story's composition.[8] The implication is that such issues mattered during the antebellum period but were less important, or even unimportant, in the 1950s. Despite their helpful attention to the political backsliding of the cold war era, accounts like Nadel's and Foley's either explicitly or implicitly accept Dickstein's assertion that following World War II "economic fears were largely put to rest."[9]

This book argues, by contrast, that economics and class remained central to postwar writing, belying our standard assumptions about the irrelevance of such matters in the postwar period. Of course, there is good evidence for these assumptions. Statistics compiled by the business historian Jeffrey Madrick make it clear that the postwar years were indeed prosperous ones, and not just in comparison with the lean years of the Depression. Along with the fact that "family incomes doubled . . . between 1947 and 1973,"

> By 1970 four out of five American families owned at least one car, two out of three had a washing machine, and almost all families had a refrigerator. About 65 percent of American families owned their own homes, and almost all had flush toilets and running water. The proportion of white males who had graduated from college rose from 6 percent in 1947 to 11 percent in 1959 and to about 25 percent in the 1980s. More than half of working Americans had a private pension, compared with only about 15 percent after World War II, supplementing Social Security benefits, which themselves were only a generation old.[10]

As Paul Krugman and others have noted, moreover, the postwar economy not only grew at a remarkable rate, but its fruits were—by the standards of either pre-Depression America or our own time—remarkably evenly distributed.[11]

Given such real and relatively widespread prosperity, the elision of economic matters in accounts of postwar writing seems understandable. As early as 1962, to be sure, Michael Harrington had called into question the assumption that "the basic grinding economic problems had been solved in the United States."[12] In *The Other America* Harrington argued that postwar social criticism's focus on "the emotional suffering taking place in the suburbs" (1) belied the existence of an "invisible land" (1) inhabited by "the dispossessed workers, the minorities, the farm poor, and the aged" (17). But Harrington's objection to such criticism was that it disregarded those who remained on the margins, not that it misrepresented the mainstream. Similarly, recent accounts of the postwar period, such as George Lipsitz's *Rainbow at Midnight* (1994), Alan Wald's *Writing from the Left* (1994), and *The Other Fifties* (1997), edited by Joel Foreman, have turned from the mainstream to the various class and racial subcultures that existed during this period.[13] But while such revisionist accounts usefully remind us that not everyone in the fifties had equal access to the fruits of the economic boom, they leave untouched our sense that those who did have such access somehow transcended the economic realm.

This assumption is reinforced by the fact that while postwar prosperity is generally associated with a particular class, it is one that is traditionally understood in the United States as classless. This idea of American "middle-classlessness" has proven especially compatible with our understanding of the postwar boom,[14] as Jack Beatty's account of the boom suggests:

> The expanding middle class had in it two distinct kinds of workers: white-collar and blue-collar. Back then, thanks to the wages won for him by his union, the blue-collar man (the gender specification is unavoidable) could live next door to the white-collar man—not to the doctor, perhaps, but to the accountant, the teacher, the middle manager. This rough economic equality was a political fact of the first importance. It meant that, in a break with the drift of things in pre-war America, postwar America had no working class and no working-class politics. It had instead a middle-class politics for an expanding middle class bigger in aspiration and self-identification than it was in fact— more people wanted to be seen as middle-class than had yet arrived at that state of felicity. Socialism in America, the German political economist Werner Sombart wrote in 1906, foundered upon "roast beef and apple pie," a metaphor for American plenty. The expanding middle class of the postwar era—property-owning, bourgeois in outlook, centrist in politics—hardly proved him wrong.[15]

The myth of America as a classless—because universally or at least potentially universally middle-class—nation has a long history, as Beatty's reference to Sombart suggests. But in its current incarnation it is inseparable from what Krugman calls the "middle-class interregnum" that lasted from the New Deal thirties through the late seventies, and has been succeeded by a "new Gilded Age" characterized by a vast and growing gap between rich and poor.[16] The postwar middle class, Beatty argues, "muted the class conflict that Marx had prophesied would one day destroy capitalism" by providing "a reproof to the very idea of class" (65).[17]

We might expect accounts of the middle-class dimensions of postwar literature and culture to undermine this conception of the middle-class as a nonclass. Yet these accounts, while usefully skeptical about what Dickstein calls the "deep discomfort at the core of American affluence and power" (16), tend—by reading the middle class solely in the light of privilege—to affirm its putative transcendence of the economic. "This was a time," Barbara Ehrenreich writes in her 1983 study *The Hearts of Men*, "when the educated middle class worried about being *too* affluent."[18] Jackson Lears, reading some of the same texts as Ehrenreich, argues that " 'a new class' of salaried managers, administrators, academics, technicians, and journalists" achieved cultural hegemony in the postwar period by identifying its "problems and interests with those of society and indeed humanity at large."[19] Through frequently popular works of social and cultural criticism, Lears argues, this class falsely universalized its own concerns about "the bureaucratization of bourgeois individualism in America" (46–47), in the process rendering others' concerns "marginal or even invisible to the wider public culture" (50). Catherine Jurca, finally, imputes a similar disingenuousness to postwar accounts of middle-class "suffering" and "discontent," which she views as self-interested counterfeits designed both to ratify middle-class affluence vis-à-vis less fortunate groups, and to allow individual members of the middle class a sense of distinction vis-à-vis their less self-aware counterparts.[20] While properly chary toward "exaggerated claims about postwar affluence" (139), Jurca is not chary about such claims as they relate to the middle class.[21]

To a certain extent, these accounts all continue—from a perspective more sophisticated about race, gender, and, less decisively, class—the project of the social criticism they describe, which in the words of one intellectual historian was preoccupied with "the problems of prosperity."[22] Thus William H. Whyte writes in *The Organization Man* (1956)—a locus classicus of postwar social criticism cited by Ehrenreich, Lears, and Jurca—that "it is not the evils of organization life that puzzle [the organization man], *but its very beneficence.*"[23] More concretely, Whyte argues that the comfort and security enjoyed by the members of the middle class blunt their ambitions and render them all the more susceptible to the pressures toward conformity that characterize the organizations in which they work and, increasingly, do almost everything else. While some critics continue to see the problems of prosperity as authentic, and others have redescribed them as strategies for achieving or maintaining cultural dominance, most concur that they were not "material."[24]

Richard Ohmann's 1983 essay "The Shaping of a Canon: U. S. Fiction, 1960–1975" at first glance seems to belong in this category, although Ohmann departs from the consensus about the middle class's transcendence of the economic in a crucial way. Ohmann argues that middle-class gatekeepers in the publishing industry, the media, and the academy awarded "precanonical" status to fiction that translated middle-class insecurity into the narrative of individual breakdown that he calls the "illness story."[25] He thus concurs with Lears that the middle class exercised cultural hegemony by falsely universalizing its specific concerns, which for Ohmann, too, have to do with the pressures exerted by society on the individual. But Ohmann understands the resulting cultural products not simply as an expression of privilege, but also as symptomatic registers of the middle class's less than fully dominant role in the postwar economy. The postwar middle class, in

Ohmann's account, was a "subordinate but influential class" (397) that exercised control over the content of postwar culture at the discretion of the "ruling class" that actually "own[ed] the media and control[led] them formally" (386). Ohmann, to be sure, emphasizes the novel authority of the middle class—or what he calls, following Barbara and John Ehrenreich, the "Professional–Managerial Class" or "PMC"—at this juncture. In the Ehrenreichs' influential description, the PMC is the class of "salaried mental workers" that "emerged with dramatic suddeness [sic] in the years between 1890 and 1920" and that constitutes an authentically new class with interests opposed to those of both owners and workers.[26] Drawing on the Ehrenreichs' essay, Ohmann insists that his account "turns upon class but not just upon the two great traditional classes" (387), though his own reference to ruling-class media-owners suggests that at least one of the two traditional classes was alive and well.

Moreover, with the demise of the postwar boom (which began faltering shortly before the mid-seventies end date Ohmann selects for his study), the members of the middle class have increasingly entered the other great traditional class of those who sell their labor. Beatty and Krugman both extol the postwar middle class in contributions to the crisis-of-the-middle-class genre that has been a journalistic staple (with the exception of a brief hiatus during the late nineties tech boom) for several decades. As such accounts suggest, this crisis has taken the form not simply of the disappearance of median incomes, but also of white-collar workers' new vulnerability to the sorts of workplace exploitation traditionally associated with those who work for a living. As Robert Seguin succinctly puts it, "with the recent downsizing of middle management, the increasing technological displacements of engineers and architects, and the sessionalization/detenuring of university departments, positions and locations once regarded as concrete evidence of Marx's errors are today under an intense pressure of proletarianization" (13). To say this is not, as Seguin hastens to add, by any means to deny the differences between the members of what is still called the middle class and the members of either the traditional working class or the new service class. To assert this would be absurd: it's still far better to work in an office than to clean it, and some people who work in middle-class occupations—lawyers, brokers, executives—still do quite well in the so-called New Economy.[27] But even a New Economy booster like Robert Reich admits that the well-paid, nonhierarchical, creative jobs he ascribes to "symbolic analysts" coexist with the far less appealing kinds of work he categorizes under the headings "routine production services" and "in-person services."[28] In addition to software engineers and cinematographers, the global economy employs (far more) data-entry clerks and phone-service representatives (and, as Andrew Ross points out, the hype over the former jobs helps to inculcate an ethos of overwork within the high-tech workforce more generally).[29] There is, in this regard, a kind of false pastoralism in accounts of the postwar middle class as the embodied refutation of Marxism. If subsequent events have contradicted the circumstances that presumably proved Marx wrong, then perhaps we shelved our copies of *Capital* too early. The fate of the middle class in recent years if anything seems to confirm Marx and Engels' assertion that "society as a whole is more and more splitting . . . into two great classes directly facing each other": those who own capital and those who must sell their labor at the former group's terms.[30] The postwar middle class did well, but the fate of the middle class since the seventies suggests that this had more to do with the postwar boom and the redistributive policies of the mid-century welfare state than with the inherent nature of the postwar economy.

Of course, it is one thing to worry about contemporary white-collar workers subject to downsizing, or the assault on the forty-hour week, or capital's perpetual flight to cheaper labor pools, and quite another to worry about postwar white-collar workers whose comfortable jobs putatively threatened their individuality. But while the well-off members of the postwar middle class seem like the antithesis of their successors in terms of income, security, and other factors, their situations share an important element if we consider the rise of the postwar middle class in structural terms. In the first half of the twentieth century "the rise of corporate and bureaucratic structures" triggered a process of "remarkable growth and meta-morphosis" through which "managers and white-collar workers" replaced "independent entrepreneurs" as the prototypical members of the American middle class.[31] Historically the basis of middle-class status in the United States had been the ownership of small property. Of course, the American middle-class ideal mutually embodied in the otherwise very different figures of the Jeffersonian free-holder and the Franklinian entrepreneur was from the start mostly limited to white men, and even for them this ideal began to break down early on.[32] But it was the changes brought about by industrialization—the growth of corporations, the elaboration of their managerial strata through vertical integration, the expansion of finance capital and the professions—that really accelerated the shift from entrepreneurship to white-collar employment.[33] The PMC emerged in the final decade of the nineteenth century as the first middle-class generation not to define itself through (the increasingly limited possibility of) property ownership, instead attempting to shift the basis of social authority onto management.[34]

The advent of the PMC, however, did not immediately or completely reconfigure the structure of the middle class as a whole. Throughout the first half of the twentieth century, the PMC coexisted with the small-property-owning middle class whose national political role had climaxed with Populism but which remained significant—albeit increasingly on a regional rather than a national scale—at least through the 1930s.[35] The PMC was, however, on the side of history, growing alongside the increasingly more complicated managerial structure of early twentieth-century monopoly capitalism as its scale received successive boosts from the rise of industrial trusts, the economic impetus of the World War I, and the merger movement of the 1920s.[36] During this period, the PMC relied upon the ideology of professionalism to bolster its members' agency within "large bureaucratic entities."[37] The thirties, and the New Deal, initiated a significant transition for the middle class, as for capitalism more generally. On one hand, PMC ambitions reached a high point with the New Deal implementation of limited forms of centralized planning: here at last managerial oversight was deployed to save capitalism from its own obvious failures, for the good of all. At the same time, however, the New Deal represented much more of an accommodation with big business than Progressive-era policies ever had. It was "managerial," but less in the sense of articulating an overall vision of society than of attempting to balance various conflicting interests, and marked a shift from "moralism" to "opportunism" on the part of Progressivism's increasingly technocratic heirs.[38] Concurrently with this shift in attitude at the highest levels of the PMC, at least some white-collar employees in the education system, the culture industry, and the new state bureaucracies began to conceive of their work not in professional-managerial terms but as a form of routinized mental labor.[39] These two shifts taken together—the decline of PMC faith in the managerial ideal, and an increasingly negative understanding of mental labor within large organizations—anticipate the new middle-class consciousness that would assume its definitive shape following World War II.

The war itself provided another huge boost—the largest yet—to the processes of corporate expansion and centralization. The hundred largest American corporations' share of manufacturing grew from 30 percent to 70 percent between 1940 and 1943 alone.[40] By the end of the war, there were over 500,000 fewer small businesses than at its start,[41] and over 1,600 mergers had taken place, "nearly one-third of which involved corporations with assets of $50 million or more taking over smaller enterprises."[42] By "1948, the corporate sector held almost 60 percent of national income-producing wealth."[43] The governmental sector, and the corporate-government nexus, also expanded in this period, as World War II defense spending gave way to the even more feverish outlays of the cold war and the federal government pursued a Keynesian program of spending and regulation designed to promote permanent growth.[44] The white-collar workforce grew apace, and in a frequently cited statistic white-collar workers surpassed blue-collar workers as the largest segment of the nonfarm workforce in 1956.[45] By this point, moreover, even the remaining small-property owners could not avoid "constant interaction with corporate and bureaucratic America."[46]

Postwar descriptions of the middle class forged in this context largely abandon the PMC's more positive understanding of organizations and the sense of agency—both individually and as a class—that this understanding enabled. For figures as diverse as Edward Bellamy, Charlotte Perkins Gilman, and Thorstein Veblen, the overall organization of society had seemed like the cure for the poor management of specific institutions.[47] For Whyte—who sees Progressivism as the enemy because it replaced the Protestant Ethic with a "Social Ethic" that "ma[de] morally legitimate the pressures of society against the individual" (6–7)—the problem is not so much specific organizations as the all-encompassing abstraction that he calls "The Organization." As Timothy Melley argues in his study of late twentieth-century fiction and social criticism *Empire of Conspiracy* (2000), Whyte and his contemporaries engaged in a discourse of "agency panic" that posed a reified, "all-or-nothing conception of agency" against an equally "monolithic conception of 'society' (or 'system,' or 'organization')."[48] Taking my cue from Lears' and Ohmann's arguments about the universalization of middle-class concerns, I argue that this discourse of constrained agency is best understood as a product of the transition from small-property ownership to white-collar employment as the basis of middle-class status. In brief, the postwar period constitutes a tipping point in the history of the middle class, when PMC efforts to rewrite individual and class agency in managerial terms give way to skepticism about organization as such and nostalgia for the putative autonomy of the property-owning old middle class.

This understanding of what it means to be middle class poses dispossession in abstractly individualized terms. Nonetheless, it reconfigures middle-class status around employment in ways that not only depart from the PMC's activist self-conception but also point toward the more concrete forms of dispossession experienced by the contemporary middle class. Descriptions of the organization man's threatened individuality, this book argues, simultaneously obscure and reveal concerns about downward class mobility. This occurs, for instance, in Whyte's discussion of "the use of psychological tests" as "symptomatic" of the organization man's situation:

> Originally, they were introduced by the managers as a tool for weeding out unqualified workers. As time went on, and personality tests were added to aptitude tests, the managers began using them on other managers, present and prospective, and today most personality testing is directed not at the worker, but at the organization man. If he is being hoist, it is by his own philosophy. (42)

Beneath this passage's ironic deflation of the PMC project of managing workers lies a submerged parable of the managers' own fate: if they are now subjecting themselves to the personality tests once reserved for workers, the unacknowledged implication is that they themselves have become workers.

What the *Fortune* editor Whyte only alludes to, C. Wright Mills makes explicit in his still influential 1951 study *White Collar*.[49] For Mills white-collar work exhibits the same sort of rationalization that had been central to the Fordist transformation of the factory in the early twentieth century:

> Even on the professional levels of white-collar work, not to speak of wage-work and the lower white-collar tasks, the chance to develop and use individual rationality is often destroyed by the centralization of decision and the formal rationality that bureaucracy entails. . . .
>
> The introduction of office machinery and sales devices has been mechanizing the office and the salesroom, the two big locales of white-collar work. Since the 'twenties it has increased the division of white-collar labor, recomposed personnel, and lowered skill levels. Routine operations in minutely subdivided organizations have replaced the

bustling interest of work in well-known groups. Even on managerial and professional levels, the growth of rational bureaucracies has made work more like factory production. The managerial demiurge is constantly furthering all these trends: mechanization, more minute division of labor, the use of less skilled and less expensive workers. (226–27)

Here Mills understands the threat to agency not as some generalized specter of conformity but rather as the concrete loss of control in the workplace that, as it earlier had for factory workers, precedes and underwrites other kinds of proletarianization (one can be replaced with less expensive workers).

Thus while Mills acknowledges the variations in income, status, and workplace power within what he calls white-collar pyramids (70–76), his overarching historical narrative stresses "the centralization of small properties" (xiv) that has structurally proletarianized the middle class by placing its members "in exactly the same property-class position as the wage-workers" (71):

> In the early nineteenth century, although there are no exact figures, probably four-fifths of the occupied population were self-employed enterprisers; by 1870, only about one-third, and in 1940, only about one-fifth, were still in this old middle class. Many of the remaining four-fifths of the people who now earn a living do so by working for the 2 or 3 per cent of the population who now own 40 or 50 per cent of the private property in the United States. Among these workers are the members of the new middle class, white-collar people on salary. For them, as for wage-workers, America has become a nation of employees for whom independent property is out of range. Labor markets, not control of property, determine their chances to receive income, exercise power, enjoy prestige, learn and use skills. (63)

To make this point is not to deny the real prosperity enjoyed by the postwar middle class and the upper levels of the unionized working class. Nor is it to confuse white-collar workers with the members of the traditional working class, or to obviate the (ongoing) differences between those at different levels of white-collar pyramids. But it is to impute a structural priority to the middle class's loss of its historical control over property, which in a capitalist economy rendered it vulnerable *as a class* to future losses of income and job security.

While it is a staple of discussions of Mills to cite his alleged transcendence of Marxism, this is a fundamentally Marxist argument. In this case Mills owes an insufficiently acknowledged debt to a book he mentions only briefly in a long list of sources, Lewis Corey's 1935 *The Crisis of the Middle Class* (Mills, *White* 357). Corey, too, had argued that economic concentration had transformed "the old middle class of small producers" into a " 'new' middle class of salaried employees."[50] No doubt one reason that Corey's argument has traveled less well than Mills's is his Depression-era claim—made with an eye to contemporary events in Germany—that the members of the dispossessed middle class should be encouraged to identify with and as workers lest they become recruits to Fascism. But if the postwar boom (thankfully) invalidated this thesis, Mills's appropriation of

Corey suggests that it did not invalidate Corey's underlying claim that the transformation of the middle class symptomatized the increasing binarization of the U.S. class system.[51] While this seems to contradict our standard understanding of the postwar period as an era of redistribution, Adolf Berle's preface to the 1968 edition of his and Gardiner Means's classic 1932 study of economic concentration, *The Modern Corporation and Private Property,* suggests that it need not do so. Berle points out that the commonplace understanding of redistribution in fact conflates two separate meanings of "wealth." While "individually owned wealth has enormously increased" in the postwar era, he acknowledges, "relatively little of it is 'productive' property—land or things employed by its owners in production or commerce." Instead, the largest amount is invested in "owner-occupied homes" and the next largest in "consumer durables" such as "automobiles and home equipment."[52] On one hand, then, a relatively equal distribution of *income* during the postwar period created a large class of people, white-collar workers and otherwise, who enjoyed a middle-class standard of living. On the other hand, however, this process concealed an ongoing concentration of *capital* continuous with the current unequal distribution of wealth.

Good middle-class incomes and an active welfare state, not to mention cold war strictures against anything smacking of Marxism, rendered the concentration of capital difficult to see in the postwar period. But postwar representations of the middle class nonetheless found a substitute narrative of declension in the story of the middle class's fall from its golden age of property-owning autonomy. Lipsitz argues the concentration of property during World War II undermined "the ideal of small-business ownership [that] constituted a popular symbol of freedom in the United States,"[53] although this is only partly true. Following Melley's account of agency panic—which he argues conserved individualism discursively by continually describing it as threatened—we can argue that the postwar decline of property ownership as a material reality in fact led to its ascendancy as "ideal" and "symbol." Mills, for instance, invokes the classic terms of property-owning liberal individualism alongside his more Marxist narrative of structural proletarianization.[54] In the past, he writes,

> since few men owned more property than they could work, differences between men were due in large part to personal strength and ingenuity. The type of man presupposed and strengthened by this society was willingly economic, possessing the "reasonable self-interest" needed to build and operate the market economy. He was, of course, more than an economic man, but the techniques and the economics of production shaped much of what he was and what he looked forward to becoming. He was an "absolute individual," linked into a system with no authoritarian center, but held together by countless, free, shrewd transactions. (9)

Eschewing his skepticism elsewhere in *White Collar* about "sentimental versions of historical types that no longer exist, if indeed they ever did" (xiii), Mills here reproduces the classic terms of American (white, male, middle-class) self-making.

In contrast with this golden age, he writes, "The decline of the free entrepreneur and the rise of the dependent employee on the American scene has paralleled the decline of the independent individual and the rise of the little man in the American mind"(xii).

Despite the obvious difficulties with such liberal nostalgia, however, it still provides a way of thinking about the pervasive anxieties of the postwar middle class in class terms rather than individual ones, and historically rather than existentially. Even in works lacking Mills's Marxist perspective, like Whyte's *Organization Man* and David Riesman's *The Lonely Crowd* (1950), this narrative of decline provides a sedimentation of class history usefully at odds with the countervailing pressure toward an existential narrative of conflict between individual and society.[55] Whyte's invocation of the Protestant Ethic to describe a lost era of middle-class ambition and creative endeavor, for instance, functions in this manner. Less obviously, Riesman postulates an emergent shift within contemporary society from "inner-direction" (in which guidance comes from goals implanted early in life by parents and other adult authorities) to "other-direction" (in which it comes from the continuously changing signals sent by peers and the media).[56] While Riesman subtitles *The Lonely Crowd* "The Changing *American* Character" (my emphasis), he notes that

> if we wanted to cast our social character types into social class molds, we could say that inner-direction is the typical character of the "old" middle class—the banker, the tradesman, the small entrepreneur, the technically oriented engineer, etc.—while other-direction is becoming the typical character of the "new" middle class—the bureaucrat, the salaried employee in business, etc. (20)

Riesman sees the rise of other-direction, that is, at least in part as a class phenomenon, one conditioned by the loss of the private property that served, during an earlier "era of private competitive capitalism," as "a kind of exoskeleton" separating "the individual self" from "other people" (114).

Riesman and Whyte are typical postwar authors, then, not insofar as they understand the crisis of individualism in terms that verge on the existential, but rather insofar as they deploy such terms in ways that simultaneously mask and reveal the historical transformation of the American middle class. It is worth noting, however, that not all postwar texts need to be teased into giving up their economic engagements; as Ohmann's essay on postwar fiction makes clear, middle-class dissatisfaction does not so much determine the production of this fiction as guide what gets canonized. The classic realist account of the dismantling of the American middle class is Ira Wolfert's largely neglected 1943 novel *Tucker's People*. Here I mean classic realism in the sense theorized by Georg Lukács, in his discussion of "the classic form of the historical novel," which for him "portray[s] the struggles and antagonisms of history by means of characters who, in their psychology and destiny, always represent social trends and historical forces."[57] Such fiction, neither "romantically monumentalizing the important figures of history

[nor] dragging them down to the level of private, psychological trivia" (47), instead offers types of "the inter-relationships between the psychology of people and the economic and moral circumstances of their lives" (40). This sort of fiction, epitomized for Lukács by Walter Scott's historical novels, arises with "the class struggles between nobility and bourgeoisie . . . whose last decisive stage was the . . . French Revolution" (27–28), and comes to an end with the bourgeois reaction to the failed but nonetheless threatening revolutions of 1848. Fredric Jameson has observed that this chronology, which lays the groundwork for Lukács' well-known critique of modernism as inherently apolitical, leaves out "writers and whole cultures which lay outside Lukács' personal interests and background."[58] While Jameson is concerned to recover various versions of politically progressive modernism, we might also apply his argument, in the American context, to writing that remained outside the canons of experimental modernism. *Tucker's People*, later filmed as the Abraham Polonsky noir *Force of Evil* (1948), starring John Garfield, tells the story of a gangster's efforts to consolidate the numbers rackets in New York City. But the novel can also be read as an allegory of the traditional middle class's disappearance in the face of an increasingly large-scale capitalism. *Tucker's People*, we might say, continues to operate as Lukácsian classic realism, although coming at the opposite end of the historical trajectory initiated in Great Britain by Scott, it records not the triumphant emergence but the ignominious decline of the small bourgeoisie.

As the novel opens the small businessman Leo Minch is reluctantly entertaining a proposal from another character named Samson Candee to go into the numbers business in Harlem. Minch has just lost his garage business because his landlords have turned him in for allowing his brother Joe to store liquor trucks owned by his bootlegger boss Ben Tucker. In fact, they had merely used Leo's indiscretion as a pretext to recover the property, whose value "Leo's success with his business had increased."[59] This is not the first, nor will it be the last, time that Leo loses his business to larger operators. Leo's story, Wolfert makes clear at the end of book 1, is a historically typical one:

> He had been born in the time of Rockefeller. He had spent his business life being hounded from the woolen business to butter-and-egg routes to real estate to the garage business to policy. He had run from place to place, looking for one place where he could hole up and be overlooked and at peace in a world of expanding big business. But all his running had done was advance him towards the time of Hitler, when big business and its creatures, when trusts and monopolies and their methods, having grown powerful and hungry in the hunt, were foraging even among the rabbit holes. (71)

Repeatedly driven from businesses whose very growth attracts bigger players and makes it impossible for him to compete, Leo accepts Candee's proposition, and builds a successful policy operation in Harlem. Unbeknownst to Leo, however, Ben Tucker is planning to take over and consolidate the New York numbers business. He does this by arranging for a certain popular number to hit so that Leo and his colleagues will have to pay out all their assets and he can buy them out, a "method," Wolfert writes, that "was simple and had a long tradition among monopolists" (74). Leo finally surrenders his organization to Tucker in exchange for a top managerial position, in a deal that has been brokered by Leo's brother. When Joe asks Leo if he "begin[s] to see the possibilities" in this arrangement, Leo replies—in words that might serve as the epitaph of the small-property-owning old middle class—"I see that I had a business when I came up here and now I'm working for Tucker for salary" (143).

Wolfert reinforces this point with another story of middle-class expropriation, the family history of Tucker's lawyer, Henry Wheelock. In a chapter whose title ("An American Hero's Son") invokes the national heritage of liberal individualism, we learn that Wheelock's father was a hotel manager in a small town built by the "big lumber companies" in "western timber country" (147). Like Leo Minch, Roger Wheelock lies at the end of the line for the old middle class, in a world shaped by big capital. When the lumber companies had "plundered the forests and got theirs out of it" (147) they moved on, precipitating a general economic collapse: "The sawmills nearest town started closing and the branch of the furniture company that advertised 'From Forest To You' moved away and the railroad cut its passenger train schedules in half" (149). The elder Wheelock, who "had known what the big lumber people were up to" and had paid off the mortgages on the hotel in the hopes that "if he owned [it] all free and clear, then he would be safe" (148), finds himself stuck with a useless business. Eventually the bank repossesses the hotel and asks Roger Wheelock "to stay on as manager" (155), thereby completing his transition from old middle-class independence to white-collar employment. Henry, who at the time is struggling to find work as a lawyer in New York City, meditates on his father's life:

> Roger knew the end, his son thought, the minute the big lumber companies started working on the forests. He saw the day and he tried to prepare for it. He got his hotel all paid off and he thought that would be the rock he would stand on. Then the rock began to sink and he had to fight to hold the rock up. It was a hopeless fight. He was a man holding up something that was holding up him. The old man must have known it would be hopeless and must have known it was hopeless, but he kept right on with it. It was heroic. It was a life to which music should be played. (153)

The experience of seeing his father ruined by men who "had no thought of people as people or as anything but tools or opponents" (147), the novel suggests, drives Henry to his position as Tucker's amoral, cynical lawyer. *Tucker's People* analogizes crime and business, not simply because "Tucker's organization [is] like that of any many-sided management corporation geared to absorb new businesses" (175), but more importantly because "business—without thought of anything but money—could destroy the lives of great numbers of people. . . . The murderer was the same kind of personality in either case, whether he was a big man and sat in a corporation's office . . . or whether he was a small man and had to supervise everything himself" (174).

Although he thus treats business as no better than gangsterism, Wolfert's politics have less to do with Marxism than with the politics of small property that, Mills notes, have generally taken the place of class politics in the United States (55). Leo, for instance, loses his first business when the expanding woolens industry attracts speculators who drive "prices . . . up and down violently without regard to value," causing "a steeply falling market" that catches Leo "with shelves loaded" (9). He uses what's left of his credit to pursue "an opening . . . in butter-and-egg routes in the suburbs" (9), but this leaves him dissatisfied because "he had been a merchant all his life, providing goods—not merely service. To sell service, somehow, seemed false" (10). Later, he becomes a successful real estate speculator himself, but the methods he must employ—"loss leaders and premiums, doing things for good will that a man who was there to make a living out of running the store itself could not have afforded to do"—only make him feel more "dissatisfied and insecure" (10). Retrenching, he buys two apartment houses with the goal of "pay[ing] off the mortgages and own[ing] them outright," as well as leasing the garage that he is "determined to run as a business, not as a mere squeeze-box for squeezing out profits" (11). Leo's victimization at the hands of speculators and his desire to run his businesses for their own sake rather than for the sake of profit echo the agrarian-producer ethos of the Populist-Progressive era.[60] One would not be surprised, in this regard, to see Frank Norris's farmer-turned-businessman Charles Cressler take the stage and assert, as he does in Norris's 1903 *The Pit*, that "the Chicago speculator . . . raises or lowers the price out of all reason, for the benefit of his pocket," "gambling" on its eventual price to the detriment of farmers because, unlike them, he "don't care in the least about the grain."[61] But the novel's politics are not simply anachronistic. Leo's preference for goods over services also resonates with the postwar understanding of white-collar work as a field where members of the middle class no longer "manipulate *things*" but instead "handle *people* and *symbols*" (Mills, *White* 65; Mills's emphases), where "the 'softness' of men rather than the 'hardness' of material . . . calls on talent and opens new channels of social mobility" (Riesman, *Lonely* 127). In this respect, *Tucker's People* provides a bridge between the small-property-owning politics of Populism and its descendants on the contemporary left[62] and right.[63]

Wolfert's main investment in old-middle-class ideals lies, however, in his idealization of the relationship between Leo and his employees. By no means perfect—he cuts Candee out of their numbers business before it becomes successful, for instance—Leo nonetheless knows and treats each of his employees as an individual, in explicit contrast to big business's tendency to treat people as "tools" or "opponents":

Leo admired the placid way in which Mr. Middleton took his hard luck and used to give him a cigar once in a while. He listened to Juice's story sympathetically several times and once had Edgar take the door off his car to see if that would help Juice stay in it. It didn't. He was sorry for Delilah and secretly proud to have a college graduate working for him. He found her some pupils to tutor on Saturday mornings when she did not go to school and told her that if she got enough pupils, she would not have to work for him. (92)

The novel reinforces this point formally by providing detailed back-stories for each of Leo's employees, something that we only get in the case of Tucker's big organization for his inner circle. In classic old-middle-class terms, Leo's treatment of his employees epitomizes the coincidence of decency and profitability. On one hand these employees, many of them former "domestic servants or charwomen in offices and hotels" (87), are "grateful for their jobs and happy in them" (92): "He felt they all loved him . . . and, actually, they did" (92). On the other hand, Leo's practices are "copied by other bankers because the methods were profitable" (65). Self-consciously collapsing two different definitions of "good," the novel notes that "Leo, who was a 'good' man, could make it a 'good' business" (65). Despite its seemingly evenhanded exposure of Leo's character flaws, *Tucker's People* ultimately romanticizes the small employer; indeed, its attention to these flaws only reinforces the idea that small business is inherently ethical despite the motivations of any particular businessman.[64] It is thus not a proletarian novel, since it views events not from a working-class but from an old-middle-class perspective. Its working-class characters never become collective historical agents in their own rights, but remain the objects of a history told from the perspective of people like Leo Minch and Roger Wheelock.[65]

Nonetheless, Wolfert's invocation of old-middle-class ideals transcends nostalgia insofar as he understands these ideals as casualties of the historical process of middle-class expropriation. Wolfert makes this point clear in the scene where Leo negotiates with Wheelock and Tucker the terms under which he will transfer his business to Tucker. Wheelock questions, for instance, why Leo pays much more for one of the apartments he uses as a drop-off station for policy slips, and learns that the renter is "a boy who worked with [Leo] to put himself through college" and now "can't find what's fit for him to do." Leo "pay[s] half his rent" because "a college boy with a wife has to have a place that's nice to live" (130). Wheelock thinks, "There were a lot of things like that, . . . sloppy things, where expenses could be cut when the business would be managed properly" (130). When Tucker arrives for the meeting he continues this line of inquiry, insisting that "things is going to be run up there on a businesslike"—by which he means profitably standardized—"basis": no more covering collectors' shortages, a lower commission for everyone, a lower payoff for customers who hit (139). Systematizing Leo's operations in this manner, Tucker trims away Leo's ability to treat employees on an individual basis, what Wheelock thinks of as Leo's inability "to get used to paying people their wages and letting them alone" (130). This produces tragic results for both Leo and his employees: Leo's bookkeeper, Frederick Bauer, unable to quit because Leo's brother Joe thinks it would be a bad example for Leo's other workers, becomes embroiled in a kidnapping scheme that leads to his shooting and Leo's fatal stroke. Leo's ability to shelter his employees from the exploitative logic of capitalism has been contingent, the novel insists, upon his control over his own capital. Thus it is no coincidence that, as the final stage in their negotiations, Tucker barely lets Leo retain his $31,000 cash reserve, letting Leo know that he knows about it and making it clear that he allows him to keep it only to bind Leo more closely to him (142). Granted the return of what was previously his own capital at his new employer's sufferance, Leo—and by extension the American middle class he represents—loses the autonomy that property grants, bringing an era of history to a close.

From the perspective of postwar literary history, the realism of *Tucker's People* was a dead end. But the transformation of the middle class that Wolfert's novel takes as its explicit historical backdrop shapes all postwar fiction in one way or another. The middlebrow novels of middle-class life popular in the fifties, for instance, translate the shift from entrepreneurship to employment into generational conflicts whose successful resolution phantasmatically negates this shift's worst effects. Elizabeth Long has argued that Sloan Wilson's 1955 *The Man in the Gray Flannel* Suit enacts a shift "from entrepreneurial adventure to corporate-suburban compromise," in which the protagonist Tom Rath rejects his employer Ralph Hopkins's single-minded devotion to business, "in favor of a balance between work and privatized familial happiness."[66] But the contrast between Hopkins and Rath is not simply a contrast between workplace and domestic forms of satisfaction: it is also a contrast between a founder of a company and one of his employees, played out in the form of an Oedipal relationship. As Jurca's reading of the novel suggests, its true fantasy is not a retreat into the family but Rath's unexpected recovery of entrepreneurial status thanks to his grandmother's bequest of valuable Connecticut real estate (139–42). Rath repudiates Hopkins and still gets to have what he has; what Hopkins has, crucially, is not income but capital. Cameron Hawley's 1952 *Executive Suite* similarly fantasizes reversing the middle class's historical trajectory through the medium of a successfully resolved generational conflict, although Hawley, unlike Wilson, attempts to do so within the corporate context. *Executive Suite*, whose epigraph is "the king is dead . . ." (Hawley's ellipsis), begins with Avery Bullard, the owner of a furniture company, collapsing on a New York sidewalk in the midst of reluctantly searching for the executive vice-president demanded by his investors. It concludes with the succession of a young engineer named Don Walling to Bullard's position. Walling thus takes Bullard's place as King, reassuring the novel's readers that upward mobility still exists. But this is not the whole story, since the novel also suggests that Walling brings to his job an emphasis on personnel matters that marks him, in Whyte's reading, as a typical organization man (Whyte, *Organization* 83–84).[67] In the terms that we earlier saw employed by Mills and Riesman, Walling exemplifies the white-collar middle class in that he is less interested in making furniture than in managing furniture-makers. At the same time Walling, who has come up through the firm as an actual designer of furniture, epitomizes old-middle-class values. In a climactic speech he even suggests that it was Bullard who first abandoned these values by okaying a training film emphasizing profit over workmanship and greenlighting an inferior line of furniture.[68] *Executive Suite* thus transposes the transformation of the middle class from the economic to the moral realm, insisting that as long as men like Walling exist this transformation remains reversible. Like *The Man in the Gray Flannel Suit*—and unlike *Tucker's People*—Hawley's novel incorporates the transformation of the middle class only to offer a fantasy of its reversal.

At a further remove from Wolfert's explicit concern with the fate of the middle class, Mickey Spillane's 1947 *I, the Jury* characterizes its hero's agency as a function of his residually entrepreneurial work. In the opening pages of the novel, Spillane's detective Mike Hammer responds to the advice of a policeman friend not to "go off half-cocked" with the following speech:

> From now on I'm after one thing, the killer. You're a cop, Pat. You're tied down by rules and regulations. There's someone over you. I'm alone. I can slap someone in the puss and they can't do a damn thing. No one can kick me out of my job. Maybe there's nobody to put up a huge fuss if I get gunned down, but then I still have a private cop's license with the privilege to pack a rod, and they're afraid of me.[69]

This passage employs the distinction between private detection and police work as a symbol for the distinction between old and new middle classes. Spillane can claim some historical and generic justification here. Police work had become a more regularized, white-collar profession during the first half of the twentieth century, giving rise around the same time as Spillane's career took off to a new genre—the police procedural—dedicated to detailing the bureaucratized work of officers like Pat.[70] Hammer's ability to do what he wants derives from the fact that he is an entrepreneurial businessman, while Pat must "follow the book because [he's] a Captain of Homicide" (Spillane 6). Pat's individual agency, that is, is overridden by the role he must play, precisely as the organization man's is.

I, the Jury thus provides, like *The Man in the Gray Flannel Suit* and *Executive Suite*, a fantasy of entrepreneurial agency in a white-collar world. It is with Spillane, however, that we can begin to see the factor that distinguishes postwar fiction from its modernist predecessors, and that allows us to read such fiction as shaped by the reconfiguration of the middle class even when this event does not comprise one of explicit topics. Fundamental here is the way in which postwar fiction equates the agency of characters with the agency of authors. This move bears the traces of the transformation of the middle class insofar as postwar commentators understood white-collar work as a system for constraining the autonomy of mental laborers. Because authors themselves perform mental labor, the question of agency cannot be constrained within the horizon of content, but leaks into the form of literary work understood as the material embodiment of the author's own mental labor.

In Spillane's case—as in that of his colleague and admirer Ayn Rand, as we will see in chapter 1—this equation functions positively, with Hammer's entrepreneurial agency echoing and reconfirming that of his creator. Sean McCann has recently argued that Spillane evolves his particular brand of populism in response to the perceived transformation of the welfare state from "the realization of mass democracy" to "a system of bureaucratic institutions and individual alienation."[71] But as my reading of *I, the Jury* suggests, the degradation of "personal agency" at issue here has to do not only with "the displacement of local community by a procedural state" (McCann 223) but also with the transition from entrepreneurship to employment. McCann's own point that Spillane understood his high sales as a victory over the literary-critical apparatus (203–4) suggests as much. Spillane, like Hammer, does what he wants without regard to the "rules and regulations" of the organization men who serve as literary gatekeepers; like Hammer, he is an entrepreneur whose justification comes from success on the market. Spillane, like Rand, could lay claim to a level of entrepreneurial success that to some degree compensated for the genre writer's typically vexed relationship with the arbiters of literary prestige.

What distinguishes the postwar period, however, is the adoption of this same stance by authors who are not excluded from critical success or the institutions of literary prestige. Saul Bellow provides a perfect case in point: early recognized as a major author, he also becomes the first fiction writer of his stature to make his living within the academy *and* a bitter, life-long critic of the university.[72] I take up Bellow's attacks on "the literary intelligentsia"[73] of the university and the "culture-bureaucrats"[74] of the publishing industry at greater length in chapter 3, but here we can note that Bellow, like Spillane, turns to public success as the antidote to the constraints these institutions impose upon the author. According to his biographer James Atlas, Bellow "yearned to be—and tended to think of himself as—a 'great-public' writer, whose reach extended far beyond the modernists he admired for their high seriousness but disdained for the 'difficulty' that estranged them from a wider audience."[75] Bellow's antiacademicism has, to be sure, become an all too common stance among university writers with far less claim to public success. What's worth noting in the present context, however, is the extent to which Bellow's desire for public success distinguishes him from previous generations of American authors, for whom the market signified not freedom from constraint but precisely the opposite. Michael Gilmore has shown, for instance, how the American Romantics understood the market as "a site of humiliation where the seller has to court and conciliate potential buyers to gain their custom," and in response evolved protomodernist "strategies of difficulty and concealment" designed to "forestall easy consumption" of their work.[76] On one hand, American authors' early aversion to the market in comparison with the rest of the middle class anticipates the managerial turn taken by the PMC in the late nineteenth and early twentieth centuries.[77]

But because they defined themselves at least partially in opposition to the rest of the middle class, they developed a form of professionalism designed to protect their authority as much from the public as from the institutions of corporate capitalism.[78] Subsequent generations of authors with canonical pretensions, abetted by their comparatively less direct contact with corporate capitalism, retained this residual mode of professionalism well into the period of the PMC's rise and consolidation. Thus in the Progressive Era Jack London turns to professionalism as a means of bolstering his agency in relation to both the publishing industry and the sorts of compromises associated with "public approbation" and "success with a middle-class readership."[79] And as Thomas Strychacz suggests, modernism's cultivation of "esoteric forms of discourse" can be seen as a version of the professional's "disciplinary codes" designed to enhance the authority of the artist by excluding the mass public from his or her work.[80] Although modernists' disdain for the market often concealed a canny attention to promoting and selling their work, modernist marketing was aimed at small, self-consciously elite publics rather than the public at large.[81] Thus Timothy Materer notes that when Ezra Pound took over editorship of *The Little Review* he "decided that avant-garde literature could only be marketed though [*sic*] a magazine that appealed to an elite," in contrast to Harriet Monroe's effort "to market poetry that appealed to a wide, democratic audience." In response to Monroe's use of Whitman's "To have great poetry we must have great audiences" as *Poetry*'s masthead, *The Little Review* under Pound's editorship declaimed "Make No Compromise with the Public Taste."[82]

Bellow, by contrast, wants to make exactly this compromise, or more to the point, he sees satisfying the public taste as entailing no compromise at all. This is because in the postwar period the middle class has come to see organization—and particularly, the sorts of organizations in which one performs mental labor—in unremittingly negative terms. In contrast, the market of public taste comes to seem like not only a comparative refuge but indeed the very place where intellectual virtues per se can be realized. The authors of the 1930s, writing in the context of earlier concerns about the bureaucratization of mental labor, anticipate this turn. One way to understand late modernism, Michael Szalay implies, is as authors' attempts to reconfigure themselves in old-middle-class terms (as makers of things) in contrast to the New Deal regime of authorship as salaried mental labor.[83] But authors like Ernest Hemingway and Gertrude Stein retain a residual modernist commitment to complexity designed "to forestall the market valuation of experts by a nonexpert public."[84] Bellow self-consciously forgoes this commitment in favor of the same romanticized regard for the market that shapes postwar accounts of middle-class life more generally.

Numerous postwar intellectuals share this regard with Bellow. Mills, for instance, proclaims that

the eighteenth-century intellectual stood on common ground with the bourgeois entrepreneur; both were fighting, each in his own way, against the remnants of feudal control, the writer seeking to free himself from the highly placed patron, the businessman break-ing the bonds of the chartered enterprise. Both were fighting for a new kind of freedom, the writer for an anonymous public, the businessman for an anonymous and unbounded market. (143)

For Mills, the heroic age of the intellectual coincided with the heroic age of the entrepreneur because both are at their best when satisfying public tastes on the market. A similar nostalgia for the classic period of market society surfaces in the art critic Harold Rosenberg's well-known critique, in his 1959 *The Tradi-tion of the New,* of kitsch as art that "follows established rules."[85] While this formulation might seem to demonstrate kitsch's market dependence—it "has a predictable audience, predictable effects, predictable rewards" (266)—Rosen-berg's objection to kitsch is not a "question of . . . 'selling-out,' but of muscular slackness associated with finding an audience responsive to certain norms" (268). The source of these norms, for Rosenberg as for Bellow, is not the mass audience but "the new post-War employed intelligentsia" (280). Rosenberg complains that "Modern Art" has been transformed from an avant-garde move-ment to an institution dominated not by artists but by "the expanding caste of professional enlighteners of the masses—designers, architects, decorators, fash-ion people, exhibition directors" (37). Within this framework Rosenberg offers a measured but surprising—particularly in this context—endorsement of "bad art." "The first American playwrights," he claims, "could think of nothing less to compose than Shakespearean tragedies in blank verse. Had it not been for a will to bad art in order to satisfy the appetites of the street, the American theatre [*sic*] would never have come into being" (15–16). While Rosenberg remains too much of a modernist elitist to fully endorse mass tastes, he suggests that in the heyday of market society even bad art possessed a productive energy lacking in the desiccated institutional regime of kitsch.

Finally, Irving Howe's landmark 1959 essay "Mass Society and Post-Modern Fiction" mourns the passing of market society if only in its role as the object of earlier intellectuals' criticism. Howe begins his essay with a retelling of *Crime and Punishment* in which Raskolnikov, contemplating the murder of the old pawnbro-ker, receives a telegram informing him that he has won a Guggenheim to study "color imagery in Pushkin's poetry and its relation to the myths of the ancient Muscovites."[86] We might assume that Howe, who subsequently describes the new Raskolnikov as a "sober Professor of Literature" (125), regrets the character's transformation into one of the bourgeoisie that his earlier incarnation used to rail against. But this is not the case, as the rest of the essay makes clear. Rather, the problem is that the bourgeoisie against which modernism once set itself no longer exists. What characterized the pre–World War II world in which modernism came of age, Howe argues, was "a cluster of stable assumptions as to the nature of our society" (126) that made possible the modernists' revolt. Howe identifies these assumptions, tellingly, with entrepreneurial values: this society, Howe writes, was "hard, tangible, ruled by a calculus of gain" (127). The fact that this is not entirely true—as, for instance, the eponymous proto-organization man of Sinclair Lewis's 1922 *Babbitt* suggests—only makes all the more clear that Howe here indulges in nostalgia for the entrepreneurial values of the market, if only as a worthy object of criticism.

Indeed, Howe's desire for the entrepreneurial middle class as enemy rather than Bellow and Mills's—and, to a lesser extent, Rosenberg's—idealized lay audience makes clear what is at stake in postwar intellectuals' shared dislike for the institutions (whether academic, museological, or critical) of intellectual life. In the postwar period, intellectual work was definitively reconfigured as something that took place within institutions: foundations, museums, government, the media, and, most importantly, the expanding system of higher education. This process blurred intellectuals' traditionally antagonistic relationship with the middle-class mainstream in two ways: by transforming intellectuals into white-collar employees, and by transforming the rest of the middle-class into the higher-educated mental laborers that Riesman calls "demi-intellectuals" (148).[87] Whereas the modernists notoriously worked various jobs to pay the bills while they did their *real* work—as Wallace Stevens wrote to his fiancée in 1909, "I certainly do not exist from nine to six, when I am at the office"[88]—the postwar generation found employment *as* artists and intellectuals. And whereas the prewar generation could comfortably distinguish themselves from the philistinism of a small-business owner like George Babbitt, their postwar successors found themselves in the position of organization men par excellence, their employment symbolizing the ultimate degradation of creative mental labor within the white-collar workplace.

Mills sums up this new conception of the intellectual in a passage from the tellingly entitled "Brains, Inc." chapter of *White Collar*:

> Busy with the ideological speed-up, the intellectual has readily taken on the responsibilities of the citizen. In many cases, having ceased to be in any sense a free intellectual, he has joined the expanding world of those who live off ideas, as administrator, idea-man, and good-will technician. In class, status, and self-image, he has become more solidly middle class, a man at a desk, married, with children, living in a respectable suburb, his career pivoting on the selling of ideas, his life a tight little routine, substituting middle-brow and mass culture for direct experience of his life and his world, and, above all, becoming a man with a job in a society where money is supreme. (156)

In this passage, Mills's usual attention to the structural conditions of white-collar employment gives way to a far more typical assertion of the essential incompatibility of institutions and creative thought. This assertion—which, as we will see in chapter 1, links Mills with as seemingly disparate a figure as Ayn Rand—remains influential. Consider, for instance, the respectful attention accorded to its more or less uncritical reproduction in Russell Jacoby's 1987 *The Last Intellectuals*.[89] This notion arises at the moment when the institutionalization of intellectuals' mental labor renders it parallel to that of the rest of the middle class: designed to maintain intellectuals' distinction, it ironically reproduces the typical white-collar middle class response to The Organization.

Within this framework, mental labor takes on an ambivalent role for intellectuals. On one hand, it continues to signify a residual sense of self-authorship that (as Howe's account suggests) is simultaneously posed against and parallel with that of the entrepreneurial old middle class. On the other hand, however, it now becomes the site of a new, typically white-collar sense of institutional disempowerment. Mark McGurl, who understands the modernist art novel as participating in the PMC projects of "privileging . . . *intellectual* virtue" and producing "various forms of social distinction and status elevation," suggests that this trajectory reaches an impasse in the 1950s with "the institutionalization of modernism in the university."[90] To give a concrete example of the earlier paradigm, we can understand modernism's use of dialect to renovate the routinized language of Standard English as reflecting a typically PMC faith in the ability of good organization to displace bad.[91] But in the postwar period, when all organization comes to seem like a bad thing—a transition figured not so much in the institutionalization of modernism per se as in the persistent narration of this event as a bad thing—then style becomes simultaneously overvalued and associated with inevitable failure. The more idiosyncratic and activist deployment of style-as-mental-labor that McGurl associates with modernism gives way to the threat of Taylorized mental labor, even as style takes on an even greater burden of representing individuality.

This ambivalence about mental labor gives rise to the distinctive characteristics that Tony Tanner attributes to postwar fiction in his 1971 study *City of Words*. For Tanner, "The problematical and ambiguous relationship of the self to patterns of all kinds—social, psychological, linguistic—is an obsession among recent American writers."[92] He thus identifies at the heart of postwar fiction the dramatization of threatened individuality central to accounts of the white-collar middle class. But Tanner goes beyond content, arguing that this dramatized situation finds a formal analog in the author's quest for "a *stylistic* freedom which is not simply a meaningless incoherence, . . . a stylistic form which will not trap him inside the existing forms of previous literature" (19; Tanner's emphasis). The writer's "paradox," Tanner argues, lies in the fact that

> if he wants to write in any communicable form he must traffic in a language which may at every turn be limiting, directing and perhaps controlling his responses and formulations. If he feels that the given structuring of reality of the available language is imprisoning or iniquitous, he may abandon language altogether; or he may seek to use the existing language in such a way that he demonstrates to himself and other people that he does not wholly accept nor wholly conform to the structures built into the common tongue, that he has the power to resist and perhaps disturb the particular 'rubricizing' tendency of the language he has inherited. Such an author—and I think he is an unusually common phenomenon in contemporary America—will go out of his way to show that he

is using language as it has never been used before, leaving the visible marks of his idiosyncrasies on every formulation. (16)

The brilliance of this passage, we might say, lies in its dramatization of the situation that it seeks to describe. The writer's efforts to transcend the constraining effects of language as a social system ultimately fail, just as Tanner's own abstract and ahistorical staging of this conflict give way to his admission that it is particularly prevalent in postwar fiction. One explanation for this prevalence—the most convincing, to my mind—is that Tanner's formal paradox (language provides the only means for expressing the individuality it constrains) corresponds to the situation of the postwar intellectual for whom mental labor is the site of both transcendence and disempowerment. Or, in the terms with which this introduction began, it is the place where the presumed irrelevance of the economic actually becomes the economy's textual trace.

The opening paragraph of Saul Bellow's first novel, *Dangling Man* (1944), exemplifies the way in which style encodes authors' relationship to the transformation of the middle class, and the economy more generally. "There was a time," Bellow's novel begins,

> when people were in the habit of addressing themselves frequently and felt no shame at making a record of their inward transactions. But to keep a journal nowadays is considered . . . in poor taste. For this is an era of hardboiled-dom. Today, the code of the athlete, of the tough boy . . . is stronger than ever. Do you have feelings? There are correct and incorrect ways of indicating them. Do you have an inner life? It is nobody's business but your own. Do you have emotions? Strangle them. To a degree, everyone obeys this code. And it does admit of a limited kind of candor, a closemouthed straightforwardness. But on the truest candor, it has an inhibitory effect. Most serious matters are closed to the hardboiled. They are unpracticed in introspection, and therefore badly equipped to deal with opponents whom they cannot shoot like big game or outdo in daring.[93]

Here hardboiled style, which Bellow implicitly links to Hemingway and his imitators, functions not as a means of resistance to literary rules and regulations but, on the contrary, as a form of systemic constraint imposed upon the "truest candor" of the authentic self. To the extent that Bellow here criticizes the regime of the hardboiled "tough boy," this passage might seem like a preemptive critique of Spillane. But in fact it plays out precisely the critique of bureaucracy that animates Mike Hammer's rejection of "rules and regulations," on the terrain not of professional institutions but of what Tanner calls "the existing forms of previous literature" (19).

Insofar as Bellow understands inherited literary forms as deindividualizing embodiments of institutional logics, the opening paragraph of *Dangling Man* provides an explicitly thematized formal equivalent to his more direct attacks on the academy and the publishing industry. At the same time, this move cannot be reduced to the merely formal; it understands preexisting literary forms as institutional constraints upon individual creativity and autonomy and thus—however insistently disguised—as versions of the white-collar workplace. Bellow himself, as I discuss in chapter 3, will pose his third novel, *The Adventures of Augie March* (1953), as a stylistic revolt against his own first two novels, which he will come to see as exemplars of a facile modernist alienation that he identifies with the university. Similarly, much postwar poetry stakes its claims to innovation against modernism as an ossified bureaucratic system. "At mid-century, accepted, even celebrated, by the Luce Corporation, the modernist revolution might well seem finished," James E. B. Breslin writes, leading poets like Allen Ginsberg and critics like Leslie Fiedler to turn to "recuperated versions of the modernists . . . as civilized ideals against which to judge the 'anarchic' work of the present."[94] It would be a mistake to understand these phenomena solely in literary-historical terms, as a revolt against modernism. *Dangling Man* poses one form of modernism (Dostoyevskyan self-exposure) against another (the minimalism Hemingway learned from Stein). And Bellow's friend Ellison turns toward modernism (including Hemingway) as part of his own stylistic revolt against Richard Wright's naturalism. What matters in these cases is not the specific target but the way that any inherited form can become an avatar of the "social institutions which by their bureaucratic planning and mathematical foresight usurp both freedom and rationality from the little individual men [or in this case little individual authors] caught in them" (Mills, *White* xvii).

The ultimate irony here is that because no particular style can successfully avoid this fate, the burden shifts from the lineaments of style itself to the act of opposing the previous style (any style). What looks like a commitment to form in opposition to repetitive mental labor itself becomes a repetitively assumed stance. Thus Mills argues, in his suggestive comments on style near the conclusion of his "Brains, Inc." chapter, that the "cult of alienation" in literature (like the "fetish of objectivity" in the social sciences) (159) becomes the formal equivalent of intellectuals' superficiality "in an age of organized irresponsibility" (160):

> Simply to understand, or to lament alienation—these are the ideals of the technician who is powerless and estranged but not disinherited. These are the ideals of men who have the capacity to know the truth but not the chance, the skill, or the fortitude, as the case may be, to communicate it with political effectiveness. (160)

In some branches of postwar fiction, this becomes a self-conscious commitment to antistyle: for instance, Kerouac's (highly polished, as we now know)[95] efforts to appear spontaneous.

While postwar authors' engagement with stylistic innovation thus links their work to the transformation of the middle class, it does not necessarily constitute a politically desirable response to this transformation. On the contrary, the inherently individual and formal nature of such stylistic interventions necessarily forecloses the sorts of collective struggle and organization that a political response to the transformation of mental labor would call for.[96] Moreover, postwar fiction projects an essentially middle-class experience of capitalism's negative aspects and thus reinforces the putative universality of middle-class problems. It is, in this regard, a particularly middle-class idea—conditioned by traditional doctrines of individual upward mobility and the autonomy that derives from property ownership—that the worst aspect of mental labor is the threat that it poses to one's individuality. Nonetheless, understanding postwar authors' stylistic revolts as responses—however displaced—to the expansion and ultimate proletarianization of mental labor does give the lie to our understanding of the era's novels as rejecting political and economic concerns in favor of individual and psychological ones.

In this regard, even as putatively hermetic a novel as Vladimir Nabokov's *Lolita* (1955 France; 1958 United States) engages the postwar transformation of the economy not in spite of, but to the extent that, it announces itself as a pure expression of individual style. We can begin to see this by considering how the standard understanding of the novel as a self-contained exercise in formal innovation leads Nabokov's biographer Brian Boyd—normally a meticulously careful reader of textual details—to a clumsy mistake. Boyd, who argues that the Nabokovian aesthetic privileges "the uniqueness of [the artist's] invented world" over the "philosophical, social, and historical generalizations so customary in literary criticism,"[97] writes of *Lolita* that "no other novel begins so memorably: 'Lolita, light of my life, fire of my loins. My sin, my soul. Lo-lee-ta: the tip of the tongue taking a trip of three steps down the palate to tap, at three, on the teeth. Lo. Le. Ta' " (228). These alliterative lines, the first paragraph of chapter 1, not only engage in the verbal play that is Nabokov's trademark, but also perform the subsumption of content by form—the transformation of "Lolita" from a girl into a series of syllables—that is the function of such play in the Nabokovian aesthetic. The only problem is that the novel does not actually begin with these lines, but with the fictional foreword that Nabokov appends to Humbert Humbert's narrative over the signature "John Ray, Jr., Ph.D."

This foreword functions as a tutorial in precisely the reading of *Lolita* that Nabokov wants us to avoid, the sort of reading that he elsewhere associates—in terms that should by now be familiar to us—with the categorizing imperatives of the paraintellectuals who staff institutions of culture. In the commentary that accompanies his translation of Alexander Pushkin's long poem *Eugene Onegin*, Nabokov complains that

> there are teachers and students with square minds who are by nature meant to undergo the fascination of categories. For them, "schools" and "movements" are everything; by painting a group symbol on the bow of mediocrity, they condone their own incomprehension of true genius. (qtd. Boyd 345)

It is precisely these categorizing habits—against which Nabokov promotes "the quiddity of individual artistic achievement" (qtd. Boyd 345)—that the fictional John Ray exemplifies. Ray explains that he was given the manuscript of "Lolita" by his friend, the lawyer of the pseudonymous narrator Humbert, on the basis of his Poling Prize–winning article "Do the Senses make [*sic*] Sense," a treatise on "certain morbid states and perversions."[98] Yet Ray, as befits the winner of the Poling Prize (with its suggestions of demographic rather than individual, quantitative rather than qualitative, standards), ultimately justifies the manuscript on the basis not of its pathological, but of its representative, status. Thus he tells us "that at least 12% of American adult males," according to a colleague of his, "enjoy yearly, in one way or another, the special experience 'H.H.' describes with such despair" (5). Ray recognizes both the singular nature of Humbert's actions and the aesthetic value of his account. While Humbert is "abnormal" and "not a gentleman," Ray writes, "how magically his singing violin can conjure up a tendresse, a compassion for Lolita that makes us entranced with the book while abhorring its author!" (5).

Within his scheme of values, however, the text's individual properties—either as the record of a specific event or as a unique aesthetic object—take a back seat to its synechdochic relationship to a larger social whole. Thus, while "as a case history, 'Lolita' will become, no doubt, a classic in psychiatric circles," and "as a work of art, it transcends its expiatory aspects," its primary value resides in

> the ethical impact [it] should have on the serious reader; for in this poignant personal study there lurks a general lesson; the wayward child, the egotistic mother, the panting maniac—these are not only vivid characters in a unique story: they warn us of dangerous trends; they point out potent evils. (5–6)

Ray, that is, understands the worth of "Lolita" to inhere in the way in which its merely "personal" and "unique" aspects dissolve into a more "general" narrative, in which Humbert, representing the 12 percent of the adult American male population who engage in pedophilia, provides an object lesson for "all of us—parents, social workers, educators—[engaged in] bringing up a better generation in a safer world" (6). If "our demented diarist [had] gone, in the fatal summer of 1947, to a competent psychopathologist," Ray proposes, "there would have been no disaster; but then, neither would there have been this book" (5). While he acknowledges, that is, that psychological intervention would have cured Humbert at the cost of silencing his "singing violin," he accounts this a reasonable trade-off. And if Ray were discussing real life events, it might well be. As a discussion of a work of art, however, Ray's reading errs not only in giving the didactic precedence over the aesthetic, but—even worse—in endorsing the anti-individual logic of norms, trends, general lessons, types.

Before we get to the (undeniable) formal excellences of Humbert's narrative, then, we must travel through the terrain of intellectual labor transformed into white-collar work. That Nabokov begins in this way suggests some anxiety on his part about whether the "quiddity of individual artistic achievement" can be understood other than in opposition to the intellectual labor performed in institutional contexts. As Alfred Kazin puts it, "The non-Nabokov world must always be shown up as unnecessary to Nabokov's freedom."[99] The irony here is that with the inclusion of Ray's foreword parodying social scientific methods, *Lolita* ends up producing the same model of individuality as the postwar sociology of white-collar work. Whyte, for instance, insists in *The Organization Man*'s introduction that his book "is not a plea for nonconformity":

> We must not let the outward forms deceive us. If individualism involves following one's destiny as one's own conscience directs, it must for most of us be a realizable destiny, and a sensible awareness of the rules of the game can be a condition of individualism as well as a constraint upon it. The man who drives a Buick Special and lives in a ranch-type house just like hundreds of other ranch-type houses can assert himself as effectively and courageously against his particular society as the bohemian against his particular society. He usually does not, it is true, but if he does, the surface uniformities can serve quite well as protective coloration. The organization people who are best able to control their environment rather than be controlled by it are well aware that they are not too easily distinguishable from the others in the outward obeisances paid to the good opinions of others. And that is one of the reasons they do control. They disarm society. (11–12)

For Whyte, as for Nabokov, individuality can only be gestured toward as the ineffable residue left over after one accounts for all the social forces shaping the individual (be it the individual person or the individual novel). Of course, it might seem mistaken to align Whyte's disregard for "outward forms" with Nabokov's anti-Freudian investment in "the pulsating surface."[100] Whereas Whyte rejects form, for Nabokov form is everything. Thus even Ray's foreword defines *Lolita* in formal terms, albeit the implicit and negative ones of "not sociology" and "not psychology."

Yet on some level the preference for form is, for Nabokov, indistinguishable from the rejection of form: what defines literature and distinguishes it from other forms of writing is not its particular form but its essential formlessness. "On a Book Entitled *Lolita*," the essay Nabokov wrote for the novel's American debut and that has since been appended to some editions as an afterword, seemingly sets out to distinguish *Lolita* in formal terms from the pornography some had accused it of being. Pornography, Nabokov asserts, "must consist of an alternation of sexual scenes"; "passages in between must be reduced to . . . logical bridges of the simplest design"; "the sexual scenes . . . must follow a crescendo line"; and so forth (313). When it comes time to describe his own novel, however, he abandons such formal specificity in favor of simply listing specific images: "Mr. Taxovich, or that class list of Ramsdale School, or Charlotte saying 'waterproof,' or Lolita in slow motion advancing toward Humbert's gifts" (316), and so on. This suggests that the distinction between pornography and literature lies not in their different formal structures, but in the fact that pornography has a formal structure while literature does not. In contrast to pornography's devotion to "Old rigid rules" (313), art is characterized by its resistance to any coercive structure beyond the level of the individual image. Thus Nabokov can no more describe what makes a good novel than Whyte can describe what makes an individual. "I happen to be the kind of author," Nabokov writes, "who, when asked to explain [a book's] origin and growth, has to rely on such ancient terms as Interreaction of Inspiration and Combination—which, I admit, sounds like a conjurer explaining one trick by performing another" (311). Nabokov in this respect practices what he preaches in decrying others' interpretive efforts: "everybody should know that I detest symbols and allegories (which is due partly to my old feud with Freudian voodooism and partly to my loathing of generalizations devised by literary mythists and sociologists)" (314). As this capacious dismissal—which links literary critics with social scientists and clinicians like John Ray—reminds us, Nabokov's preference for ineffability arises out of the same context as Whyte's. Both feel that the transformation of the middle class (including intellectuals) into white-collar employees continually raises the possibility that what they think of as "their" ideas—or even "their" identities—may in fact originate in the systemic framework in which they perform their mental labor. Nabokov's only way to protect the products of his own mental labor from this possibility is to refuse to describe them, to refuse to give them a form that might then turn out to be a product of The Organization. But this then involves these products in the catch-22 that they can only be described negatively, as *not* products of The Organization, in a way that ultimately grounds them in the very social framework that Nabokov seeks to transcend.

As Frederick Whiting argues in his brilliant reading of *Lolita*, the novel's claims to transcend the social aesthetically thus mirror its content, which consists of Humbert Humbert's equally unrealizable efforts to produce his individuality over against the constraining forces of the social. Humbert's career as a pedophile theoretically flies in the face of social norms and thus constitutes a kind of perverse individualism, a claim that Humbert plays up in his descriptions of himself as a monster of sensuality. In practice, however, these very descriptions insistently return Humbert to the legal and cultural norms that constitute the pedophile as a member of a pathological category and thus not an individual at all.[101] In this way, Humbert ends up seeming like nothing so much as a prototypical organization man. Humbert tells us, for instance, that

> overtly, I had so-called normal relationships with a number of terrestrial women having pumpkins or pears for breasts; inly, I was consumed by a hell furnace of localized lust for every passing nymphet whom as a law-abiding poltroon I never dared approach. (18)

In this passage Humbert declares his separation from the "so-called normal" yet admits that in his behavior at least he cleaves to social norms. The distinction between inner desire and outward behavior, as we saw in the quote from Whyte above, is central to the understanding of the organization man as a conformist. If there was no such distinction, then the organization man could not be said to be sacrificing his individuality to the Social Ethic. Elsewhere Humbert notes (speaking of himself in the third person), that "under no circumstances would he have interfered with the innocence of a child, if there was the least risk of a row"

(19–20). In this regard Humbert might well be following the advice of an executive cited by Whyte who remarks that "the ideal . . . is to be an individualist privately and a conformist publicly" (172). Humbert's pursuit of nymphets does, it is true, assume a more outward form when he begins sleeping with Dolores Haze. But even then his activities remain publicly conformist to the extent that he pursues them under cover of his masquerade, first as the devoted husband of Lolita's mother, then as her widower father. In thus performing socially approved roles to cover his sexual relationship with Lolita, Humbert exemplifies the behavior of "the other-directed person [who] gives up the one-face policy of the inner-directed man for a multi-face policy that he sets in secrecy and varies with each class of encounters" (Riesman, *Lonely* 139).

Here one might reasonably object that Humbert's status as a European émigré prevents us from reading his story in the class terms that I have claimed are central to postwar fiction's engagement with narratives of threatened individuality. Nabokov grounds Humbert's questionable individuality, however, in the fact that he makes his living as a critic and sometimes teacher of English and French literature.[102] The author of such papers as "The Proustian theme in a letter from Keats to Benjamin Bailey" (16) and a devoted Freudian, Humbert is like his redactor John Ray a member of the "employed intelligentsia" that Nabokov and others saw as the prototypical organization men of the world of ideas. Moreover, Humbert embarks upon this career in explicit departure from his family's history as property owners: his father, he tells us, "owned a luxurious hotel on the Riviera," while his father's "father and two grandfathers had sold wine, jewels and silk respectively" (9). Despite his European background, then, Humbert's family history recapitulates the story of the American middle class's transition from entrepreneurship to employment.

Humbert's story differs in this detail from his creator's, although this difference may be less significant than it at first seems to a consideration of *Lolita*'s resonance with postwar narratives of lost middle-class autonomy. Nabokov, unlike Humbert, was a descendant not of the bourgeoisie but of the aristocracy, the child of an official who was forced to take his family into exile following the Bolshevik Revolution.[103] As Boyd tells this story, it recapitulates not the narrative of new-middle-class descent but, on the contrary, the classic myth of old-middle-class ascent in the New World. "[B]orn into an old noble family and stupendous wealth," Nabokov "at seventeen . . . inherited the most splendid of the family manors," but lost it when his family fled Russia. Thereafter he made a tenuous living as a writer for "a fragmented and destitute émigré audience of less than a million readers," eventually emigrating to the United States where he supported his wife and young son by teaching literature at various colleges. "In America life was easier but still modest until the success of *Lolita* turned Nabokov again, at sixty, into a wealthy man." Quitting his last teaching job, at Cornell, he retired to Switzerland where he and his family lived "in a luxury hotel, waited on by a retinue of liveried attendants." But this event marks not so much Nabokov's return to aristocratic ease as his transformation from employed intellectual to bourgeois entrepreneur, since *Lolita's* success freed him, in Spillane-esque fashion, to "carry on with his writing undisturbed."[104] As we have seen, this same transformation provides the counterhistorical fantasy of middlebrow novels of middle-class life like *The Man in the Gray Flannel Suit* and *Executive Suite*.

During the early fifties, however, Nabokov could not see this outcome and thus perhaps identified more with figures like Humbert and Timofey Pnin—the hapless Russian teacher who is the protagonist of the academic comedy Nabokov wrote after *Lolita*—than the story of his later triumph might suggest. *Lolita* and *Pnin* (1957), we might say, translate Nabokov's experience of his family's expropriation into the American narrative of middle-class expropriation, even as his background attunes him particularly well to the core of loss and nostalgia that catalyzes the crisis of the organization man. Recognizing this, we can see how *Lolita*, so far from simply reproducing the postwar narrative of threatened individuality, indirectly critiques this narrative on both logical and ethical grounds. Central to this critique is the fact that Humbert relates to Dolores Haze not as a person in her own right but as a form of property over which he can retain control only by rigorously isolating her from all social contact. In doing so, he of course violates the necessarily alienable nature of middle-class property, becoming as Marx says of the miser "a capitalist gone mad."[105] His sexual perversion, which he traces to his unconsummated adolescent affair with the Poe-derived Annabel Lee, is thus equivalent to his perversion of property, his refusal to allow Lolita to circulate paralleling his refusal of adult sexual partners:

> "Whose cat has scratched poor you?" a full-blown fleshy handsome woman of the repulsive type to which I was particularly attractive might ask me at the 'lodge,' during a table d'hôte dinner followed by dancing promised to Lo. This was one of the reasons why I tried to keep as far away from people as possible, while Lo, on the other hand, would do her utmost to draw as many potential witnesses into her orbit as she could. (164)

Seeking to remain forever on "that intangible island of entranced time where Lolita plays with her likes" (17), Humbert becomes the real Dolores Haze's jailer. In this respect his narrative parallels that of the postwar middle class, whose fascination with its lost property becomes an ethos of antisociality at odds with the very forms of exchange that, Mills notes, underwrote the old-middle-class world of "countless, free, shrewd transactions" (9). Humbert thus undermines his own project, though more importantly he mistreats Dolores. The novel's ethical judgment against Humbert derives not from an investment in normative definitions of pedophilia but rather from the fact that, in his need to shape the world around him to his own specifications, Humbert displays "disregard for the live reality" of other people, particularly Lolita.[106] This becomes jarringly clear in those moments where Humbert's narration either intentionally or naively allows Lolita's personhood to leak through: Lolita's "wild, intense, hopeful, hopeless whisper" pleading to talk to a family she recognizes (157); her "weeping in my arms" after sex

(169); "her sobs in the night—every night, every night—the moment I feigned sleep" (176). As Whiting puts it, "the elements of Lolita's subjectivity that [Humbert] must will himself to ignore in pursuit of [his] fantasy are not confined to her failure to desire him but extend to all aspects of her subjectivity."[107]

Lolita is, in this regard—and however much Nabokov himself might have disliked this characterization—a surprisingly feminist novel. In his 1976 *Capitalism, the Family, and Personal Life* Eli Zaretsky proposes the historically oversimplified but nonetheless usefully counterintuitive notion that "proletarianization gave rise to subjectivity."[108] By this he means that the proletariat, by definition lacking property, could only cultivate the subjective " 'property' " of "our inner lives and social capabilities, our dreams, our desires, our fears, our sense of ourselves as interconnected beings" (76). For Zaretsky this elaboration of subjectivity carries a revolutionary potential whose ability to register "universal feelings and experience" is degraded, in "modern art," into something "obscurantist and remote from actual human concerns" (120–21). This account, whatever its historical value, corresponds quite well to the stereotype of Nabokov as an apolitical writer. But what distinguishes *Lolita* from other postwar books in which style simply becomes a reified marker of distinction is that Nabokov, through the unreliable narrator, Humbert, also parodies this stance and undermines its pretensions to singularity by alluding to Dolores's viewpoint. As a result, Nabokov produces something like the second-wave feminist critique of the family that Zaretsky dialectically attributes to the postwar hypervaluation of the family as the site of personal life.

Nabokov thus participates, surprisingly, in what I will describe in chapters 3 and 4 as the production of identity politics out of the encrypted class politics of the organization-man discourse. *Lolita* retains the traces of this encryption in the way that Humbert treats Dolores not only as an object but also—in terms that are particularly loaded in any discussion of the white-collar middle class—as a member of a category. This, Humbert makes clear, is what a nymphet is: "Now I wish to introduce the following idea. Between the age limits of nine and fourteen there occur maidens who, to certain bewitched travelers, twice or many times older than they, reveal their true nature which is not human, but nymphic (that is demoniac); and these chosen creatures I propose to designate as 'nymphets' " (16). Humbert thus tries to do to Dolores precisely what society threatens to do to him: to transform her from an individual into a member of a species. In this way, *Lolita* returns us—more than a little unexpectedly—to the account of dehumanization that appears in *Tucker's People*. Wolfert's novel understands dehumanization as a historical process, contingent upon the expanding reign of "business" (that is, centralized property) that not only transforms the formerly autonomous members of the middle class into agency-less employees but also sees its "victims" more generally not "as people" but "merely [as] opposition" (174). Thus Leo Minch's death comes about when, absorbed into Tucker's operation and no longer able to use his status as a " 'good' man" to make his numbers business a " 'good' business," he denies Bauer's request to quit and precipitates the bungled kidnapping scheme that kills them both. From the perspective of Bauer, whose only encounter with Tucker's top management is a few run-ins with Leo's brother Joe, Leo is the enemy because he makes the decision that keeps Bauer imprisoned within the numbers business. From Leo's own perspective, however, he has no control over these decisions, and it is "torture to have to do to Bauer what Joe had done to him" (310).

Lolita has absolutely no explicit concern with the history of economic concentration within which *Tucker's People* grounds this situation, yet Nabokov's novel reproduces this dilemma structurally in Humbert's relationship with Lolita. Just as Leo's lack of agency looks like tyranny to Bauer, what looks like Humbert's crisis of agency from his own narrating perspective becomes from Lolita's perspective his tyrannical enforcement of *her* lack of agency. In this way, *Lolita* depicts nothing less than the historical situation of the American middle class at the middle of the twentieth century. Threatened with proletarianization through the loss of its property to big capital, the middle class translates this loss into narratives of individual dispossession that enforce its cultural dominance rather than seeking a potentially more useful affiliation with those already outside the magic circle of capital. The insufficiency of this strategy has become apparent as the problems of the employed middle class have migrated from compromised individual agency to more practical forms of dispossession like overwork and tenuous job security. Within this framework, big capital exploits the ongoing resonance of traditional American middle-class values even while it proves increasingly able to dispense with an actual middle class. The contemporary United States is haunted by a specter: the specter of the middle class. To exorcise this ghost we must return to the culture of the 1950s, and unravel how the specific class interests of the middle class were translated into cultural forms predicated on their supposed ahistoricity and classlessness.

CHAPTER ONE

Ayn Rand and the Politics of Property

IT WASN'T TOO LONG AGO that Ayn Rand, despite her enormous and ongoing popularity, was all but invisible in the criticism and history of twentieth-century American fiction, although that has begun to change. Sharon Stockton and Michael Szalay have recently demonstrated the centrality of Rand's conception of brain work to the Depression Era in which she wrote her first bestselling novel, *The Fountainhead* (1943).[1] In what follows I make a case for her ongoing relevance in the postwar era, focusing primarily on her 1957 novel, *Atlas Shrugged.* Unlike many of the authors I deal with in this study, Rand writes books whose engagement with the questions of mental labor central to the postwar reorganization of the middle class is self-evident, if not as simple as her reputation might suggest. Rand's conception of mental labor, and the politics to which it gives rise, are much more complicated (if in many ways no less conservative) than we usually give them credit for being. Rand's absence from the critical canon is, in this respect, continuous with the evasion of the economic that continues to structure our readings of postwar fiction. Thus this study begins with Rand, although it will do so by way of an initial detour through Lionel Trilling.

Trilling hardly seems like the best person with whom to think about the relevance of economic issues to post–World War II American literature. Yet Trilling's 1948 essay "Art and Fortune," later reprinted as the centerpiece of *The Liberal Imagination* (1950), memorably credits what Trilling sees as a crisis in the novel to the declining social significance of subjects traditionally associated with business. If, as Trilling begins his essay, "It is impossible to talk about the novel nowadays without having in our minds the question of whether or not the novel is still a living form,"[2] this is in part because "money and class," two of the novel's "defining conditions," no longer "have the same place in our social and mental life that they once had" (1275). While Trilling's reference to class clearly invokes the standard postwar belief in the imminent classlessness promised by the then-new economic boom—"the conflict of capital and labor," he writes, "is at present a contest for the possession of the goods of a single way of life, and not a cultural struggle" (1276)—his allusion to money is more mysterious. In 1948, personal income in the United States totaled $210.4 billion, up from $68.6 billion ten years earlier and two-and-a-half times higher than its pre-Depression peak of $85.8 billion in 1929.[3] Likewise, median family income in the United States was $2,854 in 1947, more than double the 1939 figure of $1,231.[4] The same abundance widely credited with ending class struggle, that is, meant that there was far *more* money in circulation when Trilling wrote his essay than at any time previously. Trilling's assertion that "money of itself no longer can engage the imagination as it once did" (1275) thus seems to depend on conditions precisely the opposite of those making for class's declining importance. It is not because of money's absence, but on the contrary its profusion, that people no longer have to spend quite so much time thinking about it.

While money and class both serve as "defining conditions" of the novel, then, they do not define the form in the same way. If class provides the stable social frameworks that the novel critiques, money—in an argument Trilling borrows, we might note, from Marx and Engels—furnishes the "impious" and corrosive social energy that breaks these frameworks down (1274). Postulating that "the real basis of the novel" was the erstwhile "tension between a middle class and an aristocracy which brings manners into observable relief" (1275), Trilling credits the form with the same historical genesis and revolutionary agency that Georg Lukács had a decade earlier in *The Historical Novel* (1937). The novel, for Trilling as for Lukács, does the same work in the cultural sphere as money does in the economic sphere, breaking down inherited social roles and forging new ones in support of the bourgeois revolution. The "falling-off in the energy of mind that once animated fiction" (1277) thus parallels the falling off of the energy of money, which having "lost some of its impulse and certainty" is "on the defensive" because it "must compete on the one hand with the ideal of security, and on the other hand with the ideal of a power that may be more directly applied" (1275). In typical cold war fashion, Trilling equates the threat of direct power with the horrors of totalitarianism unleashed during the war (1278–79) and now allied with communism (1275), thereby foreclosing the possibility of a proletarian revolution to succeed the bourgeois one. Contra Thomas Schaub's reading, however, Trilling's cold war liberalism lies not in his opposition to revolutionary social change per se, but rather in his belief that such change was only possible and/or desirable in the era of the insurgent middle class.[5]

Trilling's invocation of "the ideal of security" might likewise be read as referencing the threat of totalitarianism, but in this context it perhaps more interestingly indexes a range of postwar texts about business that likewise describe the waning of the middle class's once-abundant energies. Perhaps most famously, Whyte's *The Organization Man* argued that the Protestant Ethic of the nineteenth century was being replaced by a new Social Ethic that emphasized group consensus over individual achievement, to the detriment of those qualities of ambition and drive that once powered American business. Whyte, who based his book largely on ethnographic research among the members of the postwar middle class, describes college seniors in terms that echo Trilling's account of social malaise:

> While they talk little about money, they talk a great deal about the good life. This life is, first of all, calm and ordered. Many a senior confesses that he's thought of a career in teaching, but as he talks it appears that it is not so much that he likes teaching itself

as the sort of life he associates with it—there is a touch of elms and quiet streets in the picture. For the good life is equable; it is a nice place out in the suburbs, a wife and three children, one, maybe two cars (you know, a little knock-about for the wife to run down to the station in), and a summer place up at the lake or out on the Cape, and, later, a good college education for the children. It is not, seniors explain, the money that counts. (78)

Whyte's ironic suggestion that his interview subjects' studied indifference to money masks their desire for expensive things does not undermine but reinforces the parallel with Trilling. Whyte's seniors are able to eschew money because they will find corporate jobs that provide "security *and* opportunity both" (79). In an environment where opportunity is no longer at odds with security, the middle class has lost touch with the ethos of individual achievement—a situation that, for *Fortune* editor Whyte, sentences the corporation to the same lingering heat death that Trilling predicts for the novel.

The crisis of the middle class described by Trilling and Whyte receives its fullest exposition—albeit not as such—in *Atlas Shrugged*. In Rand's novel, a group of industrialists, inventors, and sympathetic artists goes on strike—the working title of the novel was "The Strike"[6]—to demonstrate to the world what happens when they withdraw the productive energies that politicians, intellectuals, and ungrateful employees simultaneously denounce and exploit. The symbol of this band of renegades, stamped on their own personal brand of cigarettes and cast in a three-foot gold statue suspended on a granite column in their Rocky Mountain hideaway, is the dollar sign. As one of the strikers explains to Dagny Taggart, the railroad executive who shares their values but who resists joining them until the final pages of the novel, they have adopted the dollar sign as their ensign in defiance of its common use as "the one sure-fire brand of evil," preferring instead to understand it as a badge of "achievement, . . . success, . . . ability, [and] man's creative power."[7] Like Trilling and Whyte, Rand understands money as the symbol of a productive energy belonging to an idealized past. Informing her that the dollar sign "stands for the initials of the United States," one striker tells Taggart that the United States "was the only country in history where wealth was not acquired by looting, but by production, not by force, but by trade, the only country whose money was the symbol of man's right to his own mind, to his work, to his life, to his happiness, to himself," but has lost its way because it has turned "its own monogram [into] a symbol of depravity" (630).

The strikers' regard for what another of them calls the "one magnificent century" in which the United States "redeemed the world" (711) presumably finds a sympathetic audience in Dagny, who shares their nostalgia for nineteenth-century American capitalism. In Dagny's case, this nostalgia finds its focus in her ancestor Nat Taggart, the founder of the family company for which she now works. Nat Taggart's career stands in salutary opposition to his descendant's work as Taggart Transcontinental's Vice-President of Operations. Where Dagny must continually deal with a company whose executives—exemplified by Taggart's president, her brother Jim—are timid, hyperconscious of bureaucratic restraints, and more interested in engineering profitable government regulations than in running trains, her forebear worked blessedly alone:

> He was a man who had never accepted the creed that others had the right to stop him. He set his goal and moved toward it, his way as straight as one of his rails. He never sought any loans, bonds, subsidies, land grants or legislative favors from the government. He obtained money from the men who owned it, going from door to door—from the mahogany doors of bankers to the clapboard doors of lonely farmhouses. He never talked about the public good. He merely told people that they would make big profits on his railroad, he told them why he expected the profits and he gave his reasons. He had good reasons. Through all the generations that followed, Taggart Transcontinental was one of the few railroads that never went bankrupt and the only one whose controlling stock remained in the hands of the founder's descendants. (62)

Rumored to have murdered a state legislator who tried to use regulatory chicanery to make a profit on his failure, Nat Taggart is his successor's antisocial *beau ideal*. Passing his statue in the concourse of the Taggart station she feels "a moment's rest . . . as if a burden she could not name were lightened and as if a faint current of air were touching her forehead" (63). John Galt, the organizer of the strike, makes clear the connection between Dagny's reverence for her ancestor and the strikers' ideals when he tells her that she can signal her willingness to join them by "chalk[ing] a dollar sign on the pedestal of Nat Taggart's statue—where it belongs" (884–85).

Rand notes of Galt's home in the strikers' refuge of Atlantis that it has "the primitive simplicity of a frontiersman's cabin, reduced to essential necessities . . . with a super-modern skill" (655); likewise, one of his lieutenants lives in a home "like a frontiersman's shanty thrown together to serve as a mere springboard for a long flight into the future" (710). Nor is it an accident that she situates Atlantis itself in the Mountain West. As a product of the postwar period, *Atlas Shrugged* participates in the celebration of frontier individualism that likewise animates works of American studies scholarship like Henry Nash Smith's *Virgin Land* (1950), R.W.B. Lewis's *The American Adam* (1955), and Leslie Fiedler's *Love and Death in the American Novel* (1960). At the same time, one of the novel's last scenes consists of a nightmarish depiction of stranded rail passengers rescued by a wagon train. For Rand, the pioneer only serves as a metaphor for her true hero, the robber baron. The moment of declension in her mythos is not the closing of the frontier that preoccupied Frederick Jackson Turner's heirs, but rather the moment when, say, Andrew Carnegie sells out to U.S. Steel or Thomas Edison's workshops institute team research—the moment, that is, when the individual owner or inventor cedes control to the collaborative organization of management and mental labor characteristic of the modern corporation. This explains *Atlas Shrugged*'s characteristic investment in such anachronisms, from the perspective of business history, as a family-owned railroad system or the head of a steel company who personally invents a revolutionary new alloy.

But although *Atlas Shrugged*'s plot focuses on the eventual conversion of Dagny Taggart and mill owner Hank Rearden, and spends a lot of time theorizing the natural aristocracy that links heirs like Taggart and copper magnate Francisco D'Anconia to self-made men like Galt and Rearden, its actual historical referent is not the American ruling class. Rather, I will argue in what follows, its ahistorical fantasies of owner-operators serve as a site for the conservation of *middle-class* agency in a period when the traditional basis of such agency—private property— had given way to a new definition of middle-class status based on white-collar employment. If Rand's heroes proudly define themselves as producers and traders, her villains reproduce the picture of white-collar self-abdication central to *The Organization Man*. Mr. Thompson, the head of state in the totalitarian government that coalesces as the strikers withdraw, is no jackbooted führer, but on the contrary "a man who possessed the quality of never being noticed":

> In any group of three, his person became indistinguishable, and when seen alone it seemed to evoke a group of its own, composed of the countless persons he resembled. The country had no clear image of what he looked like: his photographs had appeared on the covers of magazines as frequently as those of his predecessors in office, but people could never be quite certain which photographs were his and which were pictures of "*a* mail clerk" or "*a* white-collar worker," accompanying articles about the daily life of the undifferentiated—except that Mr. Thompson's collars were usually wilted. (494; Rand's emphases)

Literally embodying the triumph of the group over the individual central to Whyte's analysis of postwar business, the "undifferentiated" and explicitly white-collar Thompson likewise shares the organization man's lack of ambition: "Holding enormous official powers, he schemed ceaselessly to expand them, because it was expected of him by those who had pushed him into office. . . . The sole secret of his rise in life was the fact that he was a product of chance and knew it and aspired to nothing else" (494). Whereas Galt and his crew are self-contained, self-starting prime movers symbolized by Galt's invention of a motor that runs on atmospheric electricity, their opponents are mere conduits for an impersonal and purely reactive evil. Rand's villains, she insists, do not reveal their true natures when they stop casting their motives in terms of altruistic service and instead profess a will to power or profit. Rather, both forms of self-description serve as screens for the true horror behind their actions, a thanatopic "lust to destroy whatever was living, for the sake of whatever was not" (1052). By means of this contrast, Rand's novel allegorizes the transformation of middle-class identity central to the work of Whyte and other postwar social critics. Rand's particular value lies in her commitment to property relations, which will allow her to function for us in much the same way that Smith and Ricardo function for Marx: as a misguided but nonetheless useful register of the relations of production subtending social and cultural phenomena.

Among postwar social critics, as I argued in the introduction, Mills most forcefully and directly links middle-class malaise to the transformation of property relations. If, for Mills, the new middle-class white-collar worker is the deindividuated "cog and . . . beltline of the bureaucratic machinery" (80), this is because he lacks the old middle class's defining relationship to small capital. The possession of such capital made the middle-class entrepreneur, in Mills's most hyperbolic formulation, into "an 'absolute individual,' linked into a system with no authoritarian center, but held together by countless, free, shrewd transactions" (9). It is of course the case that this account of American economic history obscures significant disparities in who could own property, not to mention the fact that for much of this period some Americans were owned *as* property. Mills's investment in this version of the American past might, moreover, seem even more suspect when placed alongside Rand's strikingly similar sense of the market as matrix for the ideal social system. Consider, for instance, the following passage from *Atlas Shrugged*, another of the strikers' rhetorical set-pieces about money:

> Money rests on the axiom that every man is the owner of his mind and his effort. Money allows no power to prescribe the value of your effort except the voluntary choice of the man who is willing to trade you his effort in return. . . . Money permits no deals except those to mutual benefit by the unforced judgment of the traders. Money demands of you the recognition that men must work for their own benefit, not for their own injury, for their gain, not their loss—the recognition that they are not beasts of burden, born to carry the weight of your misery—that you must offer them values, not wounds—that the common bond among men is not the exchange of suffering, but the exchange of *goods*. . . . And when men live by trade—with reason, not force, as their final arbiter—it is the best product that wins, the best performance, the man of best judgement and highest ability—and the degree of a man's productiveness is the degree of his reward. (383; Rand's emphasis)

For Rand, the market is not the source of social inequality but the mechanism for eliminating hierarchical relationships, the basis for what is in effect a functioning anarchy. In the strikers' haven, there are "no laws . . . , no rules, no formal organization of any kind," other than the "custom[ ]" that forbids "the word '*give*'" (659). On this basis, the strikers erect a perfectly functioning social system that for the first time fulfills man's nature as "a social being" (690). Despite the vast gulf separating their politics, then, Rand shares Mills's vision of a society structured not around an "authoritarian center" but through a multiplicity of "free, shrewd" exchanges.

Whereas Rand sees this system as the ideal and heretofore unrealized fulfillment of human history, however, Mills sees it as a moment now irretrievably lost to the "centralization of small properties" (xiv) and the resulting concentration of economic control. The process of middle-class expropriation that culminated in the mid-twentieth-century United States, as a factor in the ongoing centralization of property, helps to explain *Atlas Shrugged*'s anachronistic investment in the managerial revolution that began in the mid-nineteenth century, and was more or less a fait accompli by World War II. The idea of a railroad still owned and managed by its founder's descendants completely belies the railroad industry's historical participation in this revolution, as those familiar with Alfred Chandler's *The Visible Hand* (1977) will recognize. Railroads, Chandler argues, played a central role in the shift from "small, personally owned and managed enterprises . . . coordinated and monitored by market price mechanisms" to large, vertically integrated organizations "monitored and coordinated by salaried employees" because they were, along with telegraph companies, the first businesses "to require a large number of full-time managers to coordinate, control, and evaluate the activities of a number of widely scattered operating units."[8] The extent and complexity of railroads' operations, that is, drove the development of precisely the forms of bureaucratic administration by professional managers that rendered owner-managers like Nat Taggart obsolete. Dagny Taggart thus fights a battle that, in a more historically accurate account, Nat Taggart would already have lost. Or perhaps even more accurately, she fights a battle against forces that Nat Taggart would himself have set in motion.

Rand's celebration of owner-managers like Taggart and Rearden might make sense, however, if we see them not as a belated generation of robber barons but rather as outsized representatives of the middle-class entrepreneur whose historical twilight had occurred more recently. And in fact, the novel itself suggests this connection insofar as the strikers give up the giant industries they are unable to run in the modern world for the life of middle-class proprietors. Dagny, having stumbled prematurely on their mountain hideaway, finds the oilman Ellis Wyatt, for instance, supervising just two workers (665), while "Calvin Atwood of the Atwood Light and Power Company of New York is making the shoes" (668) and others have opened small shops on "the valley's single street" (670), among them a former automaker whom Dagny spies "weighing a chunk of butter" at his new grocery store (670). This transformation of captains of industry into shopkeepers, while meant to highlight the dignity of free trade, suggests the historical dilemma behind Rand's simultaneous love and fear of the nineteenth-century past. Recognizing that her traders' utopia is unfeasible in the contemporary world, and able to realize it only in the terms of a nostalgic regression, Rand cannot depict the new world of large industry *and* individual trade that the strikers promise to build after the old system's failure. The novel ends with Galt announcing, "We are going back to the world" (1074), unable actually to show what happens when they do.

In its form, then, *Atlas Shrugged* reveals the problem inherent in its own celebration of the capitalist producer and trader: the way in which capitalism itself, by continually concentrating property in larger and more complex forms, leads to the disenfranchisement of individuals that Rand abhors. Ever more centralized property, and not external controls, undermines the market of free individuals that can only be restored through an artificial return to smaller-scale capitalism. This is not, however, to suggest that Rand's investment in a (by mid-century) largely residual mode of property ownership likewise marks her politics as residual. On the contrary, Mills for one stressed the durability of "the ideology suitable for the nation of small capitalists" in a United States "transformed from a nation of small capitalists into a nation of hired employees" (34). For Mills, the persistence of the politics of small capital, "as if that small-propertied world were still a going concern" (34), ironically served the big business interests responsible for small capital's difficulties:

> at the same time that small firms are being driven to the wall, they are being used by the big firms with which they publicly identify themselves. This fact underlies the ideology and the frustration of the small urban capitalist; it is the reason why his aggression is directed at labor and government. (51)

Big business, Mills argued, uses "small businessmen [as] shock troops in the battle against labor unions and government controls," thereby "exploit[ing] in its own interests the very anxieties it has created for small business" (53). *Atlas Shrugged* exemplifies this process, blurring the distinction between small and large capital by stressing what Rand sees as their shared conflict with government.[9]

Rand's decision to make Dagny Taggart a railroad executive makes sense insofar as by 1957 the railroad industry exemplified the industrial decline that *Atlas Shrugged* imputes to the economy as a whole. Here, too, though, Rand fails to get her business history exactly right. At one point during a press conference held to discuss the opening of a new rail line, Dagny tells the assembled reporters that "the average profit of railroads has been two percent of the capital invested" (220). Assuming that *Atlas Shrugged* does in fact take place in the late fifties, this statistic slightly undershoots the actual figure, even for what had been lean years for the industry. According to John F. Stover's 1961 *American Railroads*, "the four largest railroads had a net income of only 2.9 percent" in 1957, although the figure for the industry as a whole since 1945 had "ranged from 2.76 per cent to 4.31 per cent" and "averaged . . . 3.64 per cent."[10] More important than the actual figure, however, is the way in which Rand implicitly poses this particular industry as a representative of the postwar economy more generally. There is no doubt that the railroads were in trouble in the late fifties, and in fact had been in decline since rail mileage had peaked in 1916.[11] In *Atlas Shrugged*, however, the progressive decline of Taggart Transcontinental emblematizes an economy more like that of the Depression thirties than the boom fifties. The reader's introduction to Dagny, riding a Taggart train diverted by a broken switch and halted by a faulty signal light, anticipates a world in which—even before the total collapse that sets wagon trains in motion—goods are scarce, machines are breaking down and cannot be fixed, and streets are filled with empty storefronts.[12] But of course the railroad industry's difficulties were not typical of the postwar economy. In the same year, for instance, airlines posted a 7.75 percent return on their investments,[13] and much of the railroads' troubles in these years was the result of competition from both the airlines and the equally well-off trucking industry.

This is not to endorse the market-based analysis of the railroads' vicissitudes that have governed the most recent round of attacks on what is left of U.S. rail service, however. As Amtrak's proponents have pointed out in response to attacks on its inefficiency, the carrier receives only a small percentage of the government funding devoted to highways and the infrastructure of the aviation industry.[14] This pattern was already established by the late fifties, belying Rand's sense—which, of course, remains central to conservative rhetoric—of government as the purely negative enemy of business. In the postwar period railroads were, to some degree, victims of aggressive government regulation left over from their glory days in the late nineteenth century.[15] At the same time, however, the industry's competitors benefited not only from the absence of similar regulation but also from positive government action, including massive direct funding for highways, airports, and other facilities.[16] As Kim McQuaid has pointed out, World War II and the cold war led to a new symbiosis between government and big business, with the state more and more exerting its financial, regulatory, and even diplomatic and military powers in the interests of business.[17]

On one hand, *Atlas Shrugged* fully acknowledges this new corporate-state intimacy through its depiction of executives like Jim Taggart and the steel maker Orren Boyle, who devote their time to engineering government regulations that allow them to ruin their competitors and steal their products. Indeed, Rand's description of Boyle reads, in the post-Enron world, like a left indictment of corporate welfare and the CEO star culture:

> Orren Boyle had appeared from nowhere, five years ago, and had since made the cover of every national news magazine. He had started out with a hundred thousand dollars of his own and a two-hundred-million-dollar loan from the government. Now he headed an enormous concern which had swallowed many smaller companies. This proved, he liked to say, that individual ability still had a chance to succeed in the world. (49)

Here Rand's novel seems to dramatize Mills's sardonic comment six years earlier that "nobody talks more of free enterprise and competition and of the best man winning than the man who inherited his father's store or farm" (36). *Atlas Shrugged* is filled with similar critiques of businessmen who spend their time "running to Washington" rather than "running . . . mills" (283). Such depictions at times make it seem as though the novel is as opposed to big business as to Rand's more expected government and union targets.

But this is not the case, insofar as Rand sees men like Taggart and Boyle as abberations from capitalist business practice rather than its norm. Rand's insistence, driven home by Taggart's final breakdown, that such men act out of a perverse death-drive rather than self-interest highlights her flawed picture of postwar capitalism. In her world, as we have seen, steel companies prosper because their owners invent new metals, not because Taft-Hartley and other legislation weakens the labor movement or because the Korean War generates sharp demand for steel while accelerated depreciation encourages steel companies to expand.[18] Likewise, oil companies succeed because the young "prodig[ies]" who run them discover "rich new oil field[s], at a time when the pumps were stopping in one famous field after another" (16–17), not because the U.S. government exerts its power to open up Middle Eastern oil fields to American companies.[19] This is not to say that the federal government, after World War II, became simply the tool of big business. In fact, both big oil and big steel endured regulatory incursions from antimonopolist legislators from the South and West. Even these legislators were operating, however, not in the interests of public service but rather in those of small producers in the same field who briefly managed to swing the ideology of small capital in their favor.[20] In *Atlas Shrugged*, by contrast, government action is only inimical to business, and companies thrive best in an atmosphere where, as one character says of the temporarily booming state of Colorado, government "does nothing . . . outside of keeping law courts and a police department" (254).

Rand's own brief history of the railroads, first published two years after *Atlas Shrugged*, makes clear how her understanding of government as purely antagonistic to business requires her to blur the distinction between small and large capital. In "Notes on the History of American Free Enterprise" (1959), Rand reduces the early history of the railroads to a battle between individualistic capitalists and coercive government regulations, arguing that "the evils, popularly ascribed to big industrialists, were not the result of an unregulated industry, but of government power over industry."[21] This argument is most convincing when she contends that Cornelius Vanderbilt only engaged in stock market manipulation because city and state politicians reneged on promises of favorable action, hoping to make a profit by selling Vanderbilt stock short (105–6). Elsewhere, however, the lines between business and government get blurrier, and can only be maintained by the same problematic distinction that she makes in *Atlas Shrugged* between proper and improper businessmen—or, as she calls them in "Notes on the History of American Free Enterprise," "free enterprisers" and those who "achieve[ ] power by legislative intervention in business" (104). As in the novel, Rand's investment in the free market leads her to claim not just the moral but the strategic high ground for businesses that go it alone, arguing that "the degree of government help received by any one railroad, stood in direct proportion to that railroad's troubles and failures. The railroads with the worst histories of scandal, double-dealing, and bankruptcy were the ones that had received the greatest amount of help from the government" (103). Yet Rand's own description of the eminently successful Central Pacific on the subsequent page belies her claim not to have discovered any "exceptions to this rule" (103):

> The Central Pacific—which was built by the "Big Four" of California, on federal subsidies—was the railroad which was guilty of all the evils popularly held against railroads.

For almost thirty years, the Central Pacific controlled California, held a monopoly, and permitted no competitor to enter the state. It charged disastrous rates, changed them every year, and took virtually the entire profit of the California farmers or shippers, who had no other railroad to turn to. What made this possible? It was done through the power of the California legislature. The Big Four controlled the legislature and held the state closed to competitors by legal restrictions—such as, for instance, a legislative act which gave the Big Four exclusive control of the entire coastline of California and forbade any other railroad to enter any port. During these thirty years, many attempts were made by private interests to build competing railroads in California and break the monopoly of the Central Pacific. These attempts were defeated—not by methods of free trade and free competition, but by *legislative action*. (104; Rand's emphasis)

What is most interesting here is not that Rand contradicts her assertion that recourse to government leads inevitably to business failure, although that is certainly the case. Rather, it is the way in which she is enabled to do this by the implication that the Central Pacific's manipulation of the legislature originates not with the railroad but with the legislature itself—that it is legislative and not corporate "action" that is at issue here. This sleight of hand enables Rand to transform what might otherwise be described as a conflict between small and large capital—with the latter employing legislative action among its weapons against "competing railroads"—into a conflict between business per se and government per se. Lining up the sides in this way obscures the distinction between big and small capital.

If there is no distinction between big and small capital, then the conflict "between holders of small property . . . and holders of larger property" (Mills, *White* 55) that those like Corey and Mills saw as central to pre-twentieth-century U.S. history likewise disappears. The ills of small business, many of them caused in both the long and short term by big business, become the imagined ills of big business; the defense of big business against the very state that it just as often employs to its own ends becomes small business's duty. No longer anchored in actual socioeconomic conditions as they had been through the Progressive Era, the politics of small capital became more powerful than ever following the war, when they were pressed into the service of the large capital that had been small capital's historic enemy. It makes sense that the politics of small capital would continue to appeal to the remants of the petit bourgeoisie, even if they were being manipulated in the interests of another class. Less logical is why they would appeal to the structurally proletarianized—*and therefore no longer really middle class*—mass of white-collar workers for whom a more traditional class politics might make more sense.

One obvious answer is the enormous political pressure deployed against class politics throughout U.S. history, particularly during the cold war. Another is the fear of downward mobility through being identified with the working classes that Mills notes in his discussion of why white-collar workers do not unionize

(301–23). In Mills's time, many white-collar workers enjoyed remuneration for their labor far superior to that of their small-capitalist parents. Their inheritors, as we have already noted, continue to enjoy significant advantages in pay, status, and authority that depend upon their distinction, however phantasmatic from a structural point of view, from others who must sell their labor in the contemporary economy. Finally, less obviously, capital continues to seduce the "disappearing middle" with things like home and stock ownership that blur the distinction between property and capital,[22] or between capital and capital that matters, thereby keeping white-collar workers invested in the ideology of property as such.[23]

But Rand suggests an additional avenue whereby white-collar workers are kept affectively routed into a politics of small capital that no longer serves their interests. This is through a structure of feeling that makes them continue to refight the lost battle of small capital as though it were continually happening again in their own work lives. We began with the sense, indexed in such disparate places as Trilling's postmortem for the novel and Whyte's lament for the Protestant Ethic, that the middle class had lost the dynamic energies that characterized its role since the beginnings of modernity. Rand, by rewriting American business history as a struggle between capitalist rationality and the death-drive expressed in senseless government regulations, reinstates the bourgeois revolution as a battle yet to be won. The coup de grace of *Atlas Shrugged*'s regulators is Directive 10–289, a governmental order that forbids people to change jobs, or to invent new products, or to make either more or less money in a given year than they did in the one in which the rule went into effect. The ostensible purpose of this ruling is to temporarily freeze the economy and thereby prevent it from worsening in a time of crisis, though as Jim Taggart's semihysterical reaction makes clear, its actual purpose is to impose the stasis associated in the history of the West with feudalism:

> We'll be safe for the first time in centuries. Everybody will know his place and job, and everybody else's place and job—and we won't be at the mercy of every stray crank with a new idea. . . . There's been enough invented already—enough for everybody's comfort—why should they be allowed to go on inventing? . . . Just because of a few restless, ambitious adventurers? Should we sacrifice the contentment of the whole of mankind to a few non-conformists? . . . We're through with them. We've won. This is our age. Our world. We're going to have security—for the first time in centuries—for the first time since the beginning of the industrial revolution! (504)

Another of the co-conspirators responds, a bit too frankly for his comrades' tastes, that they are thus proposing "the anti-industrial revolution" (504). But it would be more accurate to say "the antimodern revolution," since what they desire is to reverse time to a moment before the "adventurers" of the European mercantile class defied the social stability of the Middle Ages with capital as both their weapon and their goal.

Rand's own project is not to turn time back quite so far, but rather to stop it at the moment of the bourgeoisie's emergence, when the members of this class played the heroic role mourned by Trilling, Whyte, and others. The reinvigorated conflict between bourgeoisie and feudalism plays itself out throughout the novel, for instance in a scene in which Hank Rearden defies a representative of the State Science Instititue who wants him to delay placing his new metal on the market out of fear of its socially disruptive consequences. Rearden's response is to reject such concerns out of hand, relying instead on the language of pure scientific rationality: "If you have anything to say to me about the physical danger of Rearden Metal, say it. Drop the rest of it. Fast. I don't speak that language" (170). Here Rearden is Gailileo defying the Catholic Church, as well as a merchant with an eye to profit. *Atlas Shrugged*'s new Atlantis, as its name suggests, is not only a nostalgic reinvention of nineteenth-century entrepreneurial capitalism but also— with its society of capitalists, inventors, and artists—a fantasy of the Renaissance as well.

Rearden's answer to his interlocutor suggests the appeal of this second layer of the novel's historical palimpsest to postwar white-collar workers whose work was understood to be alienatingly social. In Mills's formulation, "The one thing they do not do is live by making things; rather, they live off the social machineries that organize and coordinate the people who do make things" (65). For commentators less attuned than Mills to the historical role of property ownership in maintaining middle-class autonomy, the problem with white-collar work was simply the pressure for consensus—Whyte's Social Ethic—induced by working with people rather than things. Rand's earlier novel *The Fountainhead* had mounted a strong defense of individualism against the threat of bureaucratic constraints with its story of a heroic architect, Howard Roark, who defies corporate employers, critics, and even clients in order to build what he wants.[24] Similarly, the neofeudalism that the villains seek to impose in *Atlas Shrugged* can be seen as an extreme version of The Organization, an institutional structure whose demands supersede the agency, and sap the individuality, of the men working within it. Rearden, staking his claim on the properties of things, becomes an antiorganization man whose heroism resides in his defiance of social imperatives.

Fatally attached to market exchange as the only possible basis for desirable social relations, Rand denigrates all other forms of social relatedness as inherently deindividualizing and alienating. The question is, to what end? One possible answer is that Rand provides a kind of Walter Mitty-esque fantasy for white-collar workers who can eat shit at the office while imagining themselves as steadfast Hank Reardens. David Riesman suggests as much when he argues in *The Lonely Crowd*—a book with its own suspicions of the social—that *The Fountainhead*'s Howard Roark is "the very apotheosis of the lonely success, to be admired perhaps . . . but too stagey to be imitated," a figure who allows readers to feel superior to others while remaining "quite unaware of [their] own tendencies to submission in the small, undramatic situations of daily life" (156). But to figure Rand in this way would be to confine her influence to a few lonely fans (precisely our stereotype of Rand), and to ignore the similarities between her worldview and that of postwar white-collar workers more generally—not excluding those of us who work in the academy. Rand depicts a world in which people experience intensely passionate relationships with their work, and secondarily with people who are valued, and in turn value others, on the basis of work. That is, she presents something much like Stefano Harney and Frederick Moten's description of academic work, in which academics, approaching their work through both "a nostalgic and histori-cally inaccurate view of craftwork," and an equally misguided model of "liberal individualism and market exchanges," misread their place in the social relations of production defined by capitalism.[25] If, as Andrew Ross has recently argued, academic labor provides a model for labor exploitation more generally in the new knowledge economy,[26] then we might say that capitalism has finally caught up with Rand. For Rand's novels do not simply project a fantasy of old-middle-class property ownership for white-collar employees. They also struggle to reimagine white-collar work as itself a form of property ownership and exchange—a move that requires refiguring all property as intellectual property.

If Rand's utopian vision requires a middle class restored to its heroic early strug-gle with feudalism, or to capitalism's nineteenth-century heyday, *Atlas Shrugged* indirectly acknowledges the post-middle-class present through the motif of the strike. Ostensibly, the purpose of the strike is to defy the argument "that the indus-trialist is a parasite" whose "workers . . . create his wealth" and "to show to the world who depends on whom, who supports whom, who is the source of wealth, who makes whose livelihood possible and what happens to whom when who walks out" (684). But in fact going on strike undermines the whole politics of property associated with these men and women, since it means imagining the site of agency not as property but as labor that can be withdrawn. Ironically, this is most clear not in the case of Rand's artists and intellectuals—the composers and philosophers who refuse any longer to work in the outside world—but rather in her capitalists. For these figures do not take their property with them, but rather leave their coal mines and oil fields to fall into disrepair once severed from the animating mental labor of their former owners. As the mine owner Ken Dannager says just before he joins the strike, "Why should I leave a deed or a will? I don't want to help the looters to pretend that private property still exists. I am complying with the system which they have established. They do not need me, they say, they only need my coal. Let them take it" (415–16). Likewise, Dagny is initially put on Galt's trail when she and Rearden find the remains of Galt's motor sitting on a junk pile in the now-abandoned factory where Galt built it, before leaving in protest of the employees' decision to run the factory on the principle of "from each according to his ability, to each according to his need." As Galt explains his decision,

> I looked at my motor for the last time, before I left. I thought of the men who claim
> that wealth is a matter of natural resources—and of the men who claim that wealth is a

matter of seizing the factories—and of the men who claim that machines condition their brains. Well, *there* was the motor to condition them, and there it remained as just exactly what it is without man's mind—as a pile of metal scraps and wires, going to rust. (688)

Although meant to critique (Rand's misunderstanding of) Marxism, this passage curiously comes around to the central Marxist point that property is worthless without the infusion of labor. The strikers refuse to sell the only thing that they, as workers, have to sell—their mental labor: one of them, refusing Dagny's offer of a managerial job on any terms though willing to take a menial one, tells her, "My mind is not on the market any longer" (627).

While Rand means to reorient our understanding of what counts as productive labor—giving us a world in which owners supply both capital and labor, and workers at best offer little more than loyalty—the redefinition of labor caused by the expansion of the white-collar workforce continually takes her project in unintended directions. For at the same time that the expansion of white-collar labor was transforming the middle class from owners to workers, it was also transforming labor itself from hand work to brain work. The number of mental laborers in the American economy surpassed the number of manual laborers for the first time in 1956, the year before *Atlas Shrugged* was published.[27] This shift was most deeply felt, according to Mills, in the professions, where old ideologies of autonomy and self-direction came up against the increasing prominence of salaried work for organizations (113), and Atlantis's doctor exemplifies this moment of transition. Telling Dagny that he "quit when medicine was placed under State control," he goes on to say that he could not work for politicians who wanted to "dictate the purpose for which my years of study had been spent, or the conditions of my work, or my choice of patients, or the amount of my reward" (687). Here Rand's antigovernment ideology, like that of the opponents of the Clinton health care plan, provides the thinnest of glosses over what is in essence a complaint about one's exile from the means of production—one's transformation, that is, into a worker. As recent years have made clear, capital is just as likely as the state to effect this transformation among medical professionals.[28]

If the strikers continually threaten to devolve from property owners to mental laborers—thereby replicating the fate of the contemporary middle class—Rand's solution is to reconfigure mental labor as itself a form of property ownership. Another effect of depicting Hank Rearden and Ellis Wyatt as inventors as well as industrialists is to suggest that even if they leave behind their physical property, what they have withdrawn from the world is not their labor but rather the even more valuable property embodied in their ideas. For Rand, artists practicing what Szalay has called the "politics of textual integrity"—the privileging of artistic products over the processes that generate them[29]—exemplify the recondensation of mental labor more generally into property. The artists who live in Atlantis are there not simply to offer aesthetic representations of the strikers' worldview— symphonies that "embody every human act and thought that had ascent as its motive" (20); plays about "human greatness" (723)—but because they ultimately perform the same activity as the inventors and businessmen. All three groups exchange (or refuse to exchange, where the outside world is concerned) the products of their mind. Thus the other activity, besides shopkeeping, in which the strikers most frequently and fervently participate is performance: not the performance-as-process opposed by Szalay's late-modernist proponents of textual integrity, but discrete performances for pay that reaffirm the ability of ideas to serve as alienable property. When Dagny is shocked to discover that Galt has been spending his evenings in Atlantis lecturing on physics, he tells her that the strikers, committed to denying the outside world the fruits of their intellects by working only menial jobs, spend their time together "trad[ing] the achievements of our real professions. Richard Halley is to give concerts, Kay Ludlow is to appear in two plays written by authors who do not write for the outside world—and I give lectures, reporting on the work I've done during the year [at] ten dollars per person for the course" (714). Here it is not their minds that the strikers take off the market, but the products of their minds—a crucial distinction, since it reverses the historical trajectory of the middle class by transforming them from mental laborers to owners and sellers of intangible but nonetheless real property.

Rand makes the logic behind this move explicit in her 1964 essay "Patents and Copyrights," arguing that

> every type of productive work involves a combination of mental and physical effort: of thought and of physical action to translate that thought into a material form. The proportion of these two elements varies in different types of work. At the lowest end of the scale, the mental effort required to perform unskilled manual labor is minimal. At the other end, what the patent and copyright laws acknowledge is the paramount role of mental effort in the production of material values; these laws protect the mind's contribution in its purest form: the origination of an *idea*. The subject of patents and copyrights is *intellectual* property. (*Capitalism* 130; Rand's emphases)

Rand here affirms the superiority of mental labor, which lies in its counterintuitively greater productivity. By preventing the "unauthorized reproduction of the object," she goes on to note, intellectual property "law declares, in effect, that the physical labor of copying is not the source of the object's value" (*Capitalism* 130). Physical labor does not create, but only reproduces; only mental labor, contra Mills and other theorists of white-collar work, actually makes things. Rearden, refusing the government's offer of "an impressive profit, an immediate profit, much larger than you could hope to realize from the sale of the metal for the next twenty years" (171) in exchange for not producing it, tells his puzzled interlocutor, "Because it's *mine*. Do you understand that word?" (172; Rand's emphasis). Because it is his—because, that is, its formula is his—he and he alone can make and sell the metal whose status as property lies not in its physical instantiations but in his ownership of an idea.

Rand's reconfiguration of property as ideas rather than things reveals how mainstream—if not in fact prescient—her economic thinking was. In particular, this move anticipates the key concept of Gary Becker's influential 1964 study *Human Capital*. Citing "a realization that the growth of physical capital, at least as conventionally measured, [now] explains a relatively small part of the growth of income in most countries," Becker focuses his study on "activities that influence future monetary and physical income by increasing the resources in people," especially education.[30] Becker's argument quite legitimately attempts to take into account the shift from industrial capitalism to the new form—variously called, among other things, "postindustrialism," "post-Fordism," "network capitalism," and "informatization"—"in which providing services and manipulating information are at the heart of economic production."[31] But Becker's model of human capital also implicitly elides the difference between this change in the relations of production and the less tenable assertion that the binary class system no longer applies to capitalism. It does so by fudging the definition of "capital." Insofar as he focuses on "monetary and physical income," Becker ignores the distinction—fundamental to the Marxist understanding of class—between those who own capital and those who must sell their labor to its owners. The concept of human capital thus fails to distinguish between intellectual property (an idea that one can sell for profit) and skills (that one can use to bargain for a better income from one's employer). It is no doubt true, as Becker's successor Pierre Bourdieu argued in 1984, that "a growing proportion of the ruling fraction derives, if not its power, at least the legitimacy of its power from educational capital acquired in formally pure and perfect academic competition, rather than directly from economic capital."[32] Of course, the Bush administration has reminded us that old-fashioned economic capital still goes a long way, just as Bush's Yale degree suggests the limits of Daniel Bell's 1973 assertion that "the university, which once reflected the status system of the society, has now become the arbiter of class position."[33] But more importantly, concepts such as human capital and Bourdieu's cultural capital are problematic in that—precisely through their focus on education—they make it possible to understand employed mental laborers as entrepreneurs. They do, that is, precisely what Rand's novels do.

Bourdieu himself suggests the limits of the concept of cultural capital when he notes that

> although executives and engineers have the monopoly of the means of symbolic appropriation of the cultural capital objectified in the form of instruments, machines and so forth which are essential to the exercise of the power of economic capital over this equipment, and derive from their monopoly a real managerial power and relative privileges within the firm, the profits accruing from their cultural capital are at least partially appropriated by those who have power over this capital, i.e., those who possess the economic capital needed to ensure the concentration and utilization of cultural capital.[34]

The possessors of even high-level cultural capital, that is, remain beholden as employees to those who own economic capital. If this is a problem for those at the top of white-collar pyramids, it is even more so for those lower down, for whom curtailed autonomy can translate directly into the loss of money and job security. The recent trend among downsizing companies of firing experienced white-collar workers in favor of younger, cheaper ones, for instance,[35] provides a sharp rebuke to the more celebratory accounts of human capital. Such downsized workers are free to trade their human capital precisely as workers are free to trade their labor: largely at the will of those who can purchase it. In this respect, the idea of the mental laborer as entrepreneur—which arose at a time when stable jobs were equated with ennui—now provides a fantasy of agency within an economy in which job security is increasingly tenuous. Witness, for instance, the *Wall Street Journal*'s CareerJournal.com article "Should You Stay Energized by Changing Your Job Frequently?"[36]

Such romanticized—and deeply Randian—notions of craftsmanship and liberal exchange prevent contemporary white-collar workers from understanding themselves as workers. Harney and Moten provide an example close to home when they suggest that one reason tenure-track academics are so willing to participate in the exploitation of casual adjunct labor is that they view their work through the lens of "liberal individualism and market exchanges" rather than paid employment.[37] Academics' sense that some kinds of intellectual labor (research) are superior to others because, in Randian terms, they are solitary and thus creative forestalls more collective (if less glamorous) ways of conceiving the labor done in universities. In this respect some tenure-track academics' resistance to academic unions no doubt bears out Mills's argument that the "status psychology of white-collar employees" is a major impediment to white-collar unionism (312, 301–23 passim). Academics thus prove themselves to be prototypical white-collar workers at precisely the moment when, Ross argues, white-collar workers are becoming more like academics, translating the characteristically academic-artistic investment in "nonmonetary rewards—mental or creative gratification—as compensation for work" into things like the dot-comers' heroic cult of overwork.[38] Rand's characters would be totally at home in this structure of feeling, which they would recognize depends not so much upon the Romantic conception that "*the artist cannot afford to be rewarded well*" as upon the more characteristically American notion that the artist cannot afford to be rewarded well *except by the market.*[39]

Rand's relatively novel understanding of mental labor as entrepreneurship depends upon the same free market fundamentalism, and the same shift of focus from big capital to big government, as her nostalgia for nineteenth-century small property. She has her villains, for instance, include the following language outlawing intellectual property as part of Directive 10–289:

Point Three. All patents and copyrights, pertaining to any devices, inventions, formulas, processes and works of any nature whatsoever, shall be turned over to the nation as a patriotic emergency gift. . . . The Unification Board shall then license the use of such patents and copyrights to all applicants, equally and without discrimination, for the purpose of eliminating monopolistic practices, discarding obsolete products and making the best available to the whole nation. No trademarks, brand names or copyrighted titles shall be used. . . . All private trademarks and brand names are hereby abolished. (499–500)

Here, predictably, it is the regulative state that seeks to undermine by fiat the property rights—in this case, intellectual property rights—of individuals.

The more recent history of intellectual property suggests, however, that Rand once again misses how capitalism itself undermines these rights in its relentless drive toward centralization. For Rand, as we have seen, property becomes property through the process whereby an individual realizes his or her productivity. Hence she asserts, elsewhere in her essay on patents and copyrights, that "a *discovery* cannot be patented, only an *invention*" (*Capitalism* 130; Rand's emphases). As anyone familiar with debates over the property status of the human genome will recognize, however, it is precisely the transformation of "discoveries" into property to which capitalism has turned in its latest phase. Global capital is currently reorganizing itself around what Caren Irr calls a "virtual land grab," a return to the stage of primitive accumulation whose object this time around is "the sudden and immensely profitable treatment of a vast array of existing relations as property relations":

> In this enclosure of the global textual commons, Disney has seized monopolistic hold over the folk and fairy tales of a Brothers Grimm-type European heritage; Time-Warner aims to acquire exclusive access to recent history in the form of the Zapruder tapes; pharmaceuticals companies lay claim to the biological commons of the rainforests; and corporate-funded geneticists race to see who will decode and patent the information contained in the human genome. By converting existing natural and cultural resources into certain kinds of texts, corporations are now able to claim monopolistic ownership in a range of potentially supervaluable intellectual commodities.[40]

Just as the original phase of primitive accumulation freed the lower classes from feudalism by rendering them landless laborers, so this new phase transforms knowledge and information previously held in common into the site of corporate employees' mental labor. The profits from this labor accrue not to the individual creator claiming his "right to the product of his mind" (Rand, *Capitalism* 130), but rather to the large corporations that manipulate the law to transform found materials into their property.

Within this framework, the notion that mental laborers are entrepreneurs encourages white-collar employees to identify with the corporate owners of intellectual property, just as home ownership encourages the members of the middle class to identify with the owners of property as such. In both cases, big capital benefits from a confusion between what it owns, the means of production, and what the members of the middle class own, their labor and (if they are lucky) nonproductive personal property. Just because capital has been severed from individual producers and vested in corporate entities does not mean, of course, that it has ceased to exist, or that individuals no longer benefit from it. On the contrary, as Mills argued in 1951, the fact "that the power of property has been bureaucratized in the corporation does not diminish that power; indeed, bureaucracy increases the use and the protection of property power" (111). In this regard, Rand's mistake—which I have been arguing is her failure to distinguish between an earlier model of middle-class small property and property as such—has been an enormously productive one for the last half-century of capitalism. Intellectual property law as it has been codified in recent decisions, Irr argues, promotes corporate ownership of texts not only "over public interest in the distribution of knowledge" but also over against a largely residual notion of authorship: "in the late twentieth century, the author can be construed as an almost entirely anonymous creature—faceless, factual, dispersed into the events in which he was an integral but somehow also impersonal player."[41] If the author now sounds like a classic postwar organization man, this suggests the extent to which Corey and Mills's accounts of white-collar expropriation have been fulfilled in the new era of intellectual property, in which ideas rather than things have become the characteristic object of production. The academic Left has been talking for some time now about how universities are becoming more like businesses, although for the purposes of critiquing contemporary capitalism the larger and more pressing problem may be the fact that businesses are becoming more like universities. As Ross argues, the university which during the cold war abetted capital by serving as "a medium for subsidizing or socializing capital's cost of training, research, and development" has now "become a site of capital accumulation in its own right, where the profitability of research and teaching programs and the marketability of learning products is fast coming to the fore as the primary driving force behind academic policy."[42]

Within this rapidly coalescing regime, academics' understanding of their research work as both craft labor and personal property does not just reflect a general white-collar worldview with its origins in the postwar era and authors like Rand. It also limns the shape of much more profitable sectors of the economy. Take, for instance, the recent debates over music piracy, in which the members of Metallica and other celebrity musicians argued that file sharing abrogated their property rights. At the same time, some artists lower down the record-label food chain argued that they actually profited from file sharing, insofar as most of their income came not from publishing but from touring, for which the dissemination of their music provided publicity.[43] In Corey's terms, we might see artists like Metallica as well-paid employees taking on the mantle of small-property owners for the benefit of big corporations, and to the detriment of other artists who are either more exploited employees of the labels or actual small businesspeople. In this case, the nostalgia for the market that we have tracked through Rand's work becomes the basis for the extraction of surplus value from mental laborers carrying on their backs the corpse of what we used to call "the middle class."

CHAPTER TWO

Race Man, Organization Man, *Invisible Man*

IN A FREQUENTLY cited passage near the beginning of *Invisible Man*, Ellison's unnamed narrator quotes the deathbed advice of his grandfather, a former slave, to the narrator's father:

> "Son, after I'm gone I want you to keep up the good fight. I never told you, but our life is a war and I have been a traitor all my born days, a spy in the enemy's country ever since I give up my gun back in the Reconstruction. Live with your head in the lion's mouth. I want you to overcome 'em with yeses, undermine 'em with grins, agree 'em to death and destruction, let 'em swoller you till they vomit or bust wide open."[1]

This scene strikes a keynote for the novel, many of whose major characters likewise seem engaged—to varying degrees of success and with disparate ethical valences—in the same project of somehow undermining the dominant power structure by giving it what it wants. Thus the sharecropper Trueblood manipulates the expectations of his white audiences to profit from his story of accidental incest with his daughter;[2] the Booker T. Washington-like college president Bledsoe maintains his power by catering to powerful white people; and (most ambiguously) Tod Clifton drops out of the Brotherhood to peddle dancing Sambo dolls.[3] Perhaps most importantly, the narrator himself follows this pattern in his role as what Ellison called "the Negro individualist, the personality that breaks away from the pre-individual community of southern Negro life to win its way in the jim crow world by guile, uncletomming, or ruthlessness."[4]

Critics of the novel have, with good reason, usually understood the grandfather's advice in terms of the performative strategies of resistance and survival adopted by African Americans within the racist society of the United States. As Houston Baker puts it, the grandfather, "pretending to affirm the designs of the white society around him . . . represents the trickster as subtle deceiver."[5] From the perspective of this book, however, the most interesting thing about the grandfather's model of "Negro individualism" is its intriguing resemblance to the model of individualism developed in postwar critiques of the white middle class. In *The Organization Man*, for instance, Whyte claims that potential individualists "*within* organization life" are able "to control their environment rather than be controlled by it" because they adopt "surface uniformities" as "protective coloration." "[W]ell aware that they are not too easily distinguishable from the others in the outward obeisances paid to the good opinions of others," these figures "disarm society" (12) much as the narrator's grandfather instructs his progeny to disarm white people. More generally, *Invisible Man* participates in the same reification of threatened individuality that, according to Melley, links postwar fiction to works of social criticism like *The Lonely Crowd* and *The Organization Man*. In this respect the grandfather's individualism—which, like that of the organization man, produces no external signs and thus can only be understood as internal—anticipates not only the behavior of particular characters but the narrative project of *Invisible Man* as a whole. This project is to generate a sense of embattled individuality in opposition to a world that is, as the narrator notes in the epilogue, characterized by a "passion toward conformity" that ensures that "none of us seems to know who he is or where he's going" (577). "In going underground," the narrator claims, "I whipped it all except the mind, the *mind*" (580; Ellison's emphasis).

This aspect of the novel was central to early praise of *Invisible Man* as a book that transcended race in its depiction of the modern struggle for individual identity. Robert Penn Warren, for instance, praised Ellison for being "more concerned with the way a man confronts his individual doom than with the derivation of that doom,"[6] while Saul Bellow commended Ellison's "brilliant individual victory" over the deindividualizing forces of modern society and his rejection of "a minority tone."[7] Tony Tanner nicely summarizes this reading of the novel when he argues in *City of Words* that

> it is an aspect of recent American fiction that work coming from members of so-called minority groups has proved to be relevant and applicable to the situation of people not sharing their immediate racial experience . . . ; and *Invisible Man*, so far from being limited to an expression of an anguish and injustice experienced peculiarly by Negroes, is quite simply the most profound novel about American identity written since the war. (50–51)

In the sixties this reading got Ellison in trouble with those—most notably Irving Howe and the members of the Black Arts movement—who charged him with improperly eschewing the political demands placed upon the black artist by American racism.[8] Accounts of the novel from the perspective of the African American canon remain concerned with refuting such criticism by demonstrating the novel's engagement with questions of race, while Ellison's 1994 death produced renewed assertions of the universalist premise from figures as diverse as Stanley Crouch, Sean Wilentz, and Norman Podhoretz. Kenneth Warren has recently proposed that we bypass this more or less injudicable debate by historicizing Ellison's racial politics, which remained grounded in the Jim Crow Era in a way that explains his inability to finish his second novel and renders his first in some ways irrelevant to contemporary debates.[9]

In this chapter I pursue the parallel project of historicizing the univeralist position. In particular, I argue that this dehistoricized language of threatened individuality screens—in the psychoanalytic sense of simultaneously revealing and obscuring—historically specific concerns about middle-class proletarianization and downward mobility. I thus discuss *Invisible Man* not primarily in terms of race (which others have done often and well), but in terms of class. Although, as Barbara Foley has shown, Ellison sloughs off a Marxist understanding of class in the process of composing *Invisible Man*,[10] this does not mean that the novel has no engagement with class. As Eric Schocket argues, "we need . . . to resist the easy essentialism that sees class, labor, and economic structures as the exclusive properties of racial and working-class cultural forms."[11] If Ellison abandons the form of proletarian fiction, we might attribute this not only to his political defections but also to the fact that the postwar economy was no longer legible in the terms appropriate to industrial capitalism. This was the case not, as the boom economy's boosters had it, because the class divide was disappearing, but because the site of labor was shifting from blue-collar to white-collar work.

To put this in more immediately textual terms, the cold war anticommunism that surely shapes Ellison's portrayal of the pseudo-Communist Brotherhood *does not* explain the similar animus that the book directs against every other institution in its pages. The middle-class tendency to project onto all organizations the deindividualizing white-collar workplace, however, does. At its most basic level, *Invisible Man* shares the plot of such popular treatments of white-collar angst as *The Fountainhead* and *The Man in the Gray Flannel Suit*: a man, anxious to find creative and fulfilling mental labor, instead encounters mystified, conformist organizations that threaten to rob him of his individuality, agency, and autonomy. To offer a useful oversimplification, the organization-man narrative gives form to the novel's African American content. Ellison adopts this narrative out of his frequently expressed desire to create a more three-dimensional, recognizably human African American protagonist than what he saw as Wright's dehumanized—because merely the product of his environment—Bigger Thomas. Ellison's adoption of the organization-man narrative allows him to transcend the "sociological vision of society" that he accused Howe of admiring in Wright's work,[12] even as it itself ironically reproduces another sociological vision. In this respect, *Invisible Man* and the postwar language of threatened individuality reinforced each other. Because this language was generally read in universal rather than sociological terms, it gave *Invisible Man* the broadly human resonance that Ellison sought, even as the novel's relocation of this language to a setting so obviously divorced from the world of the white-collar middle class bolstered its claims to universality. This no doubt at least partly explains the attraction of the novel to white critics who rushed to describe it in existential terms. From our perspective, however, Ellison's supposedly existential or American individualism can be understood as a version of the organization-man discourse within which the compromised agency and autonomy of the white-collar worker is misread as the plight of modern man per se.

To read *Invisible Man* in terms of the plight of the white-collar middle class seems self-evidently problematic, however, given the undeniable racial homogeneity of the white-collar workforce in the 1950s. A decade after the novel was published, a U.S. Bureau of Labor Statistics survey noted that "nonwhite workers" (approximately 95 percent of whom were African American) made up a scant 3.7 percent of the white-collar workforce, while accounting for 10 percent of the total nonagricultural workforce. Needless to say, African Americans were even less well represented in the high-paying, high-status managerial jobs that occupied the attention of figures like Mills and Whyte.[13] Indeed, the shift from blue-collar to white-collar work did not simply reflect but helped generate the new form taken by the white-black racial schism in the postwar United States. The segregation of white-collar work, higher education, and suburban housing in the forties and fifties made possible a new multiethnic white identity that, feeding back into policy decisions, accelerated the growth of the African American urban underclass.[14] Long after *Invisible Man* appeared, the white-collar middle class remained white above the collar as well.

Yet Ellison, as I will demonstrate at greater length below, persistently portrays not just his narrator but his black male characters in general in terms parallel to those in which other postwar writers portray the organization man. This does not mean, however, that he simply reproduces the organization-man discourse. On the contrary, he departs from this discourse, and its universalizing tendencies, in significant ways. For one thing, Ellison's own version of the typical postwar nostalgia for nineteenth-century American individualism differs significantly from that of figures like Rand and Mills, insofar as Ellison remains ambivalent, for obvious reasons, about the traditional equation between property ownership and liberal individualism. He grounds his praise of *Huckleberry Finn*, for instance, in the assertion that Huck's well-known decision to "*go* to hell" and help Jim escape slavery "dramatizes . . . the clash between the direct, human relationships of the frontier and the abstract, inhuman, market-dominated relationships fostered by the rising middle class."[15] Ellison's attempt here to distinguish "between property rights and human rights"[16] resonates with his efforts elsewhere to distinguish American ideals from the history of their abuse.[17] But it also seems to register, more specifically, his recognition that African Americans were excluded—by definition as slaves and in ways both de facto and de jure as freedpeople—from the property ownership that historically underwrote American liberal individualism.

Invisible Man ironically suggests, however, that this very exclusion from property ownership made African Americans into proleptic organization men. Here Ellison anticipates the sociologist E. Franklin Frazier's controversial study *Black Bourgeoisie* (1955 France; 1957 United States), which defines its subject as "those Negroes who derive their incomes principally from the services which they render as white-collar workers."[18] As the reference to service here indicates, Frazier understands his "new middle class" (as he refers to his object of study in his subtitle) in distinctly proletarianized terms. The white-collar employees who make up the black bourgeoisie are clustered at the bases of white-collar pyramids, or else they are economically disadvantaged by the fact that their work is restricted to poor African American communities. "The less than one per cent of Negroes with incomes between $4,000 and $5,000 and who are at the top of the pyramid of the Negro bourgeoisie," Frazier notes, "have incomes about equal to the median income of white-collar workers among whites" (49). Even the members of the black bourgeoisie who own businesses, Frazier argues, are clustered in such fields as "beauty shops, barber shops, cleaning and pressing places, undertakers, and shoe repair shops" that require of their proprietors something more like service labor than the free exercise of capital (51, 50–55 passim). The black bourgeoisie's economic marginality means for Frazier that they occupy a social realm characterized by "status without substance," in which "the behavior and standards of consumption which are maintained by 'society' generally lack the economic base which such activities presuppose" (162). A number of scenes in *Invisible Man* set the narrator's anomalously managerial position within the Brotherhood (which in this context does, pace Foley, remain as a residual trace of Ellison's earlier acknowledgment of Communist color blindness) against other more typical forms of service work. More generally, Ellison concurs with Frazier in seeing "the world of make-believe" (Frazier 162) as a form of ingrained role playing that among African Americans derives not from white-collar employment but rather—insofar as it substitutes status performance for actual economic power—by exclusion from it.

If *Invisible Man*, then, points in one direction toward the universalizing language of threatened individuality through which white critics (following Ellison's own lead) interpreted it, it points in another direction to the "association of race and service" that has historically characterized African American labor.[19] This association began, of course, in the antebellum period. But it was reinstitutionalized after the end of slavery, most spectacularly by the Pullman Company's decision to employ African American men (with an initial preference for former house slaves, and a more longstanding one for Southerners) in the portering service it began in 1867.[20] *Invisible Man*'s dual focus allows Ellison to intervene critically in a postwar discourse that saw black men as forerunners of organization men, and white-collar work as a form of racial downward mobility. While versions of this discourse written from the perspective of white middle-class men tended to collapse the distinctions among different kinds of nonmanual work (suggesting that even the most privileged mental laborers were like service employees), Ellison's version keeps these distinctions, and the racial hierarchies that structure them, open. This allows Ellison to critique a competing—and ultimately much more successful—discourse of race, exemplified by the work of figures like Norman Mailer and Jack Kerouac, that sees idealized forms of African American authenticity as the antidote to white middle-class alienation. *Invisible Man* thus insists that not all forms of postwar alienation are alike. At the same time, however, its (uneven) conflation of the narrative of threatened individuality with the history of black service labor encourages us—contra both Ellison's universalist proponents and more recent accounts of the novel by critics of cold war culture[21]—to think of this narrative in economic rather than existential terms.

The overdetermined nature of Ellison's representation of black male role playing makes itself felt in the episode where Trueblood describes his accidental incest
with his daughter for the white college trustee, Norton, who gives him $100. In
his influential reading of this scene Baker characterizes Trueblood as a "cosmically
rebellious trickster"[22] and a representative of "black phallic energy" (185) who
"adopts tale telling . . . as a mode of expression that allows him a degree of dignity
and freedom within the confines of a severe white hegemony" (195). Trueblood,
turning both his story and himself into a commodity, participates in a history of
"artful evasion and expressive illusion" as "traditional black expressive modes"
that provide "the only resources that blacks at any level can barter for a semblance
of decency and control in their lives" (196). Baker usefully inscribes Trueblood's
role playing within African American expressive traditions of which Ellison was
well aware, although in the fifties Trueblood's behavior would have invoked at
least two other explanatory frameworks. On one hand, Trueblood's performance
points toward the self-marketing that postwar critics understood as one of the
major problems with white-collar work. If Trueblood "is ultimately merchandiz-
ing . . . an image of himself that is itself a product" (Baker, *Blues* 193) he is
mirroring the white-collar workers for whom traditional alienated labor is compounded by a new form of "self-alienation" on the "personality market" (Mills,
White 187–88). Role playing is also central to Riesman's other-directed person,
who "tends to become merely his succession of roles and encounters and hence
to doubt who he is or where he is going." Riesman's new character type thus
eschews "the one-face policy of the inner-directed man for a multi-face policy
that he sets in secrecy and varies with each class of encounters" (139). Finally,
Whyte (although later than Riesman and Mills, whose studies both predate Ellison's novel) argues that the rise of The Organization and its accompanying
Social Ethic is creating a society in which "adaptation has become . . . almost a
constant" and organization men have become "interchangeables" (435, 437). In
the work of these social critics, role playing is a preeminent marker of white-collar
self-alienation.

On the other hand, Trueblood's performance of stereotypes for unpredictable
remuneration—he essentially works for tips—points toward the labor of Pullman
porters whose "low salaries . . . forc[ed] them to assume a persona that was at
once cautious, cheerful, even obsequious before their white patrons."[23] It is true,
of course, that Trueblood seems to embody a negative stereotype of black sexual
depravity rather than a positive one of willing servility. "I done the worse thing a
man could ever do in his family," he notes, "and instead of chasin' me out of the
country, [the local whites] gimme more help than they ever give any other colored
man, no matter how good a nigguh he was" (67). But this distinction is in fact
less important than the fact of the performance itself, which like that of "the
financially successful porter or waiter" requires him "to be both a keen student of
human behavior (assessing his customer accurately) and an actor (playing the
required part properly)."[24]

Thus while Baker is absolutely correct to frame Trueblood's performance in economic terms, he overemphasizes its positive aspects—not least its masculinizing effects, given that the phallic masculinity to which he alludes was mobilized at least partly in reaction to the demasculinizing associations of service labor. The section of *The Autobiography of Malcolm X* that deals with the then-Malcolm Little's experiences as a railroad sandwich man takes for granted the imbrication of such role playing with service labor:

> It didn't take me a week to learn that all you had to do was give white people a show and they'd buy anything you offered them. It was like popping your shoeshine rag. The dining car waiters and Pullman porters knew it too, and they faked their Uncle Tomming to get bigger tips. We were in that world of Negroes who are both servants and psychologists, aware that white people are so obsessed with their own importance that they will pay liberally, even dearly, for the impression of being catered to and entertained.[25]

Unlike Baker, however, *The Autobiography* understands such performances as empowering only within limited terms: they also contain an element of servility that later gets Little, who is unwilling to play along, fired and prepares the way for his metamorphosis into the hustler Detroit Red. That Ellison understands Trueblood's behavior as threateningly feminizing is suggested by the opening of this scene, in which the narrator and Norton, arriving at Trueblood's farm, see the farmer's wife and daughter "bec[o]me silent, their faces clouding over, their features becoming soft and negative, their eyes bland and deceptive" (50–51). Kate and Matty Lou here directly anticipate the narrator's subsequent description of Trueblood "seem[ing] to smile at me behind his eyes as he looked from the white man to me and continued" (61).

The obvious objection to this assertion, however, is that such self-masking is not gendered but racial, a point reinforced by Trueblood's look—however unwelcome—inviting the narrator into his deception. Yet this does not seem entirely correct, either. The role playing that distinguishes most of the novel's black characters, from the college president Bledsoe to the urban con man Rinehart, also extends to the white Brotherhood leader, Jack. Bledsoe, preparing to meet the upset Norton, stops before a mirror "and compose[s] his angry face like a sculptor, making it a bland mask" (102). Much later Jack, accused of racial condescension by the narrator, "grip[s] the edge of the table, spluttering and lapsing into a foreign language" (473). Although one scene portrays a character putting on a "bland mask" to cover anger and the other shows this mask breaking, both suggest that the person in question is not the person he has claimed to be. Foley notes that Jack's presumably native language is "probably Russian,"[26] although it is worth noting that the behavior she reads as a cold war stereotype of Communist duplicity is the same behavior that Baker reads in other contexts as evidence of black tricksterism. To a postwar reader, both scenes would resonate at least partially with accounts of middle-class masquerade such as Riesman's description of the other-directed person's "multi-face policy" (139).

Rather than attempting to prioritize one or the other of these seemingly op-posed readings, we might more profitably argue that *Invisible Man* treats role playing as overdetermined. A remarkable passage from Hawley's *Executive Suite*, published the same year as Ellison's novel, suggests that Ellison was not alone in positing a connection between self-alienating white-collar work and historically racialized service labor. We have earlier had occasion to discuss Hawley's book as both an allegory of the loss of property-owning independence and a fantasy of its partial recovery by the right kind of executive. But this passage focuses on one of the book's unredeemable organization men, the Treadway company's Vice-President of Sales, J. Walter Dudley. Dudley is all appearance and no substance, a "perpetual beggar of friendship" (247) whose professional success belies the fact that he is "a runner who [runs] without a goal" (132). Taking the train between Chicago and Treadway's Pennsylvania headquarters, Dudley goes into the dining car for breakfast. There the steward assigns him to "old Henry," "a waiter who looked as if he had spent most of his long life in the service of a fine old Southern family." The other waiters are glad because tips are pooled and Dudley looks like a customer "who would really shell out for the Uncle Tom act." Dudley demands "fast service" in a voice of "brusque command," whereupon Henry gives him the patter—punctuated by many "Yassuh!"s—at which he excels. He offers Dudley a piece of melon he has "been saving special" and makes the rest of Dudley's order "sound like an inspired triumph" (238–39). By juxtaposing Dudley and old Henry, *Executive Suite* draws an implicit parallel between their "acts," and suggests that Dudley himself engages in a kind of minstrelsy in his job.[27]

Such a passage indirectly acknowledges the proletarianization of the white-collar middle class while misreading such downward class mobility as a form of racialization. It suggests, in time-honored American fashion, that the worst part of white-collar self-alienation is that it forces white people to do "black" labor.[28] *Invisible Man*'s own conflation of self-alienation and black service labor works, by contrast, to forestall such easy analogies by insisting upon the narrator's exclu-sion from, as well as assimilation by, organizations. In this respect the novel reads like an extended riff on a brief, perceptive comment in Riesman's *The Lonely Crowd*: "The peer-group can decide that there are certain outcasts, in class or ethnic terms, to whom the glad hand need not be extended, or who can (like the Negro in the South) be forced to personalize without the privilege of demanding a reciprocal response" (139–40). And not just in the South, as Ellison makes clear. Unsurprisingly, *Invisible Man* most explicitly foregrounds its protagonist's ambivalent position vis-à-vis organizations when it focuses on the activity at the heart of white-collar middle-class anxieties about individuality: work. In chapter 8 of the novel, the narrator, newly arrived in Harlem, comes across a Gideon Bible in his room at Men's House and experiences a visceral rush of homesickness. But he puts the Bible and the homesickness aside with the thought, "This was New York. I had to get a job and earn money" (162). In the remainder of the chapter he distributes the letters of introduction that Bledsoe has given him, ostensibly asking the prominent businessmen to whom they are addressed to find a place for him. The responses he receives confuse him. "[V]aguely encouraged by secretaries" (168) but hearing nothing from their employers, he begins to suspect the former: "Maybe I've been wrong about the secretaries," he thinks; "maybe they destroyed the letters" (169). Paranoia sets in; the narrator experiences "a queer feeling that I was playing a part in some scheme which I did not understand" (170). He tells himself that his suspicions are "fantastic" (170), but considers the possibility that he is being tested for some arcane purpose. Unfortunately, he reflects, "they hadn't told me the rules" (170). Neither he nor, at this stage, the reader suspects the contents of the letters themselves, which warn their addressees not to hire him and ask them to say nothing about it to him, in order "that his severance with the college [may] be executed as painlessly as possible" (191).

In one sense, this passage could not be more like the standard postwar accounts of white-collar life. Consider the parallels between it and the classic organization-man narrative, Wilson's bestselling *The Man in the Gray Flannel Suit*. Wilson's novel tells the story of Tom Rath's decision to leave a low-paying but relatively comfortable job at a small foundation to go to work as a special assistant to the president of the United Broadcasting Corporation. Although he is immediately promoted to the position of assistant to UBC's chief executive, he finds his job near the heart of the corporate world just as mystifying as Ellison's narrator does his sojourn at its margins. Crucially, the world of business induces paranoia in both characters. Relieved of his first task—writing a speech for UBC's president, Ralph Hopkins—and not immediately reassigned, Rath sees before him a gulf that his anxiety immediately fills with speculation:

> Maybe that was the way Hopkins got rid of people. In this strange, polite world high in the sky above Rockefeller Center, maybe nobody ever really got fired. Maybe all Hopkins did was to give a man nothing to do, absolutely nothing to do, until he started to go out of his mind sitting uselessly in his office all day, and resigned. Maybe that was the polite, smooth way to get rid of a man nobody wanted.[29]

Although he eschews Ellison's brand of self-consciously modernist first-person narration in favor of straightforwardly omniscient narration, Wilson's story is driven by the same implications of conspiratorial knowledge outside the protagonist's purview: "rules" he has not been told. This concern not only links *Invisible Man* and *The Man in the Gray Flannel Suit* to each other, but also demonstrates their shared centrality to the arc of literary history that would shortly lead to novels like Joseph Heller's *Catch-22* (1961) and Thomas Pynchon's *The Crying of Lot 49* (1965).

The parallels between *Invisible Man* and *The Man in the Gray Flannel Suit* can be taken only so far, however. That the protagonist finds himself with "nothing to do" means something very different in the two books. Even if Ellison's narrator were not carrying Bledsoe's treacherous letters—and even if his story were set in the booming fifties, rather than in the Depression thirties—he could hardly expect to land a job like Rath's, "high in the sky above Rockefeller Center." The best job the narrator *could* find in the business world is that of the black men he sees "hurr[ying] along with leather pouches strapped to their wrists" (164). To be white-collar may mean that "you carry authority, but you are not its source" (Mills, *White* 80), but these men carry authority in a far more literal—and less lucrative—sense. Ellison's narrator's abortive efforts to enter the business world thus function as a kind of negative realism, to the extent that the novel can be read not only as an individual bildungsroman but also as a palimpsest of African American history from Reconstruction through the Harlem riots of 1943. The center of the white-collar world is as invisible in Ellison's novel as African Americans were in the mid-century white-collar workforce.

Crucially, the son of one of the businessmen to whom the letters are addressed, after tipping the narrator off to their contents, suggests the perhaps he would like to be his valet (192). In an intriguing reading of the novel's critical engagement with Hegel, Marx, and Freud's theories of modernity, Randal Doane suggests that it provides "a diligent phenomenology of work and labor" that encompasses "three different arrangements of labor and production: bondage (the college), wage labor (the factory), and communalism (the Brotherhood)."[30] Doane's taxonomy is a little too abstract to do justice to Ellison's often quite concrete and historically specific engagement with questions of labor. The section of the novel from the battle royal to the narrator's initiation into factory life at Liberty Paints has less to do with bondage per se than with the racially hierarchical, patronage-dependent, and self-effacing world of service. Although the racialized origins of this regime date back to slavery, it is obviously not bound to the South in the novel. Nor, despite these origins, and its evasion of the contract form central to wage labor (since it depends on things like tips and generosity), is it at all precapitalist. During the period of the novel's composition it still would have been associated with the Pullman system, and Ellison implicates the Boston financier Norton within it. Service work is, however, both raced and threatening to masculinity, as suggested by the young Emerson's efforts to seduce the narrator into playing— in the homophobic terms Ellison borrows from Leslie Fiedler—Jim to his Huck. Ellison elsewhere, as we have seen, identifies Jim and Huck as exemplars of "the simple, direct human relationships of the frontier," although here he implicitly acknowledges the feminized, eager-to-serve qualities of Twain's Jim.[31]

The Liberty Paints scene, then, does indeed initiate the narrator into blue-collar wage labor, in part offering a compressed version of Chester Himes's depiction of multiracial wartime factory work in *If He Hollers, Let Him Go* (1945). As numerous critics have pointed out, this section—with its paint "as white as George Washington's Sunday-go-to-meetin' wig and as sound as the allmighty [*sic*] dollar" (201–2) made with ten drops of "dead black" liquid (200)—allegorizes the simultaneously racially hybrid and superficially whitewashed nature of American history. But rather than reading this figure as a free-floating metaphor for American identity, we might instead insist on its contrast with the earlier invocation of national identity during the narrator's abortive search for a job in the business world. There the narrator, his search not going well, treats himself to a film:

> In the evening I went out to a movie, a picture of frontier life with heroic Indian fighting and struggles against flood, storm and forest fire, with the out-numbered settlers winning each engagement; an epic of wagon trains rolling ever westward. I forgot myself (although there was no one like me taking part in the adventures) and left the dark room in a lighter mood. (170)

In this scene, national identity is a projection on a flat white screen, rather than a white liquid with an invisible but nonetheless crucial black element. Black people (or more accurately, black men) can claim an (insufficiently acknowledged and remunerated) role in America's industrial workforce: "Ain't a continental thing that happens down here that ain't as iffen I done put my black hands into it," avows Lucius Brockway in Liberty Paints' boiler room (218). But its white-collar workforce is another story. Of course, the narrator himself buries his knowledge of such exclusion in parentheses, and notes that he leaves the theater "in a lighter mood"—that the scenes of nineteenth-century individualism do their ideological work nonetheless.[32]

Invisible Man takes on the task of undoing such historical repression. For Ellison, as for the sociologist Frazier, black role playing is a product not of assimilation into organizations but, on the contrary, exclusion from them. In a scene that directly anticipates Frazier, the narrator, leaving Men's House for the last time, describes among his former fellow tenants

> the business students from southern colleges, for whom business was a vague, abstract game with rules as obsolete as Noah's Ark but who yet were drunk on finance. . . . and that older group with similar aspirations . . . who sought to achieve the status of brokers through imagination alone, a group of janitors and messengers who spent most of their wages on clothing such as was fashionable among Wall Street brokers . . . who never read the financial pages though they purchased the *Wall Street Journal* religiously and carried it beneath the left elbow, pressed firm against the body and grasped in the left hand. (256–57)

Wilson's *Man in the Gray Flannel Suit* would, several years later, establish the business uniform as a symbol of white-collar conformity.[33] *Invisible Man* expresses a similar fear that clothes really do make the man, although for the Men's House tenants this is even worse insofar as it does not come with the material compensations that Tom Rath and other organization men enjoy. For the business students, janitors, and messengers loitering in the lobby of Men's House, actually having the jobs they pretend to have would be empowering rather than alienating; at the least, it would mean receiving a share of the boom economy's spoils.

To the extent that *Invisible Man* functions as an allegory of African American history, then, the protagonist's desire to find a "new role" within an organization—any organization—begins to seem more legitimate. Indeed, such ambiguity is the keynote to *Invisible Man*'s portrayal of the relationship between the individual and the organization in the Brotherhood sections of the novel, where blue-collar labor gives way to the psuedo-white-collar work of political organizing. Early in his experience with the Brotherhood the narrator imagines his membership as

> a way that didn't lead through the back door, a way not limited by black and white, but a way which, if one lived long enough and worked hard enough, could lead to the highest possible rewards . . . a way to have a part in making the big decisions, of seeing through the mystery of how the country, the world, really operated. (355)

The narrator conceives of Brotherhood membership as offering him "the possibility of being more than a member of a race" (355), that is, of granting him a role as an individual, not as a black man.

From this perspective the problem with the Brotherhood is that it *fails* to make the narrator like its other members, as he discovers following the funeral he holds for Tod Clifton. Recalled to the Brotherhood's main headquarters the narrator finds himself facing an angry Jack, who tells him, "You were not hired to think" (469). Although Jack asserts that for all of the Brotherhood's members, including himself, "the committee does the thinking[,] for *all* of us" (470; Ellison's emphasis), Invisible Man recognizes that this is untrue. "So here it is," he thinks, "naked and old and rotten. So now it's out in the open" (469). What is out in the open, of course, is that he is subordinated not only to the group, but to the group's white members, who lie on the other side of the preexisting hierarchy of race. *Some* people, to quote Riesman again, can "be forced to personalize without the privilege of demanding a reciprocal response."

This is to say that while *Invisible Man* does at times endorse the common postwar rejection of the social per se, Ellison also understands organizations to be striated by power relationships. These relationships are often but not always racial, as Bledsoe and the novel's persistent invocations of Booker T. Washington make clear. In part we can attribute this difference to the divergent take on the PMC that Ellison's focus on Washington affords him. Postwar intellectuals' rejection of the social, as I argued in the introduction, follows upon their rejection of the prewar PMC's historical optimism about the possibilities of social management, its sense that good organization can replace bad organization. But Ellison sees the problem with PMC social management in more specific terms as its imbrication with industrial capitalism's need to manage freed slaves following the Civil War:

> In order to deal with this problem the North did four things: it promoted Negro education in the South; it controlled [the Negro's] economic and political destiny, or allowed the South to do so; it built Booker T. Washington into a national spokesman of Negroes with Tuskegee Institute as his seat of power; and it organized social science as an instrumentality to sanction its methods.[34]

Bledsoe—who in explicit invocations of *Up from Slavery* (1901) "had trudged with his bundle of ragged clothing across two states" to get an education and had since become "a 'statesman' who carried our problems to those above us, even unto the White House" (116)—is Ellison's most scathing representation of Washington. Ellison's depiction of Bledsoe, we might say, anticipates latter-day critics of the PMC like the Ehrenreichs, Ohmann, and Sklansky in arguing that Bledsoe-Washington stakes out his own claim to mental labor by managing (in this case a racially specific group of) workers in the interests of capital.[35]

But the narrator, too, and those around him repeatedly invoke Washington to describe his own trajectory. "In those pre-invisible days," he notes in the battle royal chapter, "I visualized myself as a potential Booker T. Washington" (18). Much later, Jack recruits him for the Brotherhood by asking, "How would you like to be the new Booker T. Washington?" (305). Washington virtually stands in for the narrator's white-collar ambitions, in a way that suggests that, with the segregation of the white-collar workforce, politics becomes the only avenue for black upward mobility. "After all," another Brother tells the narrator in reference to his role as spokesperson, "you're one of the latest to fight his way to the top" (396). Ellison's pessimism about black protest politics, in this regard, stems from the fact that he also reversed this equation, understanding political work only as a form of careerism. Thus he exclaims, in his 1964 response to Howe's criticisms, "what an easy con-game for ambitious, publicity-hungry Negroes this stance of 'militancy' has become!"[36] Within *Invisible Man*, however, these constraints on upward mobility become the chief problem for the novel's would-be *bildungsroman*, in a way that brings the narrator's story in line with the standard dilemma of the organization man and of the postwar fictional protagonist as described by Tanner. The narrator's efforts to advance in the world, that is, threaten rather than affirm his identity, leaving him trapped between "fixed patterns" and "Protean fluidity" in a " 'border area' where author and hero alike attempt to create themselves and come into the meaning of their experience" (Tanner 63). "[T]o hell with this Booker T. Washington business," the narrator declares. "I would do the work but I would be no one except myself—whoever I was. I would pattern my life on that of the Founder" (311). The irony here is that the Founder *is also* Washington, outside of whose pattern doing the work—at least, the kind of white-collar work to which the narrator aspires—is impossible.

To extend the taxonomy we have borrowed and revised from Doane, then, *Invisible Man* takes its narrator through abortive encounters with (mostly black) service labor, (mixed but racially hierarchical) blue-collar labor, and (almost entirely white) white-collar labor to arrive, in the novel's final moments, at one last stop. This stop is not the isolation of the narrator's cellar but rather (since we are focused here on kinds of work) the intellectual labor of writing the book itself. Here the narrator merges with Ellison and—in a pattern I described in the introduction—the process of composition becomes an effort to escape the mere manipulation of inherited forms. For Ellison, this of course becomes the effort to escape

Wright's legacy, but more broadly it involves trying to think outside the terms of "sociology," a category that in his writing links the racial management of the PMC with Wright's communism. Hence his turn to the postwar narrative of alienation, which is itself sociological but less obviously so (and less obviously implicated in the tradition of racist social science). Ellison departs from the baseline novel of alienation as described by Tanner, however, to the extent that he attempts to rethink group agency not in sociological but in anthropological terms as "culture and personality."[37] As Ellison makes clear, among other places in his response to Howe's unfavorable comparison of his work with Wright's, he identifies sociology with an externally imposed understanding of African American life as pure reaction, and "culture" with an internally produced plenitude and vernacular aesthetic "discipline."[38]

Schaub misses this aspect of the novel when he contends that it "signals Invisible Man's lowest point when he 'organize[s] a drill team of six-footers [the "People's Hot Foot Squad"] whose duty it was to march through the streets striking up sparks with their hob-nailed shoes.' "[39] Schaub's reading of *Invisible Man* as a cold war text requires him to see Ellison's depiction of organized group activity as a critique of totalitarianism. But in a 1961 interview Ellison relates a biographical anecdote that calls Schaub's interpretation into question. In the Oklahoma City of his boyhood, Ellison tells Richard Stern,

> there were many Negro veterans from the Spanish-American War who delighted in teaching the younger boys complicated drill patterns, and on hot summer evenings we spent hours on the Bryant School grounds . . . learning to execute the commands barked at us by our enthusiastic drillmasters. And as we mastered the patterns, the jazz feeling would come into it and no one was satisfied until we were swinging. These men who taught us had raised a military discipline to the level of a low art form, almost a dance, and its spirit was jazz.[40]

This passage imagines the drill not as an unproblematically negative example of "military discipline," but as a form of "low art" whose "high" analog is Louis Armstrong "bend[ing] that military instrument into a beam of lyrical sound" in *Invisible Man*'s prologue (8). Ellison's reference to the drill team thus depicts art (popular art, but art nonetheless) as the product of organized *group* activity.

Schaub's misinterpretation of *Invisible Man* is itself symptomatic of an equally important, and perhaps even more persistent, legacy of the postwar period: the logic, inherited from the organization-man discourse, of condemning everything inside The Organization and celebrating everything outside it. Yet to the extent that Ellison seeks to escape this dynamic by positing an affirmative black culture, he anticipates the version of identity politics that emerges from the organization-man discourse in the 1950s. This form of identity politics, as I discuss in my next two chapters, seeks to relocate elsewhere the idiosyncrasies (group and individual) putatively stripped from the deracinated white-collar middle class. To put it in the most basic terms, difference as such becomes desirable when you think that society's main problem is that everyone acts the same. Indeed, to the extent that Ellison stresses cultural forms divorced from politics, he overleaps the version of identity politics mobilized by his sixties critics (in which cultural interventions form part of an overall political strategy) and anticipates its subsequent degradations (in which culture substitutes for politics).

In one respect, then, *Invisible Man* participates in the increasing tendency, during the course of the 1950s, of accounts of white-collar alienation to turn from small-property ownership to identification with romanticized forms of cultural identity as a balm for the ills of middle-class life. Insofar as the novel remains ambivalent about organization, however, it in fact departs from the tendency to romanticize everything outside the white-collar middle class—not least African Americans—that was also central to the postwar emergence of identity politics. Alice Echols and Eric Lott have described postwar "racial cross-dressing" as motivated by a crisis in middle-class masculinity,[41] but they have not sufficiently stressed its *structural* dependence on the pathologization of middle-class normalcy in the organization-man discourse. For instance, in Norman Mailer's 1957 essay "The White Negro," the postwar locus classicus of this tradition, the celebration of the Negro hipster gains its force through the juxtaposition of the hipster to the "Square cell[s] trapped in the totalitarian tissues of American society"—that is, organization men:[42] "Hated from outside and therefore hating himself, the Negro was forced into the position of exploring all those moral wildernesses of civilized life which the Square automatically condemns as delinquent or evil or immature or morbid or self-destructive or corrupt" (594). Mailer's impact on the current critical scene is too often underestimated: the legacy of "The White Negro" can still be discerned in the tendency of cultural studies to celebrate "transgressive" politics of style, thereby romanticizing those excluded from power rather than seeking to open power up. As this tendency increasingly comes under critique, we can learn from *Invisible Man* while learning how to read it.

Ellison presciently invokes and rejects the Mailerian dichotomy when he has his protagonist see and reject the hipster Rinehart as an alternative to the organizational world of the Brotherhood: "But what do *I* really want, I've asked myself. Certainly not the freedom of a Rinehart nor the power of a Jack, nor simply the freedom not to run" (575; Ellison's emphasis). Although a Rinehart-like manipulation of one's roles might serve as a useful "political instrument" (499), it becomes dangerous when elevated to an end in itself. The amoral manipulation of one's roles is, after all, precisely how one prospers *within* organizations. When one of the Brotherhood's theorists attempts to justify the group's tendency "to take advantage of the people," Invisible Man responds, "That's Rinehartism—cynicism " (504). To become Rinehart, then, is to become not the hipster opposite of the organization man but his reflection.

From this perspective, *Invisible Man* can be seen not as a mere displaced imitation of the organization-man narrative but as a critical reworking of it. By making his protagonist an African American organization man Ellison rejects the romanticization of those excluded from the white-collar middle class. While this move carries the potential (realized in much of *Invisible Man*'s critical reception) of subordinating the novel's racial concerns to a whitewashed existentialism, it can also be taken to reveal the racial unconscious of white-collar culture's construction of white identity. That is, the novel's narrative of alienation is subject to a functional reversibility through which its janitors and messengers who dress like executives can be read as executives who are afraid of becoming janitors and messengers.

Invisible Man suggests that the pervasive postwar desire for a romanticized African American lifestyle superior to the bureaucratized existence of the organization man overlays a deep-seated fear of racial downward mobility as the telos of organization life. Behind the white-collar desire to become black is the fear that one already *is*. The fear of racial downward mobility itself, however, simultaneously denies and expresses class anxieties that have proven well founded. Crucially, the service sector grew at a slightly *higher* rate (although to considerably less fanfare) than the white-collar sector throughout the 1950s.[43] Although the service workforce was disproportionately nonwhite at mid-century,[44] and remains so today,[45] it had in some ways become harder to distinguish such service labor from the labor of the equally though oppositely segregated white-collar workforce. Within this framework, *Invisible Man* offers a countergenealogy of white-collar alienation that explains such alienation's racial unconscious even as it undermines the peculiarly privileged position from which the organization-man discourse issues its complaints of middle-class angst. If the newness of the white-collar regime inheres in its shift of focus from the manipulation of things to the manipulation of people, the resulting, self-alienating collapse between person and thing is long established for African Americans, brought to North America as commodities to produce other commodities. Long after the end of slavery, the history of African American labor in the United States remained a history of segregation into precisely the sorts of servile occupations feared by postwar white-collar workers.

The forms of cross-racial identification that Mailer and others engaged in were never *simply* racial, to the extent that they depended upon simultaneously invoking and repressing this history. Jack Kerouac's *On the Road* (1957), for instance, provides a classic formulation of such compensatory identification in Sal Paradise's assertion that "I wished I were a Denver Mexican, or even a poor overworked Jap, anything but what I was so drearily, a 'white man' disillusioned."[46] At first glance, *On the Road* seems to have less to do with labor than with not laboring, although Sal's equation of Japanese American with overwork points toward the novel's obsession with various forms of labor, both as deterrents to individuality and, more surprisingly, as means of obtaining it. Sal becomes a sort of psuedo-organization man, for instance, when he and his friend Remi Boncoeur takes jobs as security guards in a Bay Area camp for laborers about to be shipped overseas. In contrast to the retired policemen and prison guards who "were proud of their jobs" (66), Sal hates having to play the heavy on the camp's residents: "This is the story of America," he sums up his experience: "Everybody's doing what they think they're supposed to do" (68).

But if this job seems to symbolize the internalized discipline of the organization man, Kerouac imputes to other working-class employment the same sort of masculine independence his protagonists also find in travel. Thus Sal describes Dean Moriarty's stint as a parking-lot attendant in Manhattan:

> [H]e'd finished his first fling in New York. I say fling, but he only worked like a dog in parking lots. The most fantastic parking-lot attendant in the world, he can back a car forty miles an hour into a tight squeeze and stop at the wall, jump out, race among fenders, leap into another car, circle it fifty miles an hour in a narrow space, back swiftly into tight spot, *hump*, snap the car with the emergency so that you see it bounce as he flies out; then clear to the ticket shack, sprinting like a track star, hand a ticket, leap into a newly arrived car before the owner's half out, leap literally under him as he steps out, start the car with the door flapping, and roar off to the next available spot, arc, pop in, brake, out, run; working like that without pause eight hours a night, evening rush hours and after-theater rush hours, in greasy wino pants with a frayed fur-lined jacket and beat shoes that flap. (6)

Dean's work, the opposite of Taylorized labor, epitomizes and restores the individuality of both the American man and—if we are to judge by his Kerouacian speed, breathlessness, and disregard for the niceties of superficial style ("you see it bounce")—the American artist. Kerouac, the seeming critic of the postwar mainstream, here affirms its belief that class privilege is a kind of burden—that white middle-class men have it worse than those lucky enough to "work like a dog" in a parking lot.

Kerouac's model for transcending the conditions imputed to white-collar middle-class life thus in no way requires race, although it can and frequently does involve race. Perhaps the most striking instance of this is a disturbing passage in which Sal, during his brief tenure as a migrant farm worker, admires "an old Negro couple in the field with us" who "picked cotton with the same God-blessed patience their grandfathers had practiced in ante-bellum Alabama; they moved right along their rows, bent and blue, and their bags increased" (96). Kerouac's nostalgic fantasy of slave labor provides a usefully extreme case of the historical amnesia underwriting postwar writers' turn to identity politics as the solution to the ills imputed to white-collar middle-class life. At the same time, we might speculate that Kerouac must fix on slavery—and particularly field labor—because the alternative model of African American labor running from house slavery through Pullman service comes too close to revealing the truth about the white-collar middle class: that its ills stem from a process of proletarianization that cannot be addressed through fantasies of shedding one's whiteness. This is also the point of *Invisible Man*, although one that we will miss if we read the novel in either purely existential or purely racial terms.

CHAPTER THREE

"The So-Called Jewish Novel"

ELIZABETH FREEMAN's account of the popular interactive stage production *Tony 'n' Tina's Wedding* attributes its popularity to what she calls a "double logic of ethnicity." On one hand, the disciplinary pressure on the audience "to adhere to middle-class, heteronormative, Anglo proprieties even as the actors purport to abandon them" follows the standard trajectory of ethnic assimilation. But on the other hand, the play about an Italian American wedding also promises that "a limited amount of 'acting out' will heal the wounds of generic, abstract, cultural nonbeing for audience members who are not consciously connected to an immigrant past."[1] Key to this reading—and what makes it a crucial intervention into recent critiques of identity politics—is the idea that cultural identity might appeal not only to those who imagine they are reviving their own lost identity,[2] but also to those who perceive their problem as having no identity.

This chapter offers a prehistory of Freeman's remarks, reading the postwar popularity of Jewish American fiction as a reaction to the contemporaneous emergence of the "generic, abstract cultural nonbeing" associated with the pathologized normalcy of the white-collar middle class. This concern with homogeneity itself misreads as cultural what might more productively be understood in class terms, insofar as it projects the curtailment of individual and class agency associated with white-collar employment outward as an imagined trait of middle-class culture. The final third of *The Organization Man*, in which Whyte describes "the great package suburbs that have sprung up outside our cities since the war" as "communities made in [the organization man's] image" (295), neatly exemplifies this culturalist turn. If organization men "express themselves more clearly [in suburbia] than in The Organization itself" (295) then their problem has less to do with the organization of mental labor within capitalism than with their characteristic manners, beliefs, and customs—or lack thereof.

Within this framework, Jews play an ambivalent role. On the one hand, this is the period when Jews enter the American mainstream by entering the white-collar workforce. But on the other hand, they exemplify an appealing ethnic difference, a form of identity that might support individuality in the same way that the more threatening difference of race does for figures like Mailer and Kerouac. This chapter traces the lineaments of Jewishness as "honorary ethnicity" in the fiction of Saul Bellow and Philip Roth.[3] Their work exemplifies the production of "Jewishness" as a form of identity that appeals to Jews—but not only to Jews—at precisely the moment when certain forms of Jewish distinctiveness are threatened by assimilation into the broad middle class. For both authors the figure of the Jewish intellectual provides the textual bridge between the world of white-collar work transforming Jews into generic members of the middle class and the formal innovations that enable Jewish American fiction to exemplify an appealing ethnic difference.[4]

The period following World War II was the classic era of Jewish assimilation, or incorporation into the American mainstream. Jews entered this period as nonwhite outsiders associated with foreignness, the working class, and disreputably left-leaning politics, and left it as mainstream white middle-class Americans whose politics, if still to the left of the majority, were now respectably in line with the mainstream liberalism of the era.[5] This shift in American Jews' status was a complex and overdetermined process, fed by, among other things, American reaction to the Holocaust (Brodkin 141); the delayed effect of prewar anti-immigration laws, which cut the number of foreign-born people in the United States to around 8 percent by 1945 and 5.4 percent by 1960;[6] and the "massive internal American migration" of Jews from "East Coast and rust-belt inner cities" to "local suburbias and . . . sun-belt communities across the nation" following 1945.[7] At its base, however, it was driven by the postwar boom, whose reorganization of the American economy prompted a parallel reorganization of American social difference into a newly multiethnic white majority and a black underclass associated with the inner city.[8] Unlike African Americans, who remained largely excluded from the kinds of white-collar work that underwrote middle-class status, upwardly mobile Jews benefited from the expansion of the white-collar workforce, whose personnel needs helped to override historical anti-Semitism in the job market and in higher education. Assimilation was, in this respect, a phenomenon of class as much as of ethnicity, in which the transformation of Jews from whites to nonwhites depended upon their transformation from workers and small businessmen (think Leo Minch) into members of the white-collar middle class. As one historian notes,

In the 1930s, most Jews had been employed as laborers or in low-level white-collar jobs, such as clerks and office help, but by the early 1950s over 55 per cent worked in professional or technical fields, or as managers, officials, and proprietors, compared to only 23 percent of the populace as a whole.[9]

A decade and a half later, "The percentage of Jews in white-collar jobs was nearly three times the national average, while only one Jew out of five worked in factories."[10] Jews attained membership in the white majority as a consequence of the "economic mobility . . . derived ultimately from America's postwar economic prosperity and its enormously expanded need for professional, technical, and managerial labor, as well as . . . government assistance in providing it" (Brodkin 37). They became white, that is, as they became white-collar.

Assimilation has frequently been understood negatively as deracination, "the attenuation and ultimate disappearance of Jewish identity."[11] In the fifth and final volume of *The Jewish People in America* (1992), for instance, Edward S. Shapiro acknowledges debates over the effects of assimilation, but ultimately concurs with those who postulate the "thinning of Jewish identity." "The most important aspect of recent American Jewish history," Shapiro writes, "has been the transformation of American Jews into Jewish Americans. The price of their remarkable economic and social ascent has been the attenuation of Jewish identity."[12] For Shapiro, becoming "Jewish American" by definition entails the "attenuation" of Jewish identity. The irony here is that accounts like these themselves rehearse the preoccupations of the new white-collar middle class that Jews entered through their "remarkable economic and social ascent." The postwar suburban Jewish diaspora that accompanied entry into the white-collar middle class was part of a much larger exodus of white Americans whose associations with "forced conformity" remain, Jurca reminds us, our most enduring social cliché.[13] Whyte argues that these locales gain their character from their population of continually transferred corporate employees—subjects of a policy designed, in the words of an IBM executive, to "make[ ] our men interchangeable" (305). This policy, and its suburban realization, exemplifies for Whyte "the whole drift of our society" toward greater homogeneity:

> We are not interchangeable in the sense of being people without differences, but in the externals of existence we are united by a culture increasingly national. . . . The more people move about, the more similar the American environments become, and the more similar they become, the easier it is to move about. (305)

If the suburbs were making everyone at least outwardly indistinguishable, and if Jews were moving to the suburbs, then Jews were becoming indistinguishable from everyone else—a thesis whose classic literary exposition is Philip Roth's 1959 novella *Goodbye, Columbus*.

Not everyone agreed, however, that assimilation entailed homogenization. The theologian Will Herberg, for instance, noted in his 1955 study *Protestant-Catholic-Jew* that synagogue membership was actually on the rise "in the smaller towns and in the suburbs,"[14] a phenomenon he explained by arguing that

> in the city, living in a "Jewish" neighborhood, one may unconsciously continue to accept one's Jewishness in residual terms of ethnic "belonging"; in the suburbs and in most smaller towns this is no longer possible: one must begin to think "seriously" of his Jewishness, and the only possible outcome of such thinking in present-day America is identification with the Jewish religious community, frequently leading to affiliation with the synagogue. (220n45)

Assimilation, in this formulation, was not undermining Jewish identity but, on the contrary, producing it as a particular thing, an object of conscious consideration distinct from the everyday practices and affiliations of the prewar urban Jewish community. Similarly, Nathan Glazer, who had collaborated with Riesman on *The Lonely Crowd*, argued that assimilation made Jews more visible to non-Jews as well. "[E]ven informed people," Glazer wrote in *Commentary*, "find it hard

to believe that the Jews make up only 3.5 per cent of the American population: one *sees* so many more! May not this be owing to the fact that their pursuit of middle-class activities and occupations makes Jews much more mobile and therefore more visible?"[15]

The postwar emergence of Jewish fiction as a distinct, ethnically defined genre similarly complicates any oversimplified notion of assimilation as deracination. Leslie Fiedler is wrong to suggest that "the very success of Jewish-American writers in thus becoming mouthpieces for all of America meant their disappearance as Jews, their assimilation into the anonymous mainstream of our culture."[16] In fact, Jewish fiction provided a concrete instance of Jewish visibility and the emergence of Jewishness as a form of identity. "Jewish" fiction had existed prior to the war, of course, although it was arguably always understood in terms other than its Jewishness: the immigrant novel (Abraham Cahan, Anzia Yezierska), the proletarian novel (Yezierska, Mike Gold), modernism (Henry Roth, Nathanael West). In the postwar period, by contrast, Jewish fiction becomes a generic category, while these earlier works are retroactively reconfigured into a precursor canon. The transformation of Jewish fiction thus parallels the experience of Jewish people as described by Herberg: disarticulated from particular social frameworks like the immigrant experience, radical politics, and bohemian intellectual culture, fiction by Jews is rearticulated around the reified category of Jewishness itself.

At the same time, however, Jewish fiction has been understood as transcending the particularities of ethnic identity, to the extent that it replays common American narratives and thereby takes its place as successor to the classic works of American fiction. As Ross Posnock and Michael Gilmore have recently noted, Philip Roth makes this trajectory explicit in his trilogy of historical novels from the late nineties—*American Pastoral* (1997), *I Married a Communist* (1998), and *The Human Stain* (2000)—with their effort to comprehend a particular sweep of American history and their explicit and implicit allusions to classic American authors.[17] But so far from awaiting Roth's fictional account of America since the fifties, this tendency was already present in Jewish fiction during the fifties. Thus Alfred Kazin contends, in his 1971 study *Bright Book of Life*, that Bellow's fiction, unlike "the 'minority' writing of the poignant, circumscribed novels of the 1930s," in which " 'Jewish' equals ghetto," was distinguished by "his command of a situation peculiarly American."[18] "With Bellow," Kazin writes, "an American of any experience could feel that he was in the midst of the life he knew" (130). Reflecting this ambivalence, Kazin refers to the genre pursued by Bellow and other postwar Jewish writers as "the so-called Jewish novel" (133).

Insofar as his fiction simply removes Jews from the ghetto, of course, Bellow might be taken not as inaugurating something new but rather as simply updating the theme of Americanization central to immigrant novels by Jews and others. But this is not quite what Kazin is saying. Rather, he suggests that the contents of Bellow's novels in toto are recognizably American: they do not narrate characters' movement from ghetto to "America," but rather present a Jewish experience that itself reproduces the American experience. Thus Kazin only seems to contradict himself when he argues that what distinguishes the work of Bellow and other postwar writers is its *failure* to fully integrate into the mainstream:

> The so-called Jewish novel (there really is one, though only a few Jews have written it, and those who write it are not always Jews) takes place in a world that is unreal, never *our* world. . . . The Jew is always in some uneasy relation to 'them'—he is a newcomer, parvenu, displaced person whose self-ordering becomes the issue in each book. (133; Kazin's emphasis)

Here Kazin suggests that if the so-called Jewish novel transcends the limitations of identity politics (not all Jews write it, some people who write it are not Jews), it nonetheless fails to achieve an unmarked American identity: Jewish novels offer a world that is not quite "ours"; Jews remain poised on the threshold of the mainstream, neither fully in nor fully out. Kazin, a Jewish critic of the American canon who had himself authored a memoir of boyhood in a Jewish neighborhood in Brooklyn, asserts his point formally with the pronoun shift that identifies him first with "*our*" culture against that of the Jews, then with the Jew "in some uneasy relation" to a " 'them' " whose coherence he calls into question with scare quotes.

To the extent that assimilation had as much to do with class as ethnicity, postwar Jewish fiction reflected a generically American experience by narrating a general trajectory of upward class mobility. Jews, in Kazin's terms, were not just newcomers but parvenus, upstart members of a new class when this was a widely shared experience, whether because of actual upward mobility or because the basis of middle-class status had itself shifted around its members. If "Jewish artists and intellectuals found themselves in the unusual position of speaking in public forums as white Americans for white America, but also as white critics of the culture of 1950s whiteness" (Brodkin 140), this was because they both exemplified the new white-collar middle class and embodied a certain resistance to it, to the extent that, as Jews, they remained partial outsiders.[19] Jews were particularly well poised to serve as "articulators of a larger American pattern . . . of uneasiness about American affluence and capitalist modernity" (Brodkin 140) because the figure of the Jew performed the remarkable feat of merging the organization man and the ethnic outsider. In doing so, Jews mediated between the putatively homogenous world of the white-collar middle class and the new terrain of identity politics that was emerging in response to this world's perceived deficiencies.

No text exemplifies this charged act of cultural mediation better than Bellow's 1953 novel *The Adventures of Augie March*. James Atlas's recent biography of Bellow reiterates Kazin's distinction between the so-called Jewish novel and its ethnic precursors. Whereas "In 1938"—a year before the start of World War II, six years before the publication of Bellow's first novel—"American novels written by Jews—as opposed to more ethnic Jewish-American novels such as Ludwig Lewisohn's *The Island Within* or Abraham Cahan's *The Rise of David Levinsky*— didn't exist," Bellow enabled "Jewish literature . . . to become American."[20] Atlas reinforces this claim by reworking Bellow's own description of his first two novels as apprentice work— "his M.A. and his Ph.D." (98)—into a teleological progression toward national identity:

> In his first book [*Dangling Man* (1944)], he had described the experience of his generation; in his second [*The Victim* (1947)], the experience of his people, Jews living in the shadow of the Holocaust. *The Adventures of Augie March* was his American book; it staked his claim as an heir to the country's native individualism. (194)

In this account, Bellow's early career parallels and exemplifies the contemporaneous process of assimilation, following a trajectory from an ethnic Jewishness with a questionable relationship to native American identity to a mainstream American identity whose exponent happens to be a Jew. This is a remarkably tidy story that does no harm to Bellow's position in the American canon, placing him squarely at the center of a historical transformation that not only made Jewish fiction American but also—as the foregoing argument suggests—almost required the preeminent American author to be a Jew.

At first glance *Augie March* seems to have little to do with the postwar reorganization of the middle class that made Jews representative cultural figures. The novel begins in the nineteen-teens and spends most of its time in the thirties, entering World War II only in the final seventh or so of its over five hundred pages, and the postwar period only during its last chapter. It takes place, moreover, in Chicago, New York, Mexico, and Paris. The closest it comes to the suburbs is when a young Augie March briefly works at an upscale clothing store in Evanston during the Depression. Moreover, Augie's experience is anything but white-collar: in addition to his turn in the clothing store he makes his living as, among other things, a newsstand operator, a paid companion to a small-time businessman, a wealthy woman's protégé, a failed immigrant smuggler, a dog groomer and walker, a textbook thief, an assistant in his brother's coalyard, a union organizer, a would-be eagle trainer and travel writer, a crackpot's research assistant, a merchant marine, and, finally, a businessman in postwar Europe. Even at this closest approach to middle-class status Augie remains, although well-off, a participant in "illicit dealing" who further spends more time sitting in cafés and visiting tourist sites than making deals.[21] Unlike his friend Frazer, who metamorphosizes over the course of the novel from student radical to Trotsky's bodyguard to World War II major to employee of the World Educational Fund—thereby almost parodically embodying what Atlas calls "the process of intellectual—or Jewish—assimilation" (181)—Augie remains on the margins of postwar society. As he declares early in the book, "Saying 'various jobs,' I give out the Rosetta stone, so to speak, to my entire life" (28).

Described in this manner, *Augie March* reads like what it on one level certainly is, a picaresque precursor to *On the Road* about a young man on the run from convention and conformity. Bellow himself, in a letter to Lionel Trilling, described his protagonist as an exemplar of "inner-directedness" whose singular talents leave him with no social role:

It isn't that Augie resists every function [the word was Trilling's]—that would make him a tramp; and while I would not hesitate to write about tramps if I were called to it, Augie is something different. I was constantly thinking of some of the best young men I have known. Some of the very finest and best intentioned, best endowed, found nothing better to do with themselves than Augie. The majority, whether as chasers, parasites, bigamists, forgers and worse, lacked his fairly innocent singleness of purpose. They had reached the place where they fixedly doubted that Society had any use for their abilities. (qtd. Atlas 188; Atlas's brackets)

Bellow's account of his novel, with its anticipation of Ginsberg's "best minds of my generation,"[22] casts Augie as an outsider whose ineffable individuality—"Augie is something different"—distinguishes him not only from solid citizens but even from the smaller "majority" of outsiders who find roles as tramps and criminals.

Augie's claims to individuality are not quite so clear cut, however. In the novel's opening he proclaims that "I am an American, Chicago-born . . . and go at things as I have taught myself, free-style, and will make the record in my own way" (3). Yet his assertion at the start of chapter 4—"All the influences were lined up waiting for me. I was born, and there they were to form me, which is why I tell you more of them than of myself" (43)—seems to more adequately characterize the story he tells. As this suggests, Augie—despite Bellow's comment to Trilling—demonstrates a character that is far more other- than inner-directed. If, as Augie declares (again in the opening paragraph), "a man's character is his fate" (3), his fate is linked to a character predisposed—like that of the organization man or the other-directed individual—toward following. "[T]here was," he says in recounting the wealthy Mrs. Renling's offer to make him her son, "something adoptional about me" (151). Bellow deploys this confusion to humorous effect when Augie describes another character typically anxious to provide him with direction: "He insisted that I should be going somewhere, at least that I should be practicing how to go, that I should concentrate on how to be necessary, and not be backward but energetic, absolute, and so forth. And of course I had some restlessness to be taken up into something greater than myself" (203–4). Augie's friend Clem here paradoxically pressures him to be more of an individual, while at the same time suggesting that this includes being "necessary" (and leaving to whom unspecified, so that this describes not a particular relationship but a quality of the individual). Augie, meanwhile, leaps at this advice out of a desire (altogether typical for him) to transcend himself.

One of Augie's first childhood memories, moreover, positions himself as other-directed in opposition to his inner-directed brother Simon. Describing how his family's boarder and de facto matriarch Grandma Lausch used to make him accompany his mother on trips to get free glasses from a relief agency, Augie explains that Simon's "martial true-blood pride . . . disqualified him for the crafty task to be done at the dispensary," while he was not only suited but eager: "I loved a piece of strategy. I had enthusiasms too; I had Simon's . . . and I had Grandma

Lausch's as well" (4–5). In contrast to his brother's rigid code—"a mixed extract from Natty Bumppo, Quentin Durward, Tom Brown, Clark at Kaskaskia, the messenger who brought the good news from Ratisbon, and so on" (12); "Old South honor and . . . *codo-duello* dangerous easiness" (19)—Augie displays an other-directed impressibility. The parallel with *The Lonely Crowd* could not be more precise here. It is not that Simon is individualistic and Augie is conformist. On the contrary, both have internalized codes of behavior, but whereas Augie's is elastic and constantly changing Simon's is stiff and set to the specifications provided by recognizable historical models. While Simon is a residual representative of a time when historical figures provided strict models of proper behavior,[23] Augie's relationship even to such paragons is far more flexible:

> So don't think I'm trying to put over that, if handled right, a Cato could have been made of me, or a young Lincoln who tramped four miles in a frontier zero gale to refund three cents to a customer. I don't want to pass for having such legendary stuff. Only those four miles wouldn't have been a hindrance if the right feelings were kindled. It depended on which way I was drawn. (23)

Just as Augie *can* adopt Simon's "enthusiasms," he *can* engage in seemingly inner-directed behavior, but with the crucial difference that he does so not because he has been "made" for heroic efforts in his childhood, but because he is "drawn" that way by whatever influences happen to be ascendant at the time. As his lover Thea later tells him (in a speech ironically meant to reinforce her own influence), he is too "obliging": "What makes me say these things is that I see how much you care about the way people look at you. It matters too much to you" (318).

From this perspective, Augie hardly looks like an individual at all, except in the limited sense that he attempts to create an identity by "repudiat[ing] or avoid[ing] the identities which other people seem eager to thrust upon him" (Tanner 68). Thus one of Augie's mentors, the businessman Einhorn, trying to figure out why Augie has participated in a robbery, tells him, "All of a sudden I catch on to something about you. You've got *opposition* in you. You don't slide through everything. You just make it look so" (117; Bellow's emphasis). A grateful Augie accepts Einhorn's words as the "truth" about himself: "I felt it powerfully. That, as he said, I did have opposition in me, and great desire to offer resistance and to say '*No!*'" (117; Bellow's emphasis). Yet more than Augie's pleasure at thus hearing himself defined by someone else—"The discoverer of this, who had taken pains to think of me—to *think* of me—I was full of love of him for it" (117; Bellow's emphasis)—should make us suspicious of this characterization. Insofar as Augie defines himself through opposition to others, what he thinks of as his individuality exists only as a negative quality, much like the claims to uniqueness that Nabokov both mocks and indirectly affirms in Humbert Humbert. Bellow goes Nabokov one step further, however, making explicit the fundamental reliance of such negatively defined individuality upon other people. As Tanner suggests, Augie is always in motion because his sense of individuality, which simultaneously depends upon and must reject other people, can never achieve stability.[24] And in fact, *Augie March*'s narrative momentum derives from precisely this catch-22: what links the novel's episodes together is the repeated pattern whereby Augie approaches another character, orbits him or her briefly, then breaks away—as much drawn by another character, frequently, as he is repelled by his revived sense of opposition. Tanner describes *Augie March* as a prototypical work of postwar fiction because it thus dramatizes the dilemma of the individual torn between autonomy and society.

But Bellow's novel inscribes its protagonist's openness to others' influence in something more historically specific than an existential contest between individual and society. Returning to Augie's work history, we can now see precisely the engagement with white-collar work that at first seems absent from his miscellaneous resumé. Another way of describing the novel's narrative structure is to note that in most of the episodes another character draws Augie not just into the sphere of his or her personal influence but, more concretely, into a job. Thus—to cite only a few examples—he becomes the wheelchair-bound businessman Einhorn's assistant because of his personal admiration for Einhorn, "the first superior man I knew" (60); goes to work at Simon's coalyard because he empathizes with the stresses of his brother's position ("Especially since I had heard him weeping in the can Simon wasn't easy for me to turn down" [225]); and, in the novel's longest episode, quits his job as a union organizer (likewise obtained at a friend's suggestion) and joins his lover Thea on her quest to train an eagle to hunt lizards in the mountains of Mexico. In this way his biography demonstrates the entanglement of work and "intimate traits" that Mills argues is central to white-collar labor (182): for Augie, getting a living is always connected with personal relationships, and vice versa.

Indeed, the connections that the novel draws between Augie's impressibility and his employability allows us to read it as a virtual allegory of white-collar self-commodification. Mills describes this process as a generalized logic of salesmanship. Appropriately, Augie's interview for an early job as a salesman in an upscale sporting goods store consists of a probingly intimate examination of his personal appearance by the store's owner, Renling.

> Prospective house slaves from the shacks got the same kind of going-over, I suppose, or girls brought to an old *cocotte* by their mothers for training. He had me strip my jacket so he could see my shoulders and my fanny, so that I was just about to tell him what he could do with his job when he said I was built right for his purpose, and my vanity was more influential than my self-respect. (129–30)

Sales, Augie's analogies imply, is a racially and sexually suspect form of service labor that turns persons into commodities and thereby hints at sexual as well as commodity exchange. Yet Augie's response to this scene is ambivalent, and his pleasure in being appreciated—what Thea will later criticize as his tendency to "care about the way people look at you" (318)—ultimately wins out over his discomfort.

Affirming Mills's argument that self-marketing forms the basis of white-collar employment per se, what Augie more than once refers to as his "vanity" turns out to be his most marketable trait. Although he subsequently experiences reservations about his job working for Renling, it nonetheless appeals strongly to a part of his personality that he retrospectively associates with fantasies of upward mobility:

> There was a spell in which I mainly wished to own dinner clothes and be invited to formal parties and thought considerably about how to get into the Junior Chamber of Commerce. Not that I had any business ideas. I was better than fair in the shop, but I had no wider inventiveness about money. It was social enthusiasm that moved in me, smartness, clotheshorseyness. The way a pair of tight Argyle socks showed in the crossing of legs, a match to the bow tie settled on a Princeton collar, took me in the heart with enormous power and hunger. I was given over to it. (134)

Read quickly this passage might seem to posit a desire for nice things as Augie's motivation for upward mobility. But in fact it suggests just the opposite, that—in terms familiar from the postwar critique of white-collar work—"social enthusiasm" and "smartness" of appearance, rather than "business ideas" and "inventiveness about money," have become the *sources of* upward mobility. Within the novel's fictional time frame, Augie reads like the first organization man, waiting for the world to catch up with his particular talents.

Read this way, Bellow's novel becomes less an existential contest between individual and society—as in Tanner's and, to some extent, Bellow's own readings—than a narrative structured by postwar reactions to the transformation of intellectual labor into white-collar employment. Bellow's own career offers some parallels. Bellow's contribution to Granville Hicks's 1957 volume *The Living Novel* makes it clear that he wants to understand writing as a profession unlike other professions. "Writers," Bellow asserts,

> have stood aside from the ordinary duties of their fellow citizens. I don't perhaps so much mean duties as I mean the routines of the milltowns, the mining towns, and the great cities. Others get up in the morning and ride in crowds to their work. Not the self-anointed writer. He sits up in his room, writing, a freer man. Or is he freer? Is he free? Perhaps he feels a weak and treasonable fear in his soul at doing something so hard to explain to the others, the early-morning passengers on the Milwaukee Avenue street car.[25]

Here the writer's very self-doubts attest to the individual nature of his chosen profession, for as a "self-anointed" practitioner he has no social logic, no "routines," nothing but his own decision to justify the work he does. Bellow's experience of mental labor, however, frequently contradicted this ideal. Atlas, for instance, writes of one of Bellow's own early jobs—doing research for the *Synopticon* designed to accompany Mortimer Adler and Robert M. Hutchins's *Great Books of the Western World* series—that "for Bellow, a job was simply another form of authority—submitting to regular hours and bureaucratic responsibilities was being told what to do" (93). This formulation suggests that for Bellow, employment was simply a subset of the force, inimical to individual agency, that Atlas calls "authority" and under which he elsewhere subsumes, variously, high culture (72), "European culture as an oppressively dominating institution" (146), and Bellow's brothers, who became successful Chicago businessmen. "Authority" is, however, a less flexibly existential category than it might at first seem if we understand Bellow's conception of individuality as grounded in his particular concerns about work. In this case, all of Atlas's subsets of authority—high culture and Europe no less than his brothers' example and paid employment—threaten not simply his individuality in general but his ability to enact that individuality through writing in particular. The form this threat takes is different—following in his brothers' footsteps or researching the great ideas literally take up time that might be spent writing, while the Western literary canon constitutes a pattern his own writing must struggle to escape if he is to demonstrate his originality—but the general principle is the same: all constitute forms of restraint inimical to Bellow's understanding of writing as a form of work through which the author expresses his individuality.

This principle would subsequently find expression in Bellow's long-running critique of the university as the preeminent institutional restraint upon the writer's work. Bellow, one of the first major American fiction writers to make his living as a university teacher, became a notorious critic of the same institution that "provide[d] him shelter" (Atlas 154). In his 1957 essay "The University as Villain," Bellow argued *against* the notion that the university "could not be friendly to [writers] without softening and taming them and making them fat," suggesting instead this attitude was merely "*postural*" and that—the Hemingwayesque cult of "experience" aside—writers could do as well in the academy as in "the gutter."[26] As early as 1950, however (while he was composing *Augie March*), Bellow had written Kazin that "I'd as lief work in a factory as remain in what are called intellectual millieux," declaring the latter his "heart's abhorrence" (qtd. Atlas 154). And by 1966 he had fully embraced the antiacademic posture, proclaiming in a talk to the International P.E.N. Congress that university intellectuals were "trying to appropriate literature for themselves" and in the process shaping it to their own narrow definitions: "They have projected the kinds of art and literature that suits [*sic*] them, and they have the power to recruit novelists who will meet their requirements. Novels are written which contain attitudes, positions or fantasies pleasing to the literary intelligentsia. These are, of course, given serious consideration."[27] Here the university writer becomes a classic other-directed organization man who succeeds to the extent that he is able to conform to an external template shaped by mediocre consensus.[28] Although Bellow did not restrict his criticisms of the enemies of literature to the university—indicting "editors and journalists" (Atlas 355) and "the quarterlies and the New York 'literati,' "[29] as well—the university provided his model for the institutional shape that these enemies assumed.

Augie March comes at a moment in Bellow's career when assimilation as entry into the white-collar middle class connotes both a positive sense of upward mobility—the professoriat was, we should recall, finally opening itself to Jews at this time, although the process would not be complete until the sixties[30]—and anxiety about possible threats to both individual autonomy and group identity. I have already suggested that Augie's introduction to the world of white-collar self-alienation comes under the tutelage of the Renlings, who besides presiding over the realm of salesmanship also represent the possibility of assimilation-as-deracination. German Jews, the Renlings belong to a group that had immigrated to America much earlier and assimilated much more fully than the Eastern European Jewry from which Augie derives, "los[ing] their sense of ethnic and cultural distinctiveness and [seeing] themselves as essentially a religious grouping."[31] The Renlings themselves practice the upper-class, Anglophilic manners of the suburb in which they live. Augie, describing the car trips that he and Mr. Renling would sometimes take into the country, notes that "we'd stop for barbecue chicken in some piny place, on warm sand, . . . and sip beer in the perfect clothes we wore, of sporting hound's-tooth or brown Harris tweed, carrying field glasses in cases from the shop: a gloomy, rich gentleman and his gilded nephew or young snob cousin, we must have looked" (133). Bellow crafts the Renlings, that is, as Depression-Era precursors of the Short Hills-dwelling Patimkins in Roth's *Goodbye, Columbus.* That the Renlings' lifestyle, like the Patimkins', has some vexed relationship to their Jewishness Bellow hints when Renling, sizing up Augie for the job in his store, asks "*Jehudim?*" and notes that "out there on the North Shore they don't like Jews" (129). The lessons in self-marketing that Bellow learns at the Renlings' thus involve a crucial component of passing—"Anyway," Renling goes on, "they'll probably never know" that Augie is Jewish (129)—and Augie's decision not to become a Renling thus takes on ethnic as well as personal dimensions.

This is not to say, however, that Augie rejects assimilation, but rather that he—or, more properly, the novel to which he belongs—rejects the notion of assimilation as deracination in favor of a more up-to-date notion of assimilation as entry into the white-collar middle class. The novel's presiding spirit of Jewishness as ethnic difference is the Marches' boarder, Grandma Lausch, a fallen aristocrat from Odessa who speaks Yiddish and four other European languages, smokes Murads "at a time when women did not smoke" (6), and rereads *Anna Karenina* and *Eugene Onegin* every year (11). Although "she never went to the synagogue, ate bread on Passover, sent Mama to the pork butcher where meat was cheaper, [and] loved canned lobster and other forbidden food" (11), Augie notes, she "burned a candle on the anniversary of Mr. Lausch's death" and observes various superstitions that "had nothing to do with the giant God of the Creation . . . but [were] on the side of religion at that" (12).[32] It is thus tempting to read the progressive dimming of Lausch's power—which culminates with Simon arranging with her absent sons to move her to a Hyde Park nursing home—in conjunction with the novel's bildungsroman plot as equating growing up with becoming less Jewish.

The novel does to a certain extent equate ethnic Jewishness with childhood. But it also parallels Lausch's story with that of other male characters in such a way as to suggest that its developmental narrative has as much to do with the American middle class as with Jewishness. Crucially, Bellow uses these male characters to align ethnic Jewishness with property ownership. When Augie is thirteen he leaves home for the summer to live with his cousins the Coblins and work on Hyman Coblin's newspaper route. On one hand, the Coblins exemplify the opposite of the propriety that Augie will later encounter at the Renlings'. "The filth of the house, . . . and particularly of the kitchen, was stupendous," Augie notes (19), and in anticipatory contrast to Mrs. Renling's veal kidneys with cognac (131) Anna Coblin serves "meals of amazing character . . . and of huge quantity": "Bowls of macaroni without salt or pepper or butter or sauce, brain stews and lung stews, calves'-foot jelly with bits of calves' hair and sliced egg, cold pickled fish, crumb-stuffed tripes, canned corn chowder, and big bottles of orange pop" (21). Anna's brother Five Properties, a household intimate, "spread the butter on his bread with his fingers," while "Coblin, who ate with better manners, didn't complain either and seemed to consider it natural" (21–22). This contrast suggests, in terms that might easily apply to a nostalgic reading of assimilation, that with refinement comes a certain loss of plenitude. And indeed, "Both Coblin and [Five Properties] were hipped on superabundance" (23), not only of food but of "striped silk shirts or sleeve garters or stockings with clocks" (23) or of simple bodily pleasure: at one point, Augie relates, he "walked in on [Coblin] when he was in the bathtub, lying in the manly state, erect, and dripping himself with the sponge" (22). Augie describes this scene as taking place in "the steamy, cramped steerage space of the small windowless bathroom" (22), a description that links Coblin's casual impropriety—Augie's concerns about his cousin's dignity, he realizes in retrospect, had cast the incident as "more troublesome . . . than it actually was" (23)—to immigrant Jewishness.

At the same time, Coblin and the aptly named Five Properties also exemplify other qualities usually associated with the small-property-owning middle class. "Early risers" due to their jobs (Five Properties drives a milk truck), "the Coblins went to bed soon after supper, like a farm family" and woke before dawn (26). Alongside his gustatory and masturbatory indulgences, Coblin also displays the goal orientation and subordination of pleasure that Riesman, following Max Weber and others, associates with the inner-directed middle class (109–25, passim):

> He was a solid man of relatively low current in his thoughts; he took the best care of his business and wouldn't overstay downtown to an hour that would make it difficult for him to get up at his regular time, four o'clock. He played the stock market, but that

was business. He played poker, but never for more than he carried in his change-heavy pockets. (22)

These two sides of Coblin, rather than contradicting each other, represent Bellow's efforts to depict the prewar generation of immigrant Jews as a late reincarnation of the traditional American middle class. In this sense, we might understand the bathtub scene as representing not—or better, not only—Coblin's impropriety but also his inner-directed autonomy: he does not, in this sensitive arena, care what people think. Bellow's immigrant Jews reincarnate the traditional American middle class in both their vulgarity *and* their sense of historical agency. Five Properties embodies this merger of Jewish and American petit bourgeoisie in both his life story and his accented pronunciation of his own nickname:

> It wasn't so long ago he had done a small part in the ruin of empires, driving wagons of Russian and German corpses to burial on Polish farms; and now he had money in the bank, he had stock in the dairy, and he had picked up in the Yiddish theater the fat swagger of the suitor everybody hated: "Five prope'ties. Plente money." (20).

But Bellow makes this connection between the golden ages of Jewish American and American middle-class history most strongly in chapter 5 of the novel, originally published in *Partisan Review* in 1951 as the short story "The Einhorns."[33] That this chapter appeared this early, and with only minor differences from its final form (altered paragraph breaks, isolated word changes, and so forth), suggests that it played a major role in Bellow's imagination of the novel. The chapter consists of Augie's reminiscences of William Einhorn, "the first superior man I knew" (60). Confined to a wheelchair, Einhorn nonetheless possesses "a brain and many enterprises, real directing power, philosophical capacity" (60). Einhorn fulfills the property-owning middle-class ideal hinted at in the name of the milkman Five Properties: he and his family "were the most important real-estate brokers in the district and owned and controlled much property" (61). Like Augie's cousins, the Einhorns cultivate a certain indifference to middle-class propriety: Einhorn and his father, known as the Commissioner, have trouble hitting the toilet in the bathroom that Augie sometimes has to clean (65), and "Mrs. Einhorn [is] not really a good housekeeper even though she complain[s] about the floor of the toilet and the old man's spitting" (69). In noting these things, however, Augie refers them, even more explicitly than in his description of the Coblins, to the noblesse oblige of people who have more important things to worry about. Of the bathroom, he notes that "for people of some nobility allowances have always been made in this regard. I understand that British aristocrats are still legally entitled to piss, if they should care to, on the hind wheels of carriages" (65). But Einhorn's entitlement is not so much that of the European aristocracy as it is that of the American middle class. In contrast to Tillie Einhorn's indifferent housekeeping

> Einhorn was a thoughtful proprietor and saw to it that everything was kept humming, running, flushing, and constantly improved—rats killed, cement laid in the backyard,

machines cleaned and oiled, porches retimbered, tenants sanitary, garbage cans covered, screens patched, flies sprayed. (69)

Augie here compares Einhorn to an "ancient Roman senator [who] knew of husbandry before such concerns came to be thought wrong" (69), invoking the Republican precursors of the American middle class while blending their virtues with more proximate, technological, and hygienic ones. Elsewhere, Einhorn "brag[s] about [his father] as a pioneer builder on the Northwest Side" (67) and alludes to his own paralysis "as a thing he had overcome, in the manner of a successful businessman who tells you of the farm poverty of his boyhood" (70–71). If "The Einhorns" functions as a bit of youthful nostalgia about the Jewish past, it romanticizes this past in terms of America's self-conception as a homesteading, self-reliant, middle-class nation.

The chapter already hints at its own nostalgic motives with Augie's note that he "stayed on with [Einhorn] after he had lost most of his property" (60). This occurs in a subsequent chapter of the novel as a result of the Crash of 1929, and in pushing Einhorn's story into the Great Depression Bellow aligns him with capitalism itself: "Thousands of his dough were lost [as a result of speculation] in Insull's watered and pyramided utilities" (106) and when his property has shrunken to the building in which he himself lives his tenants organize against him and precipitate Communist picketing (107). Bellow, a typical cold war, anticommunist liberal at this point, hardly embraces the long view of middle-class expropriation central to books like *The Crisis of the Middle Class* and *Tucker's People*. Nonetheless, the Depression does give him a way of thinking about the loss of property as a pivotal historical event, if not the culmination of a longer process of capitalist self-destabilization.

Augie March thus resonates with contemporaneous concerns over middle-class expropriation, but although this is interesting in its own right, what we need to be concerned with—as in the case of all the works of fiction we are considering—is how it refracts these concerns into developments in literary form. In *Augie March*'s case, the clue comes from the parallel that Bellow draws between the collapse of the Einhorns' propertied independence and the end of the regime of ethnic Jewishness represented by Grandma Lausch. The Commissioner is dying, Augie makes a point of noting in a chapter that pairs the events, at precisely the moment that Augie is installing the Marches' former boarder in a home for the elderly. The latter event, which represents a shift from the family to the institution in a way that we can take as generally symbolic of the passing of an older regime of ethnic identity, is somehow connected, Bellow suggests, with expropriation. Lausch is not allowed to keep her large trunk—"a yellow old pioneer piece with labels from Yalta, Hamburg Line, American Express" (95) that again suggests the merging of immigrant Jewish and American settler identities—in her shared room, but "had to go down to the basement where she picked out what she would need—too many things, in the opinion of the stout brown lady superintendent" (97). Lausch loses her property just as the Einhorns are about to, and her "banishment" (96), which Augie reads as the passing of the old order, immediately precedes his parallel disillusionment with Einhorn: "I was down on him occasionally, and I said to myself he was nothing—nothing. Selfish, jealous, autocratic, carp-mouth, and hypocritical" (99). Even if Augie, as he notes, "in the end, . . . every time had high regard for" Einhorn (99), he now sees his mentor's limitations. Augie's nearly simultaneous disillusionment with Lausch and Einhorn stands out in terms of what I have been suggesting is the book's rough allegory of assimilation. The coincidence of these two events suggests that rather than exchanging Jewishness for a more properly American identity, as the standard account of assimilation would have it, Augie instead divests himself of Jewishness and Americanness at the same moment. Or rather, he divests himself of specific historical forms of Jewishness and Americanness that are understood to be both parallel to each other and superseded by the new practices of self-marketing he begins learning (prepared, to be sure, by his "adoptional" character) at the home of the Renlings.

Bellow thus makes nostalgia for Jewishness congruent with a more widespread white-collar nostalgia for an earlier form of middle-class identity, both of which he sets in opposition to the self-alienating white-collar "personality market" (Mills, *White* xviii). In so doing, he not only suggests that Jews are prototypically other-directed Americans but, perhaps even more significantly, that postwar Americans are prototypically Jewish. Americans, like Jews, understand themselves to have lost something via their entry into the (new) middle class; in the terms with which we have been wrestling, they understand themselves to have assimilated. By aligning Jewishness with the property-owning autonomy that middle-class Americans fear they have lost, Bellow makes it possible for all members of the new middle class, Jewish or not, to regard Jewishness nostalgically. But *Augie March* does not understand Jewishness only in nostalgic terms; if it did, it would confirm the model of assimilation as deracination. Rather, *Augie March*'s engagement with Jewishness at the level of content is seconded by its engagement with Jewishness at the level of style. The stylistic innovations that, for many readers, have marked Bellow's true achievement in the novel show him deploying Jewishness as an individualizing marker in response to what we have seen are his (prototypical) concerns about alienated mental labor.

Praise of *Augie March*'s style has consistently linked it to the achievement of precisely the literary individualism that, for Bellow, was threatened by the university and other institutions of literary production and dissemination. Norman Podhoretz provides the most extended version of this argument, suggesting that Bellow is "the first gifted American novelist" writing in the wake of modernism "to search for another mode of operation and a more viable orientation to the world of the postwar period,"[34] and that *Augie March* fulfills this search for "a new prose style" via "the first attempt in many years to experiment with the language in fiction" (216). *Augie March*'s new style constitutes, moreover, a personal breakthrough for Bellow, who "had done his duty by the well-made novel, writing in the shadow of the accredited greats who were sanctioned both by the academy and the literary quarterlies," but who in his third novel fashions his own approach to prose fiction distinct from that of previous masters like "Flaubert, Kafka, Gide, [and] Henry James" (216). Podhoretz's sense of *Augie March*'s style as emerging out of a productive tension with a novelistic canon that "had become a burden rather than a help" (216) concretizes the idea of writerly labor as the site of resistance to the "authority" of high culture, as well as supporting Bellow's own belief that in this novel he had finally achieved something beyond the student exercises—the M.A. and Ph.D., as we saw above—of his previous books. *Augie March* constitutes Bellow's professional coming-of-age because it, unlike *Dangling Man* and *The Victim*, is not written for his teachers—not real teachers, of course, but the teachers-by-example of the well-made modernist novel circa the early 1950s. Tanner, who sees the attempt to "find a stylistic form which will not trap [the author] inside the existing forms of previous literature" (19) as a general preoccupation of postwar American fiction, contends that Augie's "ability to resist all fixed social forms" emblematizes his creator's "attempt to escape from the cramping constrictions of fixed stylistic forms": for Bellow the book constitutes at the level of form—as it does for his protagonist at the level of plot—"a bid for freedom from external patterning" (64).

At the macrolevel, *Augie March*'s primary stylistic innovation is its reinvention of the picaresque, with the introspective narrators and near plotlessness of Bellow's first two books exchanged for the new novel's "looseness of structure, . . . saltiness of language, . . . thickness of incident, [and] robust extroversion" (Podhoretz 216). In this respect Bellow's novel recalls not only Twain's American picaresque but also such earlier British models as Fielding's *Joseph Andrews*, on whose structure Bellow self-consciously drew during Augie's composition (Atlas 191).[35] The structureless structure of the picaresque serves Bellow, as I have already suggested, as the formal analog of Augie's "various jobs," and lends the novel the air of peripatetic individualism that Kerouac and others would later develop in the road novel. Yet *Augie March*'s picaresque form, like its protagonist's unorthodox work history, ultimately fails to transcend the deindividualizing world of the organization man. For both Podhoretz and Tanner, *Augie March*'s episodic structure, with its lack of linear development, downplays character in favor of setting: Augie is "a character who is curiously untouched by his experience, who never changes or develops, who goes through everything yet undergoes nothing" (Podhoretz 218); "in holding back from planning and patterning out of respect for pre-patterned 'reality', Augie comes close to disappearing into the scenes through which he passes" (Tanner 68). *Augie March*, we might say, thinks to animate the American picaresque, with its romantic focus on the individual in flight from society, and instead succumbs to the pre-Romantic *deemphasis* of individual character embedded in the form. As Deidre Lynch notes in a recent discussion of Tobias Smollet's theory of the picaresque, the picaresque protagonist (or what Smollet calls the "principle personage") is the vehicle for the narrative's representations. Complaints that he is insufficiently characterized—that he lacks individuality—miss the point. To a degree, this character is supposed to be a means for producing a sense of social context (rather than a social context counting as a means for producing our sense of a character): this character is the prosthetic device that enables readers to apprehend the comprehensive, impersonal systems that bind them together.[36]

Bellow's picaresque serves the vital function of provisionally remapping the social in a period when the transformation of the middle class has undermined its traditional American coordinates. But with its emphasis on "social context" over character, it ultimately fails as a means of affirming Augie's—and through him, Bellow's authorial—individuality.

The stylistic innovation that does function in the interests of individuality in *Augie March* is its narrative voice. Augie, unlike most eighteenth-century picaresque protagonists, but like his American antecedent Huckleberry Finn, tells his own story in what Podhoretz describes as "a new prose style, the first attempt in many years to experiment with the language in fiction" (216). This prose style, as Podhoretz's characterization suggests, constitutes the novel's other, microlevel stylistic innovation, one that works at the sentence level to give its speaker a unique voice that would come to be identified as distinctly "Bellovian." *Augie March*'s narrative voice is to some degree anticipated by that of *Dangling Man*, which as I already noted in the introduction opens with a defense of emotional self-awareness against the Hemingwayesque style that had become the mark of serious fiction by the late 1940s. It is perhaps worth looking at this passage a second time:

> There was a time when people were in the habit of addressing themselves frequently and felt no shame at making a record of their inward transactions. But to keep a journal nowadays is considered . . . in poor taste. For this is an era of hardboiled-dom. Today, the code of the athlete, of the tough boy . . . is stronger than ever. Do you have feelings? There are correct and incorrect ways of indicating them. Do you have an inner life? It is nobody's business but your own. Do you have emotions? Strangle them. To a degree, everyone obeys this code. And it does admit of a limited kind of candor, a closemouthed straightforwardness. But on the truest candor, it has an inhibitory effect. Most serious matters are closed to the hardboiled. They are unpracticed in introspection, and therefore badly equipped to deal with opponents whom they cannot shoot like big game or outdo in daring. (7)

This passage, we might now note, is marked by short, declarative sentences and a blend of tough-guy vernacular ("nobody's business"), faint Anglicisms ("that curious mixture"), and vaguely scientific-sounding prose ("an inhibitory effect") that seems to mimic the stoic language it decries. Bellow's critique of the Hemingwayesque style, that is, is not yet reflected in his own style in *Dangling Man*. For *The Victim*, his second novel, Bellow turns to third-person narration, thereby severing the link between prose style and character. When he returns to the first person for *Augie March*, he has discovered a very different style, one once again apparent in the novel's opening paragraph:

> I am an American, Chicago born—Chicago, that somber city—and go at things as I have taught myself, free-style, and will make the record in my own way: first to knock, first admitted; sometimes an innocent knock, sometimes a not so innocent. But a man's character is his fate, says Heraclitus, and in the end there isn't any way to disguise the nature of the knocks by acoustical work on the door or gloving the knuckles. (3)

Here the declarative sentences of *Dangling Man* survive only as a scaffold ("I am an American . . . and go at things as I have taught myself") on which Bellow erects a miscellaneous structure using participles, hyphens, colons, and semicolons. The resulting style seems as energetic and peripatetic as the protagonist himself, the product of a mind that if disorganized is still unwilling to be bound by constraints of a "closemouthed" hardboiled style: Augie's dictum might well be "never use one word where two—or three, or five—will do."

Podhoretz, who as we have seen finds Augie an unsatisfyingly developed character, nonetheless admits that the novel's "free-flowing style" confers upon its narrator a certain roundedness through its combination of different vocal registers. Composed, Podhoretz suggests, of "three apparently incongruous rhetorical elements—cultivated, colloquial, and American-Jewish," Augie's style suggests the multiplicity of his "character" and thereby "the new wholeness of being to which Bellow had always aspired" (218). Augie is, in this reading, a (literally) three-dimensional character. If Podhoretz likewise finds this aspect of the novel ultimately unsatisfying—"Bellow seems to be twisting and torturing the language in an almost hysterical effort to get all the juices out of it" (218–19)—his description of the novel's style bears further consideration. Insofar as he describes the "American-Jewish" character of *Augie March*'s prose as simply one element of its tripartite mixture, Podhoretz provides a reading of the novel's style that concretizes the persistent accounts of Bellow's work as transcending the "minority" status of earlier Jewish writing while remaining inseparably articulated, in Kazin's words, with "the modern Jewish experience." In particular, Podhoretz's invocation of the "cultivated" and "the colloquial" suggests precisely the upward mobility that, as we have seen, was central to "the modern Jewish experience" of the postwar period: a kind of upward mobility secured, crucially, through cultural capital.

Bellow's achievement is to imagine a way of entering the white-collar middle class without completely sacrificing one's individuality. The end of the novel seems to present Augie at his most white-collar, "in business" (530) as an agent for a man named Mintouchian. Augie's usefulness to Mintouchian derives, however, not from his other-direction, but from the novel form of worldliness that he has acquired by following through on his attractions to others. On one hand, his cosmopolitan knowledge of European language and culture fits him to do Mintouchian's business in Europe. On the other hand, his experience of various demimondes suits him for the "illicit" nature of this business (529). Augie's job at the end of the book, that is, fulfills the self-conception he articulated early on: "I was around people of other kinds too. In one direction, a few who read whopping books in German or French and knew their physics and botany manuals backwards, readers of Nietzsche and Spengler. In another direction, the criminals" (113). This typically Bellovian combination simultaneously grounds Augie's upward mobility and distinguishes it from the deindividualization thought to be the fate of the organization man. Unlike Simon and other characters in the novel who remain stuck in their respective worlds, Augie has traveled among and ultimately mastered all of them. If this distinguishes Augie from all the other characters within the novel, it likewise distinguishes him outside the novel from the faceless organization man whose entry into the middle class comes at the cost of rejecting anything that sets him apart from his colleagues.

Augie's complex relationship to cultural capital epitomizes the emergence of postwar Jewish identity from the intersection of Jewish entry into the white-collar middle-class mainstream and this mainstream's simultaneous transformation of outsider status into a positive value. In a key passage, Augie describes how, "struck by the reading fever" (193), he hangs on to the books that he is supposed to be stealing for University of Chicago students, a moment that transforms a marginal position vis-à-vis the official culture into a source of pride:

> I sat and read. I had no eye, ear, or interest for anything else—that is, for usual, second-order, oatmeal, mere-phenomenal, snarled-sholeace-carfare-laundry-ticket plainness, unspecified dismalness, unknown captivities; the life of despair-harness, or the life of organization-habits which is meant to supplant accidents with calm abiding. (194)

Augie March is, on one level, a fantasy about acquiring the cultural capital necessary for upward mobility while bypassing the putatively deindividualizing institutions responsible for disseminating it.

Within this fantasy Jewishness, as I have suggested, inhabits the site not of group identity but of individual difference. The fact that the end of the book shows Augie writing what will ultimately become the novel reminds us that these questions of mental labor have their formal analog in the book's tripartite linguistic structure.[37] Here the echoes of Yiddish in Augie's narration—"But toward women he didn't change at all" (119); "that I shouldn't be too good to do as he was doing was of enormous importance to him" (239); "a similar night for me was, years after this, on a crowded ship from Palma de Mallorca to Barcelona" (391)—persist as a linguistic trace of Augie's ethnic origins parallel to his criminal associations. They exemplify, that is, a colloquial accent that prevents Augie from being submerged within the "cultivated" side of his character. If this cultivated side links him to postwar Jewish upward mobility, his colloquial and "American-Jewish" sides prevent him from experiencing such mobility as assimilation in the bad sense of deracination. Augie retains the marks of his class and ethnic origins in his new "American" speech: new in the sense both that it represents the newly American status of Jews participating in the mainstreaming effects of white-collar culture, and that this new Jewish presence reformulates what it means to be—to sound—American.

Augie, not to put too fine a point upon it, becomes a Jewish intellectual. Although Kazin got much right about Bellow, he was wrong to claim that "Bellow's more lasting fictions will probably be those whose personae are not *exactly* as intelligent as he is—*The Victim* and *Seize the Day* [1956]" (135; Kazin's emphasis). On the contrary, Bellow's most enduring novels have been the ones built around characters most like their creator: Augie, Herzog, Artur Sammler, Charlie Citrine. In postwar Jewish fiction the Jew becomes the Jewish intellectual, because the latter figure simultaneously exemplifies the concerns about alienating mental labor central to the white-collar middle class and retains a memorializing connection to a culture and an identity understood to stand in valuable opposition to the inexorable tide of white-collar middle-class homogenization. The Jewish intellectual is the organization man with a difference: a difference, as Bellow's novels attest, that is not limited to Jewishness (it can also be Augie and Charlie Citrine's urban demimonde, or Herzog and Sammler's Western high culture), but which interprets Jewishness in this individualizing way. Bellow has proven a more lasting author than Bernard Malamud in this regard because Malamud, crafting characters unlike himself, constructs Jewishness as *simply* nostalgic, a residual culture located in urban enclaves far from the white-collar suburbs. In Kazin's formulation,

> The outside world, for which Jews can be "another," does not even reach the consciousness of Malamud's Jews. They exist for each other, depend on each other, suffer each other and from each other with an unawareness of the "world" that *is* the definitive and humorously original element—and for which Malamud has found a narrative language whose tone derives from the characters' unawareness of any world but their own. (140)

Roth, on the other hand, succeeds and even surpasses Bellow as the most accomplished author in this tradition with his own stable of autobiographical characters: Alexander Portnoy, Nathan Zuckerman, Philip Roth. In this respect, we might conclude by briefly noting how Roth's own breakout book, the novella *Goodbye, Columbus,* replicates *Augie March*'s construction of the Jew as intellectual. Roth's story maps the postwar reorganization of Jewish identity through white-collar upward mobility onto the short-lived romance between Newarker Neil Klugman and Brenda Patimkin of suburban Short Hills, New Jersey. For this purpose it develops a series of fairly obvious contrasts between Neil and his family, who represent a residual urban, working-class version of Jewishness, and Brenda and her family, who are enacting a generational drama of assimilation in the white-collar suburbs. Neil's family is extended (he lives with his aunt and uncle, his parents having moved to Arizona), Brenda's is nuclear. His lives in an apartment, hers owns a home. And whereas Brenda's household conforms to postwar gender norms, Neil's is run by his aunt, a matriarchal figure who seemingly divides her time—this is Roth, after all—between pressing food on Neil and delivering herself of Molly Goldberg-like aphorisms. Unlike the Patimkins' well-organized house-hold, that of Neil's aunt is marked by an elaborate and idiosyncratic order all her own: "None of us ate together: my Aunt Gladys ate at five o'clock, my cousin Susan at five-thirty, me at six, and my uncle at six-thirty. There is nothing to explain this beyond the fact that my aunt is crazy."[38] Unsurprisingly, however, given postwar attitudes toward organization, Roth treats such behavior not only as a source of humor but also as an appealing contrast to the Patimkin household, whose superficial placidity constantly threatens to erupt under pressure of the festering resentments, especially those between Brenda and her mother, that lie just out of sight. Ultimately, Brenda and her family serve as an object lesson in the dangers of assimilation, a threat symbolized by, among other things, Brenda's nose job and her brother Ron's nostalgia (hence the story's title) for his college days at Ohio State.

Roth's novella thus makes explicit and even schematic the more evanescent contrast between urban Jewish and white-collar worlds in *Augie March*. For Roth as for Bellow, moreover, the former is linked to small-property ownership. If Neil's aunt and uncle, who at one point make plans to attend a Workmen's Circle picnic (47), represent an increasingly residual Jewish working class, Brenda's father and her uncle Leo, whom Neil meets at a wedding, represent the pre-white-collar middle class of small-property owners. Mr. Patimkin, who, "tall, strong, ungram-matical," reminds Neil of his father (21), retains a tie to Newark through his business, Patimkin Sinks. During Neil's visit Mr. Patimkin—who works in an office hung with girlie calendars and bullies suppliers on the phone—extols hard work and tells Neil, "Here you need a little of the *gonif* [thief] in you" (94). Patimkin's brother Leo, whom Neil meets at Ron's wedding, represents a less-successful version of the pre-white-collar middle class. A traveling salesman whose light bulb business has been hurt by supermarkets, Leo envies his brother's success and longs for a similar suburban apotheosis: "This city is crazy!" he tells Neil. "If I had a little money I'd get out of here in a minute. I'd go to California" (115). Like Miller's Willy Loman, Leo represents a pathetic-because-outmoded version of sales in which "the salesman's own creativity, his own personality" played a role (Mills, *White* 185). Like his brother, he pins his hopes on his college-educated children: "You gotta use psychology. That's why I'm sending my kid to college. You don't know a little psychology these days, you're licked" (113). In *Goodbye, Columbus*, Roth depicts entry into the white-collar middle class as not merely a shift of occupation but a cultural transformation, one with a problematic relation-ship to Jewish identity. Neil's aunt asks him, "Since when do Jewish people live in Short Hills? They couldn't be real Jews believe me" (58); Mr. Patimkin himself, half admiringly noting his son's incompetence at Patimkin Sinks, tells Neil, "They're *goyim*, my kids, that's how much they understand" (94).

If the Patimkin children raise the specter of assimilation as deracination, it is Neil himself who represents another possibility—Augie's possibility—of upward mobility via the intellectual's consolidation of white-collar status and Jewish difference. If much of the novella works to align Neil with the residually more "Jewish" world of Mr. Patimkin's generation, a scene with Brenda's mother suggests that he represents an emergent form of Jewish identity superior to the Patimkins'. Caught in the same room as Mrs. Patimkin as she makes phone calls for Hadassah, Neil endures a lengthy inquisition about his own and his family's participation in Jewish activities. At one point she asks what temple he belongs to, which sets off the following exchange:

> "We used to belong to Hudson Street Synagogue. Since my parents left, I haven't had much contact."
>
> I didn't know whether Mrs. Patimkin caught a false tone in my voice. Personally I thought I had managed my rueful confession pretty well, especially when I recalled the decade of paganism prior to my parents' departure. Regardless, Mrs. Patimkin asked immediately—and strategically it seemed—"We're all going to Temple Friday night. Why don't you come with us? I mean, are you orthodox or conservative?"
>
> I considered. "Well, I haven't gone in a long time . . . I sort of switch . . ." I smiled. "I'm just Jewish," I said well-meaningly, but that too sent Mrs. Patimkin back to her Hadassah work. Desperately I tried to think of something that would convince her I wasn't an infidel. Finally I asked: "Do you know Martin Buber's work?"
>
> "Buber . . . Buber," she said, looking at her Hadassah list. "Is he orthodox or conservative?" she asked. (87–88; Roth's ellipses)

It would be a mistake to see this as a late reversal of the novella's assimilation plot, with Neil here revealed for whatever reason as *less* Jewish than the Patimkins of Short Hills. On the contrary, this passage suggests that Neil represents a different kind of new Jew, one characterized not by suburban affluence but by his connection to the Jewish intellectual world.

If Neil's citation of Buber defines him as a potentially middle-class brainworker, it nonetheless locates him outside Mrs. Patimkin's version of Jewishness as, damningly, an instance of The Organization. This passage implicitly links Neil's intellectual status—his reading of Buber—with a position outside the institutional matrix that characterizes Mrs. Patimkin's Jewishness and, according to Herberg, epitomized the postwar reorganization of American religion more generally. For Herberg, Americans had become in the postwar period "in one way, more religious than they have been for a long time . . . and yet, in other ways, . . . more remote from the centralities of Jewish-Christian faith than perhaps they have ever been" (54). Like their Protestant and Catholic colleagues, Jews had embraced their religion's institutional forms at the same time that they had eschewed its theological content:

> Virtually all Jewish children become Bar Mitzvah today, as was not the case twenty, thirty, or forty years ago, but the Bar Mitzvah is usually nothing but a lavish and expensive party, with the religious aspect reduced to insignificance, if not altogether ignored. Much of the institutional life of the synagogue has become thus secularized and drained

of religious content precisely at the time when religion is becoming more and more acknowledged as the meaning of Jewishness. (211–12)

Mrs. Patimkin exemplifies this new form of "self-identification in religious terms," whose stress on "institutional affiliation" Herberg, following Riesman, relates to "the pressures of other-directed adjustment . . . among the younger, 'modern-minded' inhabitants of Suburbia" (273). Her questions to Neil attempt to locate him in a particular temple and a particular (respectable) form of Judaism, while her work for Hadassah invokes what Herberg describes as the postwar institutionalization of American religion. Hence her chilly response to Neil's "I'm just Jewish," which for her does not parse as an answer precisely because it places Neil's religious identity—admirably, in the eyes of the book's implied reader—outside her institutional understanding of Jewishness.

Goodbye, Columbus works, like *The Adventures of Augie March*, to define its protagonist as a perpetual outsider, belonging fully to neither the residual culture of urban Jewishness nor the increasingly dominant culture of middle-class suburbia. Neil instead embodies a third position that undermines what might otherwise seem like an embrace of an oversimplified understanding of assimilation. Like the younger Patimkins he is college-educated, but at Rutgers-Newark rather than Brenda's Radcliffe or Ron's Ohio State; moreover, his job at the Newark Public Library clearly places him—as Brenda increasingly comes to complain—outside the younger Patimkins' upwardly mobile trajectory. At the same time, he does not belong to the world of Patimkin Sinks, either. When Mr. Patimkin fondly complains of his son that "he ain't got the stomach for business. He's an idealist" (94), Roth clearly intends this as a joke at the sentimental jock Ron's expense. But it is in fact Neil himself who is the classic *luftmensch*, as his imagined experience taking Ron's place supervising his father's employees hints:

Suddenly I could see myself directing the Negroes—I would have an ulcer in an hour. I could almost hear the enamel surfaces shattering on the floor. And I could hear myself: "Watch it, you guys. Be careful, will you? *Whoops*! Oh, please be—*watch* it! Watch! Oh!" Suppose Mr. Patimkin should come up to me and say, "Okay, boy, you want to marry my daughter, let's see what you can do." Well, he would see: in a moment that floor would be a shattered mosaic, a crunchy path of enamel. "Klugman, what kind of worker are you? . . . Don't you even know how to load and unload?" "Mr. Patimkin, even breathing gives me trouble, sleep tires me out, let me go, let me go." (91–92)

Unfit for either Mr. Patimkin's brand of business or the world of high-status white-collar professions—Brenda at one point sarcastically asks him, "Are you planning on making a career of the library?" (51)—Neil in fact serves as a proxy for the Jewish intellectual à la Roth. Neil confirms his intellectual role, in typical postwar fashion, through the reverse snobbery that he levels at such aspects of the Patimkins' lifestyle as Ron's record collection, with its "semi-classical" recordings by Andre Kostelanetz and Mantovani and, of course, the "Columbus record" (64).

At the same time, if Neil remains finally outside the worlds of all the other characters, he enters them at least far enough to describe them for the reader. *Goodbye, Columbus* serves, in this regard, as an allegory of the birth of the postwar Jewish intellectual who is at once inside and outside the new suburban middle-class Jewish world: inside enough to understand it, outside enough to critique it. For this figure, the subject matter of Jewishness is at once essential and immaterial, that which must be simultaneously embraced and disavowed in constructing the anti-identity at the core of the "so-called Jewish novel."

CHAPTER FOUR

Flannery O'Connor and the Southern Origins of Identity Politics

DISCHARGED AFTER A DISORIENTING STINT in the army, the protagonist of Flannery O'Connor's 1952 novel *Wise Blood* returns to his tiny Southern hometown only to find it abandoned and his childhood home picked through, with "nothing left" in the latter but his long-dead mother's "chifforobe in the kitchen."[1] He leaves a note in one of its drawers reading "THIS SHIFFER-ROBE BELONGS TO HAZEL MOTES. DO NOT STEAL IT OR YOU WILL BE HUNTED DOWN AND KILLED" (14), then leaves the house forever. Later, he buys a second-hand car, telling the preacher's daughter who is trying to seduce him that "nobody with a good car needs to be justified" (64) shortly before a policeman to whom he has talked back destroys it by pushing it off an embankment (118).

Wise Blood is thus, like so many postwar novels, a story about lost property, although unlike most of her contemporaries O'Connor treats this loss as ultimately liberating. This no doubt reflects the devoutly Catholic O'Connor's faithfulness to New Testament attitudes about property, although what Motes ultimately achieves is not only salvation but also something that, in the postwar context, looks suspiciously like individualism. On one hand, O'Connor suggests in a 1954 letter, what Motes "could not get away from" is the reality of the "fall," "Redemption," and "judgment." But in the same letter she equates this reality with individuality, describing him as a figure of "absolute integrity" whose "wise blood . . . gets him further & further inside himself where one may be supposed to find the answer."[2] In a narrative sense, at least, what Motes cannot get away from is the same thing that the narrator of *Invisible Man* cannot "whip[ ]": "the mind, the *mind*" (580; Ellison's emphasis). Thus in *Wise Blood*'s final scene the dying Motes's landlady experiences a shut-eyed vision of "him moving farther and farther away, farther and farther into the darkness until he was the pin point of light" (131). Motes here achieves in and through redemption the individual integrity toward which so many other works of postwar fiction aspire.

But if *Wise Blood* thus abandons physical property as a source of middle-class individualism, it circuitously regrounds such individualism in the intangible property of cultural identity. O'Connor's status as the preeminent Southern writer of her time derives from the way in which her religious concerns allow her to reinvent Southern identity in terms amenable to the postwar obsession with individuality. Jon Lance Bacon is correct to argue that religion provides O'Connor with a "stronghold of individualism" from which to resist national mass culture:[3] "the prophet," she writes in another letter, "is a man apart. He is not typical of a group."[4] Whereas accounts of Southern distinctiveness from the antebellum period forward had stressed the value of ordered, hierarchical community in opposition to the alienating hyperindividualism of Northern market society, O'Connor participates in the postwar rewriting of Southernness as a form of individualism. But this individualism exists in and through regional identity: if O'Connor's prophets are men apart, it is not quite true that they are not typical of a group, insofar as they are almost always poor, white, rural Southerners. O'Connor's religious concerns enable her to relocate a Southern identity threatened by the postwar boom economy in the "backwoods prophets and shouting fundamentalists"[5] whose traditionalism paradoxically comes to seem like individualism in a world dominated by the deracinated white-collar middle class.[6] In thus revising Southern identity she transforms Southern poverty from the economic phenomenon it was (mostly) viewed as in the 1930s into a cultural phenomenon, and the poor white Southerner from an economic figure into a quasi-ethnic one. Poor white Southerners become vehicles in O'Connor's writing for middle-class self-hatred and fantasies of asocial behavior, just as black men do for Norman Mailer. But whereas Mailer's fantasies inform and thereby render problematic the identity politics that emerge from the sixties left, O'Connor's underwrite what we might call the identity politics of the postsixties right. In this latter formation, the conflation of the rural-local and the religious-universal implied by a phrase like "heartland American values"[7] becomes among other things a vehicle for middle-class *ressentiment* directed at The Organization in the form of Big Government (and not infrequently its urban minority clients, as well).[8] In this respect, O'Connor's writing does not transcend the social at all, but rather anticipates yet another politically problematic form in which the postpropertied middle class has misunderstood its proletarianization. For this reason it becomes all the more urgent to identify the class and economic concerns driving O'Connor's revision of Southern identity, as I attempt to do in this chapter.

O'Connor's work in fact unfolds in reaction to major demographic and economic changes transforming the South in the years following World War II. The postwar economic boom reached into the South, bringing the region close to economic parity with the rest of the nation for the first time since the Civil War:

> Nonagricultural employment grew swiftly as the regional economy became more diversified and a revolution in the countryside brought larger, more mechanized, and more productive farms accompanied by a vast movement of farm tenants and workers from the land. By 1960 only 10 percent of the Southern population was still engaged in farm labor. New Deal labor policies and the developments of the war period ended the isolation of the southern labor market and quickened the process of integrating southern labor into the national work force. Between 1940 and 1960, the South's population shifted from 65 percent rural to 58 percent urban, and cities like Atlanta, Dallas, Memphis, and Norfolk increasingly came to resemble the great metropolitan centers outside

the South. Southern per capita income tripled during the 1940s and by 1960 had risen to about three-fourths of the national average.[9]

In his 1960 *The Burden of Southern History*, C. Vann Woodward identified this new prosperity as a threat to Southern difference, decrying the "Bulldozer Revolution" throwing up suburbs "on the outskirts of every Southern city."[10] This transformation also had distinct class dimensions that O'Connor touches upon in her essay "The Regional Writer":

> I have a friend from Wisconsin who moved to Atlanta recently and was sold a house in the suburbs. The man who sold it to her was himself from Massachusetts and he recommended the property by saying, "You'll like this neighborhood. There's not a Southerner for two miles." At least we can still be identified when we do occur.[11]

Members of the white-collar middle class—many of them newcomers imported into the region as "executives and managers" of "corporations establishing branch plants in the South"—oversaw postwar development and championed it along with their allies from the old middle class.[12] Beginning with the war "retail and wholesale trade, insurance, finance, government, the professions, and similar predominantly white-collar occupations. . . . composed the fastest growing sector of the southern labor market," expanding from a quarter of the Southern workforce in 1940 to two-fifths in 1960 and over half by 1980.[13] Employees in these fields not only "absorbed much of the South's postwar prosperity [but also] exercised an increasingly important role in public life,"[14] one associated with the breakdown of the traditional social order organized around family and community and the liberalization of social values:[15]

> They were better educated and more widely informed on public issues than southerners generally and, according to opinion polls, were more tolerant on racial matters. Their families were in the vanguard of the stampede to suburbia and of the introduction of far-reaching changes in southern life-styles. They formed the base for the open-schools movement and for the moderate position in southern politics.[16]

O'Connor was born into an old-middle-class family that was on its way to becoming part of the new middle class or at least its booster auxiliary. Her father owned real estate and construction businesses in Savannah, and became an appraiser for the Federal Housing Administration in Atlanta prior to his death of lupus in 1941. O'Connor and her mother could not make the transition to Atlanta, and the pair moved to O'Connor's mother's family farm in rural Milledgeville in 1938.[17] This move anticipated O'Connor's subsequent ideological break with the Southern new middle class and its modernizing ethos.

If O'Connor and Woodward participate in a long tradition of decrying the threat posed to Southern distinctiveness by "Northernization,"[18] Woodward's critique in particular highlights the parallels between postwar discussions of the South and of Jews. For Woodward the South faces the same threat of cultural deracination through upward mobility that the discourse of assimilation imputes to postwar Jews. In response to this threat, Woodward turns to the South's history of economic backwardness—its "long and quite un-American experience with poverty" (17)—as a residual marker of Southern difference:

> Generations of scarcity and want constitute one of the distinctive historical experiences of the Southern people, an experience too deeply embedded in their memory to be wiped out by a business boom and too deep not to admit of some uneasiness at being characterized historically as a "People of Plenty." That they should have been for so long a time a "People of Poverty" in a land of plenty is one mark of enduring cultural distinctiveness. In a nation known around the world for the hedonistic ethic of the American Standard of Living, the Southern heritage of scarcity remains distinctive. (17–18)

Needless to say, Woodward's transformation of Southern poverty into a site of Lost Cause nostalgia along with the region's other experiences of "frustration, failure, and defeat" (19) differs markedly from discussions of poverty by New Deal and proletarian writers of the 1930s. For Woodward, poverty is not a problem to be solved by state intervention or worker organization but an oddly cherished "mark of enduring cultural distinctiveness." So, too, his discussion of such poverty as a "historical experience[ ]" and the site of "memory" effaces the actual limits of postwar Southern prosperity: the fact, for instance, that Southern workers in the mid-fifties earned on average only three-quarters what their non-Southern counterparts did. Woodward's very invocation of the Southern economy is, in this respect, profoundly uneconomic, and characteristic of a more widespread shift in both Southern and non-Southern understandings of the region. As one historian has put it, this period sees the region's transformation from "the nation's number-one economic problem" into its "number-one moral problem."[19] If accounts of Northernization, pro and con, had long treated this phenomenon as "synonymous with modernization,"[20] the region's relative postwar prosperity shifted the focus of such modernization from the economic realm to the racial system left untouched by—or even embraced in defiance of—"economic and demographic changes."[21] But the increasingly noneconomic understanding of Southern difference was not only evident in Civil Rights Era racial conflict. It was also visible in the way poor white Southerners came to seem less like subjects of economic exploitation than like bearers of a particular culture.

This transformation was not entirely unprecedented: in particular, it had important roots in at least some aspects of the Agrarians' resolutely culturalist critique of Northern industrialism in their 1930 manifesto *I'll Take My Stand*.[22] Its new centrality following the war can be seen, among other places, in Erskine Caldwell's postwar transformation from a critically respected and moderately successful "proletarian naturalis[t]" like Richard Wright or James T. Farrell into an exoticist author of "comic grotesques" whose paperback reissues sell on a par with Mickey Spillane's new novels despite their explicitly leftist politics.[23] Similarly, the comic novel *No Time for Sergeants* (1954) by O'Connor's fellow Georgian Mac

Hyman follows the adventures of Will Stockdale, a rural Georgian whose life in the small backwoods shack he shares with his father is interrupted by the arrival of an official bearing a draft notice.[24] After a series of misadventures Will arrives at training camp with his newfound friend, Ben, whose diminutive stature and timid temperament threaten his wish to follow in his military-hero forebears' footsteps by joining the infantry. When Will single-handedly defeats some bullies who have been tormenting him and Ben, Ben is terrified that the two of them will acquire a reputation for not being able to "take it and keep their mouths shut,"[25] which would lead to assignments in a less desirable branch of the service. Ben's fears come true when he and Will are assigned to the Air Force, where Will's naïve inability to adapt to military organization continually generates problems for the world-weary Sergeant King. Will and Ben are eventually transferred to an incompetent flight crew as gunners, and when the pilot drunkenly crashes their plane and leaves them stranded in Houston, they make their way back to their base only to discover that they are presumed dead in the accident. Horrified to discover that they are still alive, the general officiating at their heroes' funeral concocts a scheme to claim that their deaths were faked so that they could go on a special mission for the army—whereupon they are transferred, much to Ben's delight, to the infantry.

Much of *No Time*'s humor depends upon the contrast between Will's naïve simplicity and the bureaucratic machinery of the postwar military. Compared with other characters who are superficial, incompetent, and rigidly devoted to procedural detail—the colonel obsessed with latrine inspection, the psychiatrist who insists that Will discuss his hatred for his parents—Will comes off as not only likable but likable because he is not what Whyte will subsequently label "an organization man." This transformation of the Southerner into an antiorganization man was tremendously influential within postwar culture, shaping even the television programs of the era. A mid-fifties Broadway production helped launch Andy Griffith's career, and his television hit *The Andy Griffith Show* (1960–1968) gave rise to a whole subgenre, including its spin-offs *Gomer Pyle, USMC* (1964–1970) and *Mayberry RFD* (1968–1971). As several commentators have noted about *The Beverly Hillbillies* (1962–1971), which was the most popular program on television during its first two seasons,[26] these shows simultaneously made fun of their rural characters and posed them in virtuous contrast to contemporary life.[27] As exemplars of "the moral righteousness associated with their native setting,"[28] they repeatedly demonstrated "that character was more important than appearance, that a lifestyle one could purchase was no match for simple, traditional virtues."[29] These shows' embodiments of traditional rural virtues took on a different tone as the sixties progressed and Nixon's silent majority began to coalesce, but at least initially Americans understood their rural characters in contrast to the new middle class and its organizational milieu. Such mass-cultural representations of Southern difference flesh out Riesman's suggestion that "southern rural groups, Negro and poor white," remain in the stage of "tradition-direction" and thus constitute residual pockets of resistance to the spread of other-direction (32). But whereas Riesman merely neutrally describes what he sees as a case of uneven development, these mass-cultural texts ascribe to Southern difference a positive content, treating Southern culture as a site of admirable resistance to the homogenizing imperatives represented by the new white-collar middle class.

While this mass-cultural phenomenon might seem marginal to postwar history, *No Time* suggests the deeply political ramifications that the critique of the organization would subsequently have on both the left and the right. The novel's opening scene, in which Will's father attempts to drive off the draft-notice-bearing government representatives with a shotgun, no doubt resonated among at least some readers, in the year of *Brown v. Board of Education* and afterwards, with Southern resistance to federally mandated desegregation. But in its explicit invocation of race *No Time* rather evokes the administrative progressivism of the Johnson presidency. Hyman, an Army Air Corps veteran as well as a Southerner, is authentically ambivalent about the military organization. When the milquetoast Ben leads a march, for instance, Will notes that "after a while it seemed that his voice kind of changed somehow so it sounded right powerful, and he didnt [*sic*] even look like himself no more" (67). Here *No Time*, in marked contrast with most postwar texts, understands organizational membership not as emasculating self-alienation but as masculinizing participation in the group's authority. Even more surprisingly, the military bureaucracy teaches Will how to be color-blind. Ben scolds Will for calling a black officer a "nigger," because "he's an officer, and being an officer, he's just as white as you and me, and you're supposed to stand at attention, and you're supposed to salute!" (106). The literalist Ben subsequently denies seeing a black man when the same officer walks into the mess hall, leading Sergeant King to fear that he will not be able to pass his eye exam. But if this joke suggests that antiracism might be a positive product of the bureaucratic logic of organizations, *No Time*'s other, antiorganizational side anticipates critiques of government bureaucracy on both the left and the right. On one hand, its darkly comic tone and military setting anticipate such novels as Heller's *Catch-22* and Richard Hooker's *MASH: A Novel about Three Army Doctors* (1968), whose conflation of the state and The Organization took on increasingly left-leaning implications as the Vietnam Era progressed.[30] On the other, its specifically regional resistance anticipates the Republican Party's seizure, via Richard Nixon's 1972 "Southern strategy,"[31] of attacks on Big Government. Another line runs, in this regard, from Stockdale through Forrest Gump to (the faux-Southern, possibly faux-simple-minded) George W. Bush.[32]

Despite her dislike for mass-cultural representations of the South (exacerbated by the transformation of her 1953 story "The Life You Save May Be Your Own" into a teleplay starring Gene Kelly),[33] O'Connor participates with them in the project of imagining regional alternatives to the deindividualizing organization. One of her favorite plot devices is the previously isolated poor white Southerner's encounter with the newly deracinated region, a device she uses, for instance, in

Wise Blood. Like *No Time*, *Wise Blood* makes military service the engine for this encounter, although Hazel Motes's service is far less ambivalent than Will Stockdale's. Motes experiences the army as a faceless institution whose primary function seems to be moving people around—"The army sent him halfway around the world and forgot him"—and bringing them together with strangers: Haze's "friends . . . were not actually friends but he had to live with them" (12). Motes's experience thus encapsulates the demographic changes O'Connor worried were undermining Southern difference—accurately, insofar as the South's mid-century prosperity derived in large measure from its capture of "a disproportionate number of the nation's military bases and training centers" due to "its moderate climate, abundance of open space, and congressional influence."[34] Likewise, O'Connor's, military, like Hyman's, anticipates Whyte's description of The Organization, particularly his assertion that it was undermining both individual and regional identity.[35] Fittingly, then, Motes resists the effacement of his individual identity by insisting upon his regional one:

> He meant to tell anyone in the army who invited him to sin that he was from Eastrod, Tennessee, and that he meant to get back there and stay back there, that he was going to be a preacher of the gospel and that he wasn't going to have his soul damned by the government or by any foreign place it sent him to. (12)

Unfortunately for Motes, however, O'Connor has other plans: the army discharges Motes "in a city about three hundred miles north of where he wanted to be" (13), and when he does make it to Eastrod he finds it, as we have already seen, deserted.

Wise Blood thus unfolds in a South undergoing, as in most of O'Connor's fiction, the disruptive effects wrought by assimilation to the rest of the nation.[36] In his history of massive resistance Numan Bartley suggests that many white Southerners embraced segregation as a source of "the familiar" and "continuing identity" amidst postwar changes.[37] Motes experiments with this strategy in the first chapter of *Wise Blood*, although O'Connor treats this episode ambivalently. Motes becomes angry and confused when a black porter refuses to admit that he is from Haze's home town but instead insists that he is from Chicago, the intensity of Motes's reaction clearly reflecting his dismay at finding someone who experiences dislocation as liberating rather than threatening. Susan Edmunds suggests that a minor character's speech later in the book "organize[s] the relations between people and place around the central binary home/not home: the South, economic segregation, and racial purity line up against the North, an integrated industrial work force, and miscegenation."[38] Something like this dynamic is clearly already in place in Motes's encounter with the porter. If Motes can get the man to admit that he is from his hometown, the narrative suggests, then he will have won some control over the forces that have removed him from his home, depopulated it, and then sent him off to the impersonal city. There is, in this regard, an enigmatic passage later in the novel where the narrator tells us that Motes wears "old army shoes that he had painted black to get the government off" (95). Motes, we might read this passage as suggesting, turns to race to overcome the destabilizing changes he associates with the federal government, although in the end he merely covers over what he thinks to eliminate.

Here it is unclear whether O'Connor is critiquing or simply describing this process. On one hand, she herself does at least partially equate Southern identity with a local deference to racial hierarchy, as a 1959 letter to her correspondent Maryat Lee suggests:

> No I can't see James Baldwin in Georgia. It would cause the greatest trouble and distur-
> bance and disunion. In New York it would be nice to meet him; here it would not. I
> observe the traditions of the society I feed on—it's only fair. Might as well expect a mule
> to fly as me to see James Baldwin in Georgia.[39]

On the other hand, *Wise Blood* seems committed, according to Edmunds, to a delimited critique of Southern racism informed by O'Connor's Christian principles. At the level of biography, perhaps the clearest thing to say about the story's racial politics is that they replicate O'Connor's official ambivalence about the Civil Rights Movement. While expressing guarded support with its goals she objected to many of its methods and "refrained from standing in judgment of the white South."[40]

Racism, we might thus say, is as irrelevant to O'Connor's sense of Southern difference as it is to Hyman's. In O'Connor's case, however, this is not because she thinks that Southern culture might be better off ceding its racism (which she may or may not do), but because her unwillingness to judge Southern culture on this topic reinforces its position as an identity category. If her unwillingness to judge is, on one hand, clearly Christian in nature, on the other it just as clearly anticipates what Walter Benn Michaels has described as contemporary multicul-turalism's dislike of value judgments: its insistence that different cultures' beliefs are "neither true nor false, just different."[41] O'Connor was, of course, perfectly willing to judge other aspects of postwar culture, although her disinclination to extend such judgment to what she considered her own culture anticipates the subsequent adoption by the region's partisans of the language of multiculturalism. In his 1974 *The Americanization of Dixie: The Southernization of America*, for instance, John Egerton argues that

> integration of regions into a nation—like the integration of races and classes into a
> people—can be a great achievement. But it must be based on equity, and not on any
> notions of inferiority or superiority; it must be respectful and appreciative of differences,
> not destructive of them. The success or failure of any attempt at unity depends on what
> each party gains and loses, what each gives and receives, what each surrenders and retains.
> Integration should mean neither domination nor conformity—in this instance, neither
> the domination of the North over the South nor the creation of a bland and monoto-
> nously undifferentiated Union.[42]

Egerton's rather remarkable use of "integration" to describe the plight of the South—which he variously understands as a post–Civil Rights interracial polity and as a white commonwealth burdened by racial discord—makes clear the ironies of the multicultural understanding of the South. But while it is tempting to see this understanding (and subsequent appropriations of the language of victimization by supposedly beleaguered white men) as ironic or outright hypocritical adoptions of preexisting "fashionable concepts of ethnicity and cultural pluralism,"[43] Egerton suggests a different genealogy. For him, the need to respect Southern difference arises out of the same context of homogenizing assimilation that concerned earlier writers like Woodward and O'Connor. "[I]ndustrial development . . . meant jobs and money," he writes, "but it also meant grief," bringing with it not only pollution, sprawl, and urban decay but also "depersonalization, conformity and monotony" (18). These less tangible ills he specifically identifies with the middle class, whose "capacity for coopting and assimilating tributary movements into the main current of society is both inspiring and frightening— inspiring because of its potential for creating an open and diverse society, and frightening because of its tendency to produce homogenization and conformity" (182). Here multiculturalism emerges not from outside mainstream society but internally to it, in response to the felt need to preserve difference (any difference) against the threat of homogenization.

Although antidesegregation efforts were the primary site of Southern cultural resistance in the 1950s, religion is far more important than race to O'Connor's model of such resistance. O'Connor's 1955 story "The Artificial Nigger" enacts this shift from racism to religion as the ground of Southern difference. This story, like the first chapter of *Wise Blood*, can be read as an analysis and critique of poor whites' use of racism to soften the shocks of modernity. The story describes the misadventures of the rural Mr. Head and his grandson in Atlanta, to which the elder Head has brought the younger in an effort to cure him of his rebelliousness. The trip to Atlanta constitutes the grandson Nelson's introduction to race and racism: on the train he sees his first black man, whom he does not recognize as black (O'Connor describes him as "coffee-colored") until Mr. Head triumphantly points him out as "a nigger" (215–16). Crucially, this happens just as Mr. Head is trying to initiate a conversation with a clearly uninterested man in "a light blue suit and a yellow shirt unbuttoned at the neck" (214). Any embarrassment and anger that this situation might produce is displaced onto the black man: Nelson "felt that the Negro had deliberately walked down the aisle in order to make a fool of him and he hated him with a fierce raw fresh hate" (216). Once in Atlanta the pair wanders into an African American neighborhood and misses their train. Directed by a woman to take a streetcar to the train station, they follow the tracks into a white neighborhood. There Nelson accidentally runs into an elderly woman carrying groceries, and Mr. Head, embarrassed, claims not to know him. Nelson thereafter refuses to talk to his grandfather until, in a wealthy neighborhood filled with "big white houses . . . like partially submerged icebergs" (228) they come upon "the plaster figure of a Negro" (229) that gives the story its title. Overcome by their mutual amazement at this sight, they forget their differences, adopting identical poses and "gazing at the artificial Negro as if they were faced with some great mystery, some monument to another's victory that brought them together in their common defeat" (230). Mr. Head declares, "They ain't got enough real ones here. They got to have an artificial one," and Nelson says, "Let's go home before we get ourselves lost again" (230).

As this brief account of the story and its enigmatic climax suggest, "The Artificial Nigger" repeatedly stages racism as a means for poor whites to overcome the alienation caused by urbanization and their encounters with the middle- and upper-class beneficiaries of economic development. Race, the pair's encounter with the plaster figure suggests, is an artificial product by means of which "they" distract poor white Southerners' attentions from their big houses and "wide lawn[s]" (229). Read this way, the story casts doubt on what I have elsewhere identified as O'Connor's own project, the reconstruction of a Southern identity grounded in the local ("Let's go home"). This project, "The Artificial Nigger" suggests, is an ex post facto construction that is not only bought at the price of African Americans' exclusion but also distracts attention from a properly economic reading of poor whites' situation. Hence the ambiguity about whose victory—the real one of wealthy whites or the imagined one of African Americans—produces the Heads' defeat.

Yet for all this O'Connor endorses the story's climax, within which she reads race not as a means of displacing poor whites' *resentiment* from better-off whites onto blacks, but rather as a means of displacing the story from the political into the religious realm. The story ends, in O'Connor's reading, with Mr. Head finding "redemption"[44] when he recognizes God's "mercy" forgiving him "for sins from the beginning of time, when he had conceived in his own heart the sin of Adam, until the present, when he had denied poor Nelson" ("Artificial Nigger," 230–31). Within this framework the statue serves, again in O'Connor's own words, as a symbol for "the redemptive quality of the Negro's suffering for us all."[45] Here as elsewhere in her oeuvre, O'Connor's interest in poor white characters depends ultimately not upon their socioeconomic position or their politics but upon their proximity to evangelical Protestantism. Although there are historical reasons for the prominence of evangelical Protestantism in the poor white South,[46] O'Connor turns to religion as a means of transcending history. In Bartley's succinct formulation, "In the 1930s Erskine Caldwell had written about the grotesque inhabitants of Tobacco Road and attributed their condition to a social system that could be redeemed through political and economic reform. Two decades later, Flannery O'Connor wrote about more or less the same people and attributed the condition of each to an unfulfilled longing for God's grace, which made social reform rather beside the point."[47]

O'Connor's 1953 story "A Good Man Is Hard to Find" embodies this motif. As various critics, as well as O'Connor herself, have pointed out, "A Good Man" features a decisive mid-story shift from a satiric account of the new South to a fundamentally religious drama of redemption, a shift effected by the appearance of a character named The Misfit. The Misfit embodies O'Connor's theory of the freak, a character type that she associates with religious meaning and opposes to the world of the new middle class. "Whenever I am asked why Southern writers particularly have this penchant for writing about freaks," she notes in one of her essays, "I say it is because we are still able to recognize one. To be able to recognize a freak, you have to have some conception of the whole man. And in the South, the general conception of man is still, in the main, theological." Including her standard caveat that "the South is changing so rapidly that almost anything you say about Southern belief can be denied in the next breath with equal propriety," O'Connor predicts that should "the South . . . exorcis[e] this ghost which has given us our vision of perfection," then someday "the writer from the South may be writing about men in grey flannel suits and may have lost his ability to see that these gentlemen are even greater freaks than what we are writing about now."[48] The end of the South's theological vision will be marked by the region's complete assimilation into the world of the new middle class: the presence of the freak in Southern fiction is a sign that this has not yet happened.

Yet for some reason O'Connor was unconvinced by her practice in "A Good Man." In an April 1956 letter thanking her editor at Harcourt for his advice to "drop the matter of publication" of *Wise Blood* in Poland and Czechoslovakia, she suggests that "they would probably use The Misfit to represent the Typical American Business Man."[49] Bacon is no doubt right to read this passage as evidence of the putatively apolitical O'Connor's engagement with cold war politics.[50] But this leaves unanswered the more intriguing question of why O'Connor would expect anyone—even a propaganda-crazed Soviet ideologue—to confuse The Misfit with the sort of buttoned-down exemplar of suburban normalcy played by Gregory Peck in Nunnally Johnson's just-released adaptation of *The Man in the Gray Flannel Suit*. O'Connor's apprehension that The Misfit might be mistaken for the organization man's distorted reflection points to the exemplary status of "A Good Man" in her oeuvre: exemplary because it demonstrates how O'Connor mimics the concerns of the white-collar middle class precisely through her efforts to counter its perceived hegemony.

The story opens on a Southern family—father, mother, daughter, son, baby, and grandmother—bickering over where they will go on vacation that year. The setting is O'Connor's characteristically already-deregionalized South. As Bacon notes, the household is "penetrated by one of the mass media":[51] the father, Bailey, is "bent over the orange sports section of the *Journal*" while the older children "read[ ] the funny papers on the floor." O'Connor alludes to an even more national medium (and one more readily identified with the fifties), however: in response to her brother's suggestion that the grandmother stay home, the daughter, June Star, says, "She wouldn't stay at home to be queen for a day." The mother, meanwhile, wears slacks and feeds the baby food from a jar.[52] The auto vacation is itself a standard trope of postwar middle-class life, nor is it insignificant that the family wants to go to Florida, the state that, as Schaub notes, was "then beginning to incarnate the emptiness and deregionalization of American culture."[53] O'Connor's treatment of the family also "reflects her critical perspective on the American way of life."[54] Over against her Florida-bound, sports-section-and-comic-book-reading relatives the grandmother, who wishes "to visit some of her connections in east Tennessee" (137), represents a residual—although, as we will see, problematic—connection with a "traditional southern rural" emphasis on "family, clan, church, and community"[55] at odds with the new postwar nuclear family ideal.[56] The rest of the family devotes much of their conversation to the grandmother's superfluity—"She has to go everywhere we go," June Star complains (137)—almost as though they want to erase her presence so they can more closely approximate the new ideal.

The family's trip, moreover, takes them into a rural South that is just as compromised as their home life. Shortly after they eat the lunch they have packed for their first day of driving, they stop at a restaurant called The Tower "for barbecued sandwiches" (140). O'Connor's description of this roadside stand is worth quoting in its entirety:

> The Tower was a part stucco and part wood filling station and dance hall set in a clearing outside of Timothy. A fat man named Red Sammy Butts ran it and there were signs stuck here and there on the building and for miles up and down the highway saying, TRY RED SAMMY'S FAMOUS BARBECUE. NONE LIKE FAMOUS RED SAMMY'S! RED SAM! THE FAT BOY WITH THE HAPPY LAUGH. A VETERAN! RED SAMMY'S YOUR MAN! (140)

Schaub reads this scene as anticipating a later moment in which "the family's mindless, animal appetites . . . reemerge as instances of nature's appetite, red in tooth and claw, ready to consume."[57] O'Connor's description of Red Sammy's suggests, however, that this reading is incorrect, and not simply because O'Connor would certainly have rejected Schaub's naturalism. Schaub poses "a malign and unforgiving nature" as the ground of O'Connor's universalism, and hence implies that the Red Sammy's scene foreshadows a subsequent break from the story's initial satire of middle-class life.[58] But the emphasis on advertising in O'Connor's description of the restaurant—reinforced typographically by the capitalization that makes the ads stand out from the rest of the text, just as the signs would stand out on the highway—suggests that it is merely another part of their world. The family stops not out of some natural voraciousness, but because they have been told to. The restaurant, that is, appeals to the same media-saturated consciousnessess that they demonstrated in the opening paragraphs of the story; once inside, they engage the owner and his wife in banal conversation and play the jukebox. While Red Sammy's might seem like the kind of place that Jack Kerouac would romanticize in *On the Road*, it actually has more in common with *Lolita*'s lengthy catalog of tourist traps (including "the whole gamut of American roadside restaurants").[59] A direct line runs, in this regard, from Red Sammy's to the sort of tourist attraction that Don DeLillo satirizes (with similar use of capitalization) in the scene from *White Noise* (1985) where Jack Gladney and Murray Siskind visit "THE MOST PHOTOGRAPHED BARN IN AMERICA."[60]

O'Connor thus finds the "gray new world" of the middle class in the South, although she suggests that it takes a distinctly different form on Southern soil.[61] Red Sammy's is not a product of the denatured suburban environment in which "everyone tends to look, dress, and act like everyone else, to drive the same cars, to live in the same kind of houses, and, because of the power of the mass media, even to think the same thoughts."[62] Nor does it anticipate the sort of roadside vignette, inspired by the postwar critique of the suburbs, that will become a staple of authors like Thomas Pynchon (the "printed circuit" of San Narciso as seen from the highway)[63] or indeed DeLillo (the "sordid gantlet of used cars, fast food, discount drugs and quad cinemas" the Gladneys pass while fleeing from the Airborne Toxic Event).[64] What distinguishes Red Sammy's and The Most Photographed Barn in America from such scenes is that rather than exemplifying homogeneity they exemplify the effort to produce commodified difference in its midst—to produce a reason for tourists to stop in an otherwise undifferentiated landscape. Red Sammy's is, in this regard, an icon of commodified Southernness. It is no coincidence that the mother drops a dime into Red Sammy's jukebox and plays "The Tennessee Waltz," the song "by an unknown Oklahoman, Patti Page, [that] had sold three million records in eight months and had pushed 'White Christmas' off its perennial top seller pedestal."[65] If Red Sammy's admonition to his waitress wife to "go bring these people their Co'-Colas" (142) alludes to O'Connor's favorite example of an originally Southern product transformed into an exemplar of "American consumer culture,"[66] "The Tennessee Waltz" points in the opposite direction. Country music became nationally popular in the forties and fifties, we might propose, because it appealed to the same hunger for authenticity that would later drive the Southern television show craze: unlike Coca-Cola, that is, it was not deregionalized but hyperregionalized.

Crucially, these two options correspond to O'Connor's complaints about postwar Southern *literature* in ways that allow us to read "A Good Man" not simply as a critique of consumer culture but also as an allegory of the difficulties facing O'Connor as a Southern author. In "The Regional Writer," a 1963 talk given on the occasion of receiving an award from the Georgia Writers Association, O'Connor notes that

> I read some stories at one of the colleges not long ago—all by Southerners—but with the exception of one story, they might all have originated in some synthetic place that could have been anywhere or nowhere. These stories hadn't been influenced by the outside world at all, only by the television. It was a grim view of the future. And the story that was different was phony-Southern which is just as bad, if not worse, than the other, and an indication of the same basic problem.[67]

For the Southern author, O'Connor suggests, the general postwar difficulty of engineering a stylistic escape from rationalized mental labor is compounded by the possibility that what looks like such an escape may in fact be an equally complicit assertion of a false (because externally imposed) identity.

Unlike Faulkner, who Mark McGurl convincingly argues saw commodified versions of Southernness as his entrepreneurial stock in trade,[68] O'Connor sees them as products of an institutional matrix, epitomized by the university, in which writers are transformed into proletarianized mental laborers. Here it is worth noting that O'Connor was herself a graduate of the Iowa Writer's Workshop, from which she afterwards sought to distance herself and which she described in unsurprisingly cynical terms ("I wrote Dilly to find out where you and Ann were this year and she said at Iowa. I congratulate you on your endurance").[69] In this respect her critique of the university functions, like similar comments by Bellow, to distance her from it. Her efforts in this direction go beyond the merely gestural, however, insofar as she understands the problem with being an institutional writer as having to manipulate preexisting forms rather than creating and trading her own:

> It is not a matter of so-called local color, it is not a matter of losing our peculiar quaintness. Southern identity is not really connected with mocking birds and beaten biscuits and white columns any more than it is with hookworm and bare feet and muddy clay roads. Nor is it necessarily shown forth in the antics of our politicians, for the development of power obeys strange laws of its own.[70]

Here O'Connor depicts the aim of the serious Southern writer as not reproducing the tropes associated with the region thanks to the success of previous writers: respectively, Margaret Mitchell, Erskine Caldwell, and Robert Penn Warren. This is not simply a case of the anxiety of influence, as we might more readily suspect with O'Connor's comment elsewhere that "the presence alone of Faulkner in our midst makes a great difference in what the [Southern] writer can and cannot permit himself to do."[71] The anxiety of influence as Harold Bloom defines it involves the effort to overcome a respected predecessor,[72] but O'Connor does not respect the practitioners of "so-called local color" (from which, her syntax suggests, she partially exempts Warren). Rather, she sees them as depersonalized transmitters of tropes, just as the other-directed person takes in and redistributes signals or the white-collar worker repeatedly performs "the same paper routine" (Mills, *White* xvii). In this sense, I have violated the spirit of the passage by putting names to the tropological complexes that O'Connor leaves anonymous.

In the second half of "A Good Man" O'Connor undertakes to provide a better form of Southern identity through the mid-story introduction of The Misfit. The Misfit's appearance decisively breaks the satirical frame, altering the tone of the story and violently shifting it into a new direction. After leaving Red Sammy's the family passes a dirt road that, the grandmother incorrectly imagines, leads to a plantation house that she visited in her youth. Half-unintentionally embellishing its attractions, and winning over the children with a story of family silver secreted in a hidden panel, she succeeds in getting Bailey to turn around and look for the house. On the way, however, she remembers with a start that the house she was thinking of is actually in Tennessee. This upsets the basket in which she has concealed her cat, and the animal, leaping on Bailey's face, causes an accident. Dusting themselves off afterward, the family sees a car approaching—a car that, it turns out, carries the very escaped convict against which the grandmother had warned them. The grandmother naïvely lets on that she recognizes the killer, and he has his henchman take the rest of the family off in pairs and shoot them while he remains behind to converse with her. When she, in a daze, tells him, "Why you're one of my babies. You're one of my own children!" (152), and reaches out to touch him, he leaps back and shoots her. Upon the return of his accomplices, The Misfit tells one of them that "she would of been a good woman . . . if it had been somebody there to shoot her every minute of her life." In response to his colleague's "Some fun!" The Misfit replies, "Shut up, Bobby Lee, . . . It's no real pleasure in life" (153). On that note, the story ends in characteristically enigmatic O'Connor fashion.

In her letters O'Connor claims that The Misfit's appearance challenges the Grandmother out of "her superficial beliefs" and into a recognition of Grace, which he in turn rejects when she tries to share it with him.[73] She thus sees The Misfit and "the intensity of the evil circumstances" that he introduces as the catalyst for shifting the narrative out of the banal and into the transcendental.[74] Many of O'Connor's critics have concurred with this reading. Frederick Asals, for instance, argues that The Misfit's appearance interrupts the "random exterior movement" of the first half of the story, with its focus on "the discordance and emptiness of [the family's] superficial lives," and initiates "a progressive motion toward the deepest interiors" of the grandmother and the killer.[75] Similarly, Miles Orvell claims that "A Good Man" undergoes a "sudden change in [its] atmosphere," with "a gently satirical fiction with interesting shades of local color" giving way to the second half's "brutal confrontation."[76] What this formulation does not stress enough, however, is the way in which the local color is an object of not only the first half's satire but also the second half's brutality. If the grandmother's desire to visit her "connections" links her to the Southern past in a way that differentiates her from the rest of the family, her understanding of this past is attenuated and commodified, as her subsequent joke about a plantation that is "Gone with the Wind" makes clear.[77] The grandmother, in fact, exemplifies the misplaced nostalgia that O'Connor associates with the plantation-romance variety of "so-called local color." Seeing "a Negro child standing in the door of a shack," she exclaims, "Oh look at the cute little pickaninny! . . . Wouldn't that make a picture, now?" (139). Her conversation with Red Sammy when the family stops for lunch stresses the complicity of such nostalgia with middle-class linguistic banality:

"These days you don't know who to trust," he said. "Ain't that the truth?"

"People are certainly not nice like they used to be," said the grandmother. (141)

As Asals notes, the family's "accident is not accidental at all, but the responsibility of the grandmother," and the detour that precipitates the accident—and thus the encounter with The Misfit, and thus the transition within the story—stems from her "nostalgia for an antebellum mansion."[78] In the second half of the story, as The Misfit's henchmen take the rest of the family off and kill them, the narrative narrows in on just two characters, The Misfit and the grandmother. If we read the story as a metacommentary on regional identity, this suggests that O'Connor is less concerned with the deregionalized middle class—whom she treats as comic relief, and of whom she disposes once the story becomes, from her perspective, interesting—than with those who misread Southern identity as a form of local color. It is these people, represented by the grandmother, who inspire the incommensurate aggression and discipline dispensed by The Misfit.

Moreover, the Misfit is himself an exemplar of the proper form of regional identity that O'Connor proposes as an antidote to the "phony Southern." "An identity," O'Connor insists,

> is not to be found on the surface; it is not accessible to the poll-taker; it is not something that *can* become a cliché. It is not made from the mean average or the typical, but from the hidden and often the most extreme. It is not made from what passes, but from those qualities that endure, regardless of what passes, because they are related to truth. It lies very deep. In its entirety, it is known only to God, but of those who look for it, none gets as close as the artist.[79]

Here O'Connor crucially shifts the embodiment of regional difference from the tropes of local color (which are products of mental labor) to "identity" (which is a property of individuals whether or not they write). This move gets to the heart of O'Connor's strategy for dealing with the transformation of the middle class. In brief, after toying with the possibility of treating this transformation as a change in how the members of the middle class (including writers) work, she backs away and instead transforms it into a cultural phenomenon that some people (specifically, some but not all Southerners) are able to resist.

Shifting the terms of what constitutes Southernness in this manner allows O'Connor to retain a notion of the Southern untainted by either the erosion of the "landmarks of regional identification" or by the reified nature of so-called local color.[80] As I have already suggested, she understands the grotesque as a form opposed to the world of the new middle class: O'Connor was fond of citing Thomas Mann to the effect that "the grotesque is the true anti-bourgeoise style."[81] But she also sees it as a specifically Southern literary mode via the still-theological "conception of the whole man" that enables Southerners to recognize, and write about, freaks. Her account of the grotesque, however, reveals its dependence upon discourses of new middle-class identity. Grotesque "characters" remain "alive in spite of" the "strange skips and gaps" that characterize the grotesque's relation to the social, she writes: "They have an inner coherence, if not always a coherence to their social framework. Their fictional qualities lean away from typical social patterns, toward mystery and the unexpected."[82] If the organization man is characterized by the disappearance of his individual identity amidst an overarticulated "social framework," this description of the grotesque suggests that it restores individuality by underdrawing the social. Or rather, the grotesque intimates individuality insofar as individuality, like identity, inhabits the terrain of unrepresentability that O'Connor here calls "mystery." Grotesque characters' "inner coherence," that is, emerges not in spite of but *because of* the sketchy social framework they inhabit.

Still, it is not quite right to say that The Misfit embodies the absence of the social, since he does speak from a recognizable social position: that of the poor, white, religious Southerners whom O'Connor invests with the burden of universalism. Appealing to The Misfit, the grandmother tells him, "You could be honest too if you'd only try," and appeals to him to "think how wonderful it would be to settle down and live a comfortable life and not have to think about somebody chasing you all the time" (149). This is a joke not only because he is about to kill her family but also because she is projecting her middle-class notions of decency onto someone whose speech and biography mark him as part of another social stratum. As he recounts his past to her, "I was a gospel singer for a while. . . . I been most everything. Been in the arm service, both land and sea, at home and abroad, been twict married, been an undertaker, been with the railroads, plowed Mother Earth, been in a tornado, seen a man burnt alive oncet. . . . I even seen a woman flogged" (149). This is the list of "various jobs" that Augie March aspires to, but it is more than that: mixing marital status, natural disasters, and memorable spectacles with a series of mobile, temporary jobs, it departs radically from the world of the organization man defined by his job. As John Burt argues, "We know every job the Misfit . . . has ever had, but we never feel that those jobs place him, and the list seems to be a compilation of attributes which pointedly fail to define him, an exhaustive but unsatisfactory description of the things he might have been but did not remain."[83] Moreover, while it may seem strange to identify the Jesus-denying Misfit with religion, he exemplifies exactly the understanding of Southern Protestantism that O'Connor elsewhere imputes to Hazel Motes. "Haze . . . is the ultimate Protestant," she writes, "a kind of Protestant saint" who carries the Protestant rejection of doctrine to its logical extreme with the Church Without Christ but then "transcends" Protestantism when "his nihilism leads him back to the fact of his Redemption."[84] The Misfit follows a similar trajectory, exemplifying the "do-it-yourself" aspect of "the religion of the South" that O'Connor "as a Catholic find[s] painful and touching and grimly comic" but also on some level admirable.[85]

Yet The Misfit is also, puzzlingly, characterized by the same lack of agency that characterizes the organization man. Zeroing in on the grandmother's final prepositional phrase, he ignores and thus implicitly denies her suggestion that he could take control of his life: "Yes'm," he tells her, "somebody is always after you" (149). "I never was a bad boy that I remember of," The Misfit subsequently tells the grandmother, "but somewheres along the line I done something wrong and got sent to the penitentiary" (149). When she asks if he remembers what he did "to get sent to the penitentiary that first time," he replies,

> Turn to the right, it was a wall. . . . Turn to the left, it was a wall. Look up it was a ceiling, look down it was a floor. I forget what I done, lady. I set there and set there, trying to remember what it was I done and I ain't recalled it to this day. Oncet in a while, I would think it was coming to me, but it never come. (150)

To the grandmother's suggestion that, if he does not remember his crime, maybe he was imprisoned by mistake, he replies, "Nome . . . it wasn't no mistake. They had the papers on me" (150). Although The Misfit denies the charge of "a head-doctor at the penitentiary" who "said what I had done was kill my daddy" (150), he accepts the label of criminal nonetheless. As he tells the grandmother, "I found out the crime don't matter. You can do one thing or you can do another, kill a man or take a tire off his car, because sooner or later you're going to forget what it was you done and just be punished for it" (150).

To be defined by the institution is, of course, to be an organization man. Religion, as O'Connor's most sensitive critics have pointed out, enables O'Connor to transcend the impasse between such social ascription and the performance of individualism that, for figures from William Whyte to Vladimir Nabokov, simply reaffirms the system. Burt suggests, for instance, that O'Connor's final understanding of faith mobilizes "a skepticism which keeps us free . . . to be formed by something larger than our own intellects or the intellects of those around us."[86] And in a book that reads O'Connor's fiction through her engagement with the ascetic practices of early desert fathers, Richard Giannone suggests that for Hazel Motes "to find his true self, he must cast off the rule of fabricated social and political compulsions." But because Motes, "like the culture, is so fully captivated by the power of self-will, only a stronger power outside himself can force a clean break from the world."[87] About the truth-value of such claims we can, of course, say nothing: as Burt suggests in the title of his essay on O'Connor, her power as an author lies in her fascination with "What You Can't Talk About." But this desire to delineate the inarguable is a fascination that O'Connor shares with other postwar authors. At the level of narrative her turn to religion functions in much the same way as Rand's turn to free-market fundamentalism or Mailer's Reichian turn to psychological primitivism. For all these authors, the inarguable works to forestall "the pressures of society against the individual" (Whyte, *Organization* 7), the automatic agreement that marks the organization man. "A Good Man" is among O'Connor's most interesting works, in this respect, because in not quite intentionally unmasking The Misfit as an organization man it reveals the middle-class dimensions of precisely the strategies O'Connor mobilizes against the middle class.

The Postmodern Fallacy

IN DON DELILLO'S 1982 novel *The Names* James Axton, an American risk analyst based in Athens, works for a company that sells insurance to multinational corporations doing business in the Mediterranean and the Middle East. Axton, separated from his wife Kathryn, periodically visits her and their son, Tap, on the small Greek island where she participates in an archaeological dig. During one of these trips, Axton stumbles upon what appears to be a series of ritual murders committed by a cult whose victims' initials match those of the places where they are murdered, a pattern whose blend of meaning and meaninglessness preoccupies him for the rest of the novel. Written in the wake of the Iranian Revolution and the Tehran hostage crisis, *The Names* offers a self-conscious meditation on Americans' neoimperial efforts to make sense of a newly threatening world. Axton and his expatriate friends transform the places they have visited into "one-sentence stories" in an unsuccessful effort to assimilate their strangeness:

> Someone would turn up, utter a sentence about foot-long lizards in his hotel room in Niamey, and this became the solid matter of the place, the means we used to fix it in our minds. The sentence was effective, overshadowing deeper fears, hesitancies, a rife disquiet. There was around us almost nothing we knew as familiar and safe. . . . The sense of things was different in such a way that we could only register the edges of some elaborate secret. It seemed we'd lost our capacity to select, to ferret out particularity and trace it to some center which our minds could relocate in knowable surroundings. There was no equivalent core. The forces were different, the orders of response eluded us. Tenses and inflections. Truth was different, the spoken universe, and men with guns were everywhere.[1]

As these guns suggest, Axton's efforts to decipher the mystery of the death cult parallel his work writing reports on the hostility levels of the countries that he visits. Both activities, moreover, are simply subsets of the larger epistemological project of Americans in a world in which Pakistanis "throwing away their London suits to wear traditional things" means that "our lives are in danger" (269). *The Names'* theme, we might thus say, is the globalization of the American quest for legibility whose dark side, Michael Gilmore has shown, is the tendency to project outwards the very opacity it seeks to eradicate.[2]

A mystery of a different sort unfolds during the course of *The Names*, however, coming to fruition only in the novel's final pages. Early in the book, Axton is confronted at a dinner by a Greek nationalist named Andreas Eliades, who seems to have mistaken him for someone else. Later, however, Axton learns from his friend Ann Maitland that Eliades, with whom she has been having an affair, has been asking her questions about Axton and his employer, the Northeast Group. Subsequently, Axton's superior, George Rowser, calls him to Lahore to tell him that he is resigning following his failure to predict the Iranian Revolution, and to suggest that Axton do the same. Then Ann Maitland's husband, Charles, confronts Axton with the news, which he has learned from a foreign affairs journal, that the Northeast Group has been affiliated with the CIA. Finally Axton, during his regular run, is nearby when another expatriate is shot, an assassination attempt that he believes may or may not have been intended for him. Beyond this, the narrative offers no further resolution, ending with the possibility that Axton may or may not have been working for the CIA during his years abroad. As he suggests in his role as the novel's narrator, his ignorance as to his true role makes him all the more culpable: "Those who engaged knowingly were less guilty than the people who carried out their designs. The unwitting would be left to ponder the consequences, to work out the precise distinctions involved, the edges of culpability and regret" (317).

Lacking agency within the organization for which he works—to the extent that he is unsure exactly which organization he works for—Axton is the American organization man circa 1982, who in the era of multinationals is no longer confined to the United States. "Americans used to come to places like this to write and paint and study, to find deeper textures," he notes. "Now we do business" (6). A former freelance writer who has ghosted a book for an Air Force general known for his "muddled thinking," Axton is hired by Rowser to give the material coming into the Athens office "structuring, . . . perusal by someone with intellectual range. He wanted a view that was broader than the underwriter's or statistician's" (48). If this suggests an un-organization-man-like mastery and overview, explicitly contrasting Axton's "intellectual" work with the narrower perspectives of technicians, the next sentence deflates this description: "A tallish fellow with an educated face and khaki hair might be just what he needed for the region" (48). And in fact, Axton's work partakes of the reduction of complex societies into isolated bits of information that is central to the novel's critique of multinational capitalism[3]:

> He wanted to know about Turkey. I had precise figures for nonperforming loans. I had classified telex traffic between bank branches in the region. I had foreign exchange factors, inflation rates, election possibilities, exports and imports. I had cars lined up for gasoline, daily power cuts, no water coming out of household taps, crowds of unemployed young men standing on corners, fifteen-year-old girls shot to death for politics. No coffee, no heating oil, no spare parts for combat aircraft. I had martial law, black markets, the International Monetary Fund, God is great.
>
> I'd been given the scrambled telexes by my friend David Keller, a credit head at the Mainland Bank. Much of the other material I'd been given by our control for Turkey.

The streets of Istanbul were data in their own right, the raw force, the unraveling. The rest came from our contacts at the World Bank and various research institutes. (50)

The sentence about Istanbul's streets might seem out of place here, although given the novel's skepticism about Americans' ability to read other societies—their penchants for overgeneralizations and Orientalisms—it seems no less second-hand than the rest of the data that Axton transfers from his sources to Rowser. *The Names'* international theme is thus inseparable from Axton's characteristically white-collar employment as someone who conveys and manipulates information for others.

Like the authors of the forties and fifties, moreover, DeLillo also relates the question of white-collar work to the stylistic motivations of the novel itself, in this case through the filmmaker Frank Volterra's parallel obsession with the cult. Volterra feels that filming the cult will free him from "genre crap" and the "clapped-out producers" and "lawyer-agents in Nazi sunglasses" who object to his "napoleonic" directorial style (140). The difference between DeLillo's novel and that of his predecessors is that DeLillo's sympathies are not with Volterra—whose agenda is as morally problematic as those of the CIA and the multinationals—but with Axton, who acknowledges his complicity in crimes whose precise nature he cannot specify. The novel itself has a somewhat more complicated relation to these issues, organized around the way in which DeLillo—whose own previous novels were characterized by their Volterra-like efforts to "give a sweet twist to" popular genres (140)—manipulates the conventions of the spy story.[4] An early review complained that DeLillo failed to exploit the narrative possibilities of his plot: "The cult, which is more a cerebral puzzle than a physical threat, more reported to Axton than experienced by him, and the CIA-terrorist subplot, which is evolved too late and indifferently paced, are strangely unexciting."[5] But this seems like a self-conscious choice meant to contrast with the characters' desires to romanticize their roles. Charles Maitland, for instance, is fond of saying, "It is like the Empire. . . . Opportunity, adventure, sunsets, dusty death" (7). Axton's discovery of the Northeast Group's CIA ties raises the possibility of a similar romanticization. On one hand, it implicates him in unsavory activities. But on the other hand, it potentially reorders his mundane activities into the exciting shape of the spy story—transforming Axton into James Bond, the postwar period's sexiest organization man.[6] *The Names'* style thus represents a compromise between DeLillo's efforts to achieve a fully individualized, modernist style (realized most fully in the final chapter, a supposed excerpt from Tap's novel in progress) and his borrowings from the spy novel.

Critics from Leslie Fiedler and Ihab Hassan to Fredric Jameson have, of course, identified this compromise as one of the "fundamental feature[s]," in Jameson's words, of "postmodernism."[7] What *The Names* helps us to see is the extent to which this characteristic of postmodernism remains engaged with the transformation of the middle class into a corps of white-collar mental laborers.

The novel figures this transformation both as content, through its concern with the expatriate business class, and as form, through its stylistic engagements with the genre formulas that DeLillo connects (via Volterra's conflicts with his producers) to international capital and the loss of middle-class autonomy. The fiction of the 1950s, I have argued throughout this book, is characterized by its increasingly tenuous efforts to create via style a preserve of autonomy that would distinguish the artist from the organization man. The postmodern turn comes about when artists abandon this project and instead self-consciously reimagine themselves as laboring within and through the mass-cultural forms and formulas against which their predecessors had struggled. The key figure here is, of course, not a writer but the visual artist Andy Warhol, whose project as late as the mid-sixties could still be understood in terms of the concerns about style and mental labor central to the discourse of the fifties. Ellen H. Johnson's 1966 essay "The Image Duplicators—Lichtenstein, Rauschenberg and Warhol" is concerned, for instance, to defend the artists in question from assertions—in Warhol's case, his own—that their work consisted of mechanical copies of images from mass culture:

> Warhol wants his pictures to be artless, styleless, anonymous, painted without his interference. He solemnly denies that he makes any aesthetic decisions—a pretty piece of nonsense. He selects the image in the first place, determines the size of its enlargement, how many times it will be repeated on a given work, where it will be placed each time on the canvas, whether or not he likes accidental effects and irregularities, what the color of the ground will be, how to group the colors in a composition of variously colored panels. These are just a few of the aesthetic problems that the Warhol machine faces and solves. As Franz Kline said to the man who described Barnett Newman's paintings as too simple, "Sounds very complicated to me!"[8]

Here Johnson is concerned, in the face of the seeming agencylessness of Warhol's silk-screened reproductions ("without his interference"), to restore the "complicated" aesthetic choices that qualify Warhol as an artist rather than a white-collar worker reduced to "the cog and the beltline of the bureaucratic machinery" (Mills, *White* 80). Crucially, the counter-reading of Warhol as "a machine," whose artistic output is characterized by a "lack of consciousness, [an] emphasis upon mere reproduction of the image without any understanding of its original identity,"[9] constitutes no less of a commentary on the proletarianization of mental labor. In an era when artists' and intellectuals' chief preoccupation is to assert stylistic autonomy against the formal imperatives that link them to the proletarianized middle-class, Warhol's innovation is to fully inhabit the sphere of alienated mental labor: to call his studio "The Factory" and to respond to "the challenge of automation" by claiming that he wants to "becom[e] part of it."[10]

But we can already see in these reactions to Warhol what will become the canonical account of postmodernism, figured in Jameson's own discussion of Warhol's paintings as "representations of commodity or consumer fetishism"

(158). Johnson, for instance, suggests that the subject matter of Warhol and his colleagues corresponds to a transformation in the artist's environment:

> Caught in traffic jams, packed in buses, subways, elevators, or spending a quiet evening at home, never has the human being been such a captive of the printed image, constantly changing and endlessly repeated: in books, newspapers and magazines, on the shifting world of the TV or movie screen, the blaring billboards, highway signs, giant lighted ads for hotels, theaters, stores—everywhere pictured products and pictured people beckoning, commanding and assaulting. These are the fields of Suffolk and the Fontainebleau Forest of our painters. Machine images in a machine-made world.[11]

This passage directly anticipates not only Jameson's shift from the form of Warhol's work to what is represented in it, but also the specific thing that Jameson finds represented there: not soup cans or celebrity portraiture but the process of "commodity fetishism" central to the late capitalist regime (9).

Far from wanting to ratify this aspect of Johnson's reading of Warhol, I hope to suggest that something is lost in the transition to understanding postmodernism as "the cultural dominant of the logic of late capitalism" (Jameson 46). Johnson's emphasis on the denaturalized world of Warhol and his colleagues, like Jameson's account of the postmodern that it anticipates, is at odds with her overall stress on made form. Thus she argues, later in the essay, that artists like Warhol "reveal the insignificance of their subject matter by blatantly reproducing it."[12] This might seem to anticipate Jameson's argument that what is at stake in Warhol's work, and postmodernism more generally, is not content but a transformation in the nature of capitalism signified by the process of reproduction, although Johnson in fact means something different. Johnson deemphasizes content in order to emphasize form as a site of artistic agency, and thus to keep open "the tension between anonymity and artistic individuality."[13] Insofar as this tension indexes the transformation of the American middle class into proletarianized white-collar workers, it touches upon the crucial dimension of class that is missing from Jameson's reading of postmodernism. Jameson's account of postmodernism is, I want to argue, problematically totalizing insofar as it projects onto the world at large the experience of the postwar American middle class in transition.

Most theories of postmodernism do this, although Jameson's case is particularly telling insofar as he actively works to subsume the postmodern within a Marxist reading of history. Yet to the extent that he fails to recognize the middle-class dimensions of the postmodernism he describes, his own analysis falls victim to some of the problems that he identifies in others. In particular, Jameson takes issue with theories of "'postindustrial society' . . . consumer society, media society, information society, electronic society or high tech, and the like" that, in his opinion, "have the obvious ideological mission of demonstrating, to their own relief, that the new social formation in question no longer obeys the laws of classical capitalism, namely, the primacy of industrial production and the omnipresence of class struggle" (3). In the introduction, I argued that postwar critics of the white-collar middle class like Riesman and Whyte also tend to forsake class analysis in favor of depicting modernity as a reified conflict between Individual and Society. What this move effaces—although always imperfectly, as this book has attempted to show—is the *fulfillment* of the classical Marxist paradigm that for the past fifty years has been taking place in the United States with the transformation of the traditionally independent middle class into propertiless white-collar workers. Similarly, Jameson argues following Ernest Mandel that "late or multinational or consumer capitalism, far from being inconsistent with Marx's great nineteenth-century analysis, constitutes, on the contrary, the purest form of capital yet to have emerged, a prodigious expansion of capital into hitherto uncommodified areas" (36).

This move, at the heart of Jameson's account of postmodernism, makes it infinitely preferable from a Marxist perspective to all of its more or less merely culturalist competing theories. But Jameson's invocation of commodification also marks a symptomatically postmodernist turn away from production and toward consumption.[14] As we saw in Johnson's piece on Warhol, the invocation of commodification likewise marks a turn from form to content that, in the context of intellectual labor, erases the transformation of the middle class into structurally proletarianized white-collar workers. This erasure takes an almost parodic form in another mid-sixties piece on Warhol whose author contends that

> in his commercial work, most notably in the Campbell's Soup canvases, he presents us with images which are the final reduction of the importance of the machine in our lives—art untouched by human hands. The sterility of the subject matter is magnified to such an extent in these works that they emerge ultimately as a brilliant statement on the influence of the machine on our everyday lives.[15]

Here the effacement of intellectual labor expands outward to become the effacement of labor per se, as though the ingredients in Campbell's soup were not (in the same years when Cesar Chavez became a national figure) grown on farms or canned in a Camden factory.

A similar, albeit more subtle, effacement characterizes Jameson's account of postmodernism. Jameson alludes to "the conventional feelings of First World subjects that existentially (or 'empirically') they really do inhabit a 'postindustrial society' from which traditional production has disappeared and in which social classes of the classical type no longer exist" (53). But Jameson's own focus on postmodernism as a cultural and perceptual phenomenon does little to undermine such feelings. Here I do not mean to take the cheap (although admittedly available) shot that Jameson makes the subject of postmodernity a befuddled guest in a hotel with an invisible staff—essentially, as everyone always notes, an MLA participant. He does, for instance, suggest that what we refer to as "postindustrial" capitalism might be better denominated as "multinational" capital (35), a move that at least provisionally gestures toward his more recent emphasis on globalization as, among other things, the site of "a global division of labor on an extraordinary scale."[16] Even beyond the question of the global industrial and service-worker classes, however, Jameson's stress on postmodernism as a perceptual condition effaces the question of *intellectual* labor that marks the downward mobility of the first world middle class in retreat. Jameson's figure for mental labor in this essay, cognitive mapping, remains problematically voluntary, something that one does or does not do for political reasons rather than something that one must do as the terms of one's employment. For Jameson, too, this effacement of mental labor seems somehow inevitably to circulate around Warhol. Thus he invokes the fact that "Warhol began his artistic career as a commercial illustrator for shoe fashions and a designer of display windows in which various pumps and slippers figured prominently" (9) not as an index of Warhol's relationship to mental labor but as an entrée into discussing commodification.[17]

Mike Featherstone draws on Pierre Bourdieu's notion of the new middle class as "new cultural intermediaries" to provide an alternative way of theorizing post-modernity that understands the prominence of consumption in late capitalism as a product of mental labor. In this model "marketing, advertising, public relations, radio and television producers, presenters, magazine journalists, fashion writers, and the helping professions" work to create "a general veneration for intellectual goods and the artistic and intellectual lifestyle [that] helps to create an audience within the new middle class and potentially beyond, for new symbolic goods and experiences, for the intellectual and artistic way of life."[18] To the extent that he contends this new market "could be receptive to some of the sensibilities that are incorporated into and disseminated in postmodernism,"[19] Featherstone understands postmodern commodification as the product of the mental labor of white-collar workers in an economy that has shifted from material to immaterial production. He thus anticipates Michael Hardt and Antonio Negri's more recent account of "postmodernization" as grounded in "the informatization of production" and the rise of "*immaterial labor*—that is, labor that produces an immaterial good, such as a service, a cultural product, knowledge, or communication."[20] This version of the postmodern acknowledges not only the presence of a third-world or diasporic working class but of a new—undeniably more privileged, but nonetheless structurally proletarianized—working class "in the dominant capitalist countries, and particularly in the United States, since the early 1970s," a working class whose purview "cover[s] a wide range of activities from health care, education, and finance to transporation, entertainment, and advertising."[21] In Featherstone's anticipation of Hardt and Negri, *cultural studies itself* is a form of intellectual labor involved—as the opposite side of the coin of "promot[ing] and transmit[ting] the intellectuals' lifestyle to a larger audience"—in "legitmat[ing] new fields such as sport, fashion, popular music, and popular culture as valid fields of intellectual analysis."[22] The analysis of commodification, that is, is itself a form of white-collar work aimed at creating both new products of immaterial labor and new markets for these products. DeLillo's *White Noise* exemplifies this process, although the novel's focus on traditional sites of commodification like malls and the mass media is less important in this regard than its depiction of a college professor whose work is translating Hitler into a commodity.

This does not by any means require us to accept some sort of pessimistic conclusion about the impossibility of intellectuals achieving critical distance in the postmodern era. On the contrary, it simply requires us to understand postmodernism not as an external, reified phenomenon but rather as the universalized worldview of the new white-collar middle class. Indeed, the sense that "distance in general (including 'critical distance' in particular) has very precisely been abolished in the new space of postmodernism" (Jameson 48) simultaneously generalizes the old dilemma of the organization man and effaces the class origins of this generalization. We can see this self-obscuring dynamic at work in what is surely one of the two or three most canonical works of "postmodern" fiction, Thomas Pynchon's *The Crying of Lot 49*.

Pynchon's second novel calls attention to how much has changed since the 1950s when its protagonist Oedipa Maas notes the difference between the restive Berkeley campus and the "somnolent Siwash out of her own past."[23] Even a superficial reading of *Crying* shows how deeply embedded it is in this new era, not least in the extent to which Oedipa understands the Tristero conspiracy as something like the possibility of counterculture, "another set of possibilities" (150) existing "beyond the appearance of the legacy America" (151):

> For here were God knew how many citizens, deliberately choosing not to communicate by U. S. Mail. It was not an act of treason, nor possibly even of defiance. But it was a calculated withdrawal, from the life of the Republic, from its machinery. Whatever else was being denied them out of hate, indifference to the power of their vote, loopholes, simple ignorance, this withdrawal was their own, unpublicized, private. Since they could not have withdrawn into a vacuum (could they?), there had to exist the separate, silent, unsuspected world. (101)

The fact that Pynchon makes his conspiracy an alternative postal service suggests elements of community and communication that would not figure so prominently in a novel from the fifties. *Crying*, we might thus say, offers a sixties reconfiguration of a fifties desire: a social form characterized by the possibility of "truly communicating" rather than the "lies, recitations of routine, [and] arid betrayals of spiritual poverty" of The Organization (141). The scene in which Oedipa reads a note sent by the pirate mail system of the Peter Pinguid society undercuts this idea, however. "*Dear Mike,*" it reads, "*how are you? Just thought I'd drop you a note. How's your book coming? Guess that's all for now. See you at The Scope*" (39; Pynchon's emphasis). As J. Peter Euben notes, this message "is thoroughly banal."[24] It is banal, moreover, because according to its recipient the system's users have to send one letter a week or face a fine. The one underground communication that Pynchon actually shows is thus characterized not by true comunication, but by the coerciveness and lack of meaning attributed to the social in texts from the forties and fifties. In general, however, the novel is not so much stuck in the fifties as it is "poised at the very cusp of a historical transition" between the decades.[25] Oedipa's nighttime exodus through San Francisco and Oakland on the trail of WASTE symbols, for instance, leads her to scenes of "alienation" and "withdrawal" (100) acted out by fifties-style social misfits. If indeed the WASTE system does serve as the communications network of an underground America, it seems to be an underground modeled on Inamorati Anonymous, the "society of isolates" (94) that Oedipa learns of in the bar The Greek Way. As Robert J. Hansen notes, this scene *also* extends the logic of white-collar alienation developed in the Yoyodyne scenes into a vista of ethnic and sexual subcultures familiar in "the real Bay Area of the 1960s."[26] Pynchon's belief in "a genuine society of communicants in which real information is exchanged and real diversity sustained" remains grounded, however, in a distinctly postwar logic of individualism that, to the embarrassment of left-leaning critics, seems to extend his multicultural beneficence to those on the right, as well.[27] *Crying*'s Ellisonian emphasis on withdrawal, silence, and privacy, not to mention its animus against large organizations, remind us of the ongoing resonance of fifties discourse in the 1960s, when—as we sometimes forget—the libertarian Robert Heinlein and the conservative Ayn Rand also became heroes of the counterculture.

Most importantly for our purposes, *Crying* is drenched in the postwar discourse of alienated mental labor. Inamorati Anonymous, for instance, is founded by a Yoyodyne executive who is replaced by a computer and who stumbles upon WASTE when—unable to decide whether to kill himself "without first hearing the ideas of a committee" (92)—he places a want ad seeking advice from failed suicides. Oedipa's husband Mucho Maas has quit his job as a used-car salesman because he fears being subsumed by the role, against which he has fought by anxiously dressing against type (4). Randolph Driblette, the director of the production of *The Courier's Tragedy* in which Oedipa first hears of the Tristero, plays "the colorless administrator, Gennaro" (58) in a gray flannel costume (60). And in the most extended passage on the subject, Stanley Koteks, the Yoyodyne engineer that Oedipa meets when she wanders away from her stockholders' tour group, asks her to ask management "to drop their clause on patents," which he says "stifles your really creative engineer, . . . wherever he may be" (67). When Oedipa replies "I didn't think people invented any more. . . . I mean, who's there been, really, since Thomas Edison? Isn't it all teamwork now?" (67), Koteks offers a response that could easily appear in the chapter of *The Organization Man* on "The Bureaucratization of the Scientist": "Teamwork," Koteks snarled, "is one word for it, yeah. What it really is is a way to avoid responsibility. It's a symptom of the gutlessness of the whole society" (68). Koteks wants property rights, and claims that the corporation's abrogation of those rights undermines its employees' creativity, as well as, implicitly, the American tradition of invention as a path of upward mobility. Of course, when Oedipa comes upon Koteks he "wasn't working, only doodling [the WASTE post horn] with a fat felt pencil" (67). Pynchon, typically, refuses to specify whether Koteks is a descendant of the gray-flannel protagonists of postwar fiction who enjoy the security of their jobs while railing against the middle class's shortcomings, or a Randian striker who has withdrawn his mental labor because he cannot get a fair profit for it.

But it is Oedipa who suggests what is truly at stake when Koteks attempts to explain Maxwell's Demon, the imaginary creature that James Clerk Maxwell suggested could provide perpetual motion. In Maxwell's thought experiment, the Demon sorts air molecules in a box so that the faster, hotter molecules end up on one side, creating a heat differential capable of running an engine. Koteks claims that this does not violate the Second Law of Thermodynamics—the law of increasing entropy, which states that the amount of usable energy in a system inevitably declines—because "the Demon only sat and sorted," and so does not "put any real work into the system" (68). To this Oedipa replies, "Sorting isn't work? . . . Tell them down at the post office, you'll find yourself in a mailbag headed for Fairbanks, Alaska, without even a FRAGILE sticker going for you" (68). Against Koteks's nostalgia for the lost world of the old middle class, and the language of individuality and conformity that he and others deploy throughout the novel, Oedipa asserts that sorting—which Koteks himself describes as "mental work" (68)—is a form of labor.

Oedipa's choice of example cannot be accidental in a novel whose vision of countercultural conspiracy is a pirate postal service. The lawyer Metzger suggests to Mike Fallopian, the member of the rightwing Peter Pinguid Society who receives the letter that Oedipa reads in The Scope, that a private mail service appeals to his Randian antipathy to the government-as-organization: "Of course. . . . Delivering the mail is a government monopoly. You would be opposed to that" (38). But Oedipa's comment to Koteks retroactively suggests that we should think Tristero not in terms of the standard postwar defense of individuality—which is called into question, as we have seen, by the banal contents of Fallopian's letter—but rather in terms of the labor necessary to uphold the conspiracy. In the scene at The Scope such labor takes place at the edge of the frame, an area we are well advised to watch while reading Pynchon:

> Fallopian gave them a wry smile. "It's not as rebellious as it looks. We use Yoyodyne's inter-office delivery. On the sly. But it's hard to find carriers, we have a big turnover. They're run on a tight schedule, and they get nervous. Security people over at the plant know something's up. They keep a sharp eye out. De Witt," pointing at the fat mailman, who was being hauled, twitching, down off the bar and offered drinks he did not want, "he's the most nervous one we've had all year." (38)

De Witt, far more than Koteks, provides a concrete model of the reappropriation of labor and agency from the corporation, a conspiratorial form that has value despite the fact that its contents cannot be guaranteed to be creative (when they can be apprehended at all).

The novel's central mental laborer is not De Witt or one of the WASTE carriers, however, but Oedipa, who we learn on page one has just acquired "the job of sorting [Pierce Inverarity's estate] all out" (1). Indeed, one way to read the novel is as the story of Oedipa's transformation from a stereotypical fifties housewife (the "Mrs. Oedipa Maas" who in the first sentence is returning "from a Tupperware party whose hostess had put perhaps too much kirsch in the fondue" [1]) to an independent agent by way of white-collar work. In this respect Oedipa enacts Betty Friedan's assertion in *The Feminine Mystique* (1963) that the white-collar work that putatively deprived middle-class men of agency might provide agency *to* middle-class women trapped in the home or in low status, frequently part-time pink-collar jobs.[28] Friedan stressed that such work could not be employment taken "to 'help out at home' or just to kill extra time," or the unpaid "busy-work" of "being a den mother, or serving on a PTA committee, or organizing a covered dish supper."[29] Rather, it had to "a job that [a woman] can take seriously as part of a life plan, work in which she can grow as part of society."[30] Oedipa clearly finds such work, although to the extent that postwar accounts of white-collar work depicted men's more privileged white-collar positions as equally disconnected and unfulfilling, her transformation requires a reconceptualization of white-collar work no less than of suburban domesticity. Defying standard post-war assumptions (which we still hold) about white-collar work, Oedipa imagines a version of sorting that is as creative and personalized as artistic creation:

> She had caught sight of the historical marker only because she'd gone back, deliberately, to Lake Inverarity one day, owing to this, what you might have to call, growing obsession, with "bringing something of herself"—even if that something was just her presence—to the scatter of business interests that had survived Inverarity. She would give them order, she would create constellations. (72)

Crying itself, we might say, offers a very high-level exercise in just such sorting. On the level at which the novel offers a running metacommentary on its own formal innovations, Oedipa's work points to the new—and typically postmodern—model of aesthetic labor by which Pynchon circumvents the sterile options figured by his frequent allusions to Echo and Narcissus. If Narcissus represents the overly psychologized, inward-turning modern novel, and Echo pure genre fiction that can only repeat others' utterances,[31] *Crying* and the postmodern novel more generally seek to renovate "the forms, categories, and contents of" mass culture (Jameson 2). But Pynchon goes further, using Oedipa as the focal point to anticipate Jamesonian cognitive mapping as the process by which "the individual subject [seeks] some new heightened sense of its place in the global system" (Jameson 54).

It is precisely at this point that *Crying* simultaneously achieves its admirable generality, its ability to comment on the other "legacy" that is "America" (151), and obscures its connection to middle-class concerns with mental labor. Euben not incorrectly proposes that the result of the novel's inconclusiveness and self-undermining gestures is to demand of the reader a particular kind of "labor," which he understands as the interpretive labor of the political citizen.[32] But as the novel recognizes, such labor is distinct from, and in tension with, the other form of mental labor performed by executrices and mail carriers. Early in the novel Oedipa's lawyer, Roseman, lists her duties—"learn intimately the books and the business, go through probate, collect all debts, inventory the assets, get an appraisal of the estate, decide what to liquidate and what to hold on to, pay off claims, square away taxes, distribute legacies" (10)—but of course she mostly performs such tasks off camera while performing her true work of hunting Tristero. Even at this point we might understand Oedipa performing a version of the messenger De Witt delivering pirate messages on Yoyodyne company time. But near the end of the book she realizes that her fantasy of distributing Inverarity's estate among Tristero's "nameless" members is likely to cost her not only the official job but the "shadow" one, as well. The judge would "revoke her letters testamentary, . . . slip the old man from Warpe, Wistfull, Kubitschek and McMingus in as administrator *de bonis non* and so much baby for code, constellations, shadowlegatees" (150). At this point, Oedipa's pursuit of Tristero is marked as the opposite of white-collar work, insofar as "the old man" can be trusted to do what is expected of him because, in standard postwar terms, it is his job. Here it becomes clear that Oedipa's pursuit of Tristero has been enabled all along by structural conditions very different from those of her fellow sorters in the postal service. Significantly, *Crying* never mentions whether or not she receives a fee for her probate work. She is at least potentially a volunteer who is able to engage in her hermeneutical labors because she does not have to work for someone else.

I raise this point not as the prelude to some banal denunciation of Oedipa's privilege, a move that would be as silly politically as aesthetically. *Crying*'s achievement must be understood dialectically, and from one perspective Pynchon accomplishes much by translating Oedipa's experience with estate law into "a radical challenge to the legal system that served as an accomplice to Inverarity's [capitalist] empire."[33] At the same time, however, this translation ultimately depends upon the same universalization of middle-class experience that we have seen in the novels of the fifties, in which African American public speakers, Jews with irregular resumes, and escaped Southern prisoners all serve as representatives of white-collar alienation. *Crying* carries this dynamic even further, however, not only employing Oedipa as an avatar of white-collar labor but also, through her pursuit of Tristero, transforming the world itself into a version of The Organization.

The danger inherent in this aspect of *Crying* can be seen in Stefan Mattessich's insightful but ultimately flawed recent reading. Mattessich acknowledges the novel's deep investment in what he calls, following Hardt and Negri, the "dematerialization of labor in networks of communication, information, and exchange."[34] But because he fails to specify the different registers of mental labor within the novel, or to address its universalizing tendencies, he ends up transforming the impasse of the artist-as-mental-laborer who is "constrained by a uniform and mechanical production" (52) into a trope for modern existence per se. He thus produces, as the opening paragraph of his chapter on *Crying* suggests, a postmodern update of the social criticism of the 1950s. Referring to his reading of *V.* (1960) in the previous chapter, Mattessich writes,

> The reflexive parodic mode examined in my reading of Pynchon's first novel enacts a necessary implication in the social, cultural, and industrial production of subjectivity. To be a "person" is to experience complicity in a world that effectively depersonalizes, reduces to caricature, to outline, to silhouette. What this means is that the subject in its activities, processes, or consciousness can experience its difference only as generality, or only in a certain theoretical apprehension of the ways by which singularity comes to be the reflection of a dehumanizing mode of production. This displacement of the subject (character, author, and reader) to the negative spaces around what "is," to the molded (usually plastic) stencil of being, is what Pynchon attempts to represent in his fiction—a loss of substance, of affect, of reality. Difference returns—if it returns—not in the externalization of the inhuman world but in a perception of the externalized and intrinsically discursive character of subjectivity. (43)

This passage nicely recapitulates what I have been arguing is the history of postmodernism as a concept. The subject's implication in social forms is understood here as an index of its corruption. In terms that most postwar writers would readily recognize, the socially constructed subject is depersonalized, distorted, hollow, and—in a perhaps unconscious nod to *The Graduate* (Mike Nichols, 1969)—plastic. As a result, individuality can only be defined in opposition to the social. At the same time, it can never be sustained in such opposition—the aporia, Tanner has taught us, at the heart of most postwar fiction. This aporia gives rise to a new turn, in which the subject discovers itself in its *implication* in the world, but—and this is key—a world now understood as "intrinsically discursive." In this move, the world itself is transformed into a version of The Organization in which existence consists of manipulating preexisting tropes: life as unending white-collar work. The political denouement of this reading is that Mattessich argues, against critics like Euben, that *Crying* ultimately rejects "the recovery of a dispossessed communal space" (64), which rejection he improbably sees as the political lesson of the 1960s. "The counterculture," Mattessich asserts, "did not represent a public space that either betrayed itself through its excesses or succumbed to forces of social repression. It was the discovery that *there was no public space*, and this became what had to be repressed" (64).

Nor is theoretically inflected literary criticism such as Mattessich's the only locus for this transformation of the world into The Organization. We can also see it, to cite one prominent example, in DeLillo's least social (but not coincidentally his most frequently discussed) major novel, *White Noise*. Unlike *Crying*, or even his own earlier novel *The Names*, which both at least allude to the possibility of some social horizon beyond their protagonists' alienation, *White Noise* eschews even the possibility of a social solution to its protagonist Jack Gladney's alienated, commodified existence. Beyond his performance-obsessed worklife, and his family's interpenetration by consumer goods and the media, Gladney can only imagine metaphysical solutions: the glimmer of "splendid transcendence" in his sleeping daughter's pronunciation of "*Toyota Celica*," or the possibility that "the dead speak to the living" through supermarket bar codes.[35] *White Noise* retains *Crying*'s emphasis on (the difficulty of) critically reading contemporary American culture. His comparison of his daughter's utterance with "the name of an ancient power in the sky, tablet-carved in cuneiform" (155), for instance, recalls Oedipa's belief in "a hieroglyphic sense of concealed meaning" in things like transistors and Southern Californian urban sprawl (14). But DeLillo has abandoned Pynchon's sense that the "transcendent meaning" (150) beyond "just America" (151) would have to be embodied in an actual social form, even if only a "society of isolates" (94). Here, as in Mattessich's reading of *Crying*, the hermeneutic labor persists but with no possibility that it might any longer access or lead to something outside the current system.[36]

The stress on commodification that links texts like *White Noise* and Jameson's *Postmodernism* suggests that postmodernism is the universalized worldview not just of the white-collar middle class, but of this class during the specific period when the postwar boom seemed to sever the traditional Marxist connection between class and capital. Gladney finds work to be a place of hollow performance (one of the novel's main jokes is that he is a professor of Hitler Studies who cannot speak German), while in a memorable scene he finds (temporary) fulfillment at the mall. This characteristic postmodern turn from production to consumption is underwritten, we might argue, by the ambiguous position of the postwar middle class, structurally proletarianized but not (yet) subject to the loss of income or status. In this situation, which I have described as a product of the postwar boom and the post–New Deal welfare state rather than an actual shift in the structure of class itself, the locus of middle-class identity shifts from the (intolerably deindividuating) workplace to the realm of consumption. *Crying* already exemplifies this unmooring of middle-class identity from work, offering as it does a utopian vision of meaningful mental work conducted outside the actual necessity of employment. This utopian vision is, moreover, inseparable from postwar middle-class prosperity, insofar as Oedipa's quest is made possible by that now vanished artifact of the boom economy, the single-income household. *White Noise*, coming during the postwar boom's long decline, reflects something very different. De-Lillo's narrowing of the frame of middle-class life to consumption, while meant to be critical, is to some degree complicit with the 1980s discourse on "yuppies," which functioned to obscure the actual decline of the postwar boom with anecdotes of well-off boomers who were also, not coincidentally, champion consumers.[37] As *Wall Street* (Oliver Stone, 1987) makes clear, the discourse on yuppies also promoted consumption as both a spur to and a compensation for the expansion of working time that today makes white-collar labor the frontline of efforts to overturn the forty-hour week.[38] The denouement of postmodernism, we might say, is the early twenty-first-century prominence of Ralph Nader—a consumer advocate—as the icon of the American left.

It is only recently that the decline of middle-class fortunes has grown statistically noticeable enough to render white-collar labor, and beyond that class division in the traditional Marxist sense, once again visible. One result is that we can now reread classic works of "postmodern" fiction, as I have *The Names* and *The Crying of Lot 49*, for their structuring engagement with the middle-class experience of mental labor. In addition, postmodernism itself now seems to be ceding its place as a dominant mode of fictional and theoretical production. Within the realm of theory we can see this in something like the shift from Jameson's *Postmodernism* to Hardt and Negri's *Empire*, and the accompanying shift from the difficulty of cognitive mapping to the dialectical experience of immaterial labor as the ground of contemporary subjectivity. But a similar transition is also taking place, albeit much less coherently or programmatically, in recent fiction. Perhaps the recent novel most obviously symptomatic of this change is Richard Powers's 1998 *Gain*, which tells the intertwined stories of Laura Bodey, a woman dying of cancer in the downstate Illinois town of Lacewood, and the Clare Corporation, Lacewood's largest employer. Ursula K. Heise has noted that Powers departs from the tendency of postmodern novelists like DeLillo and Pynchon to "place their protagonists in worlds that are shaped by forces and institutions they are ill-equipped to understand or combat," and through this technique to similarly challenge their readers' interpretive abilities.[39] Eschewing postmodern form, which I have suggested reflects a white-collar middle-class subject position, *Gain* offers instead paired realist narratives that suggest a link (if not a strict cause-and-effect relationship) between Laura Bodey's life and death, on one hand, and the representative history of Clare, on the other.[40] This latter narrative depicts Clare's trajectory in terms of the history of corporate concentration that forms the backdrop of this study. In its simplest terms, it is the story of an entrepreneurial, family-owned company, J. Clare's Sons, whose success transforms it into a modern, publically owned, eventually multinational corporation no longer susceptible to the control of those who founded it. As Jeffrey Williams notes,

> the first half presents a species of the mythic narrative of individual American success, a success earned through pluck, savvy, and industriousness, and in turn blessed if not by the gods then by luck. The second half thus becomes a kind of elegaic [*sic*] narrative, representing the fall of the heroic ideal of American gumption and entrepeneurial [*sic*] spirit through mass production, depersonalization, and uniformity induced by the legal fiction of incorporation.[41]

As *Gain*'s narrator puts it, "the entrepreneur's freed resources will turn on him, one by one. . . . Trade grows steadily more efficient until it everywhere holds the day. Until, at last, it cuts out all the middlemen."[42] Here it is not too great a stretch to take "middlemen" in the sense of the middle-class entrepreneurs whose very success leads to the centralization of property that ultimately eviscerates the middle class.

Heise suggests that *Gain*'s political potential is compromised by the way in which "the self-assurance of the narrator's command of the global and his transparent (though complex) language remain in tension with the scenario of individual powerlessness vis-à-vis the global power networks that the novel portrays."[43] This misses the novel's real achievement, however, which is to (almost) reveal the connection between the individual powerlessness central to the plots of American fiction of the last half-century and the loss of class agency brought home to the middle class in the same period. I say almost because Powers undermines this possibility in two ways. One is by placing the locus of middle-class powerlessness not in labor but in consumption, as indeed postmodernism more generally has. Laura Bodey works as a real estate agent, it is true, but the real meat of her story is reserved for her role as consumer. Hence the "climactic moment" (politically and narratively)[44] in which she returns from the hospital to discover her cabinets full of Clare products and realizes that she cannot conduct "a consumer boycott" because "every hour of her life depends on more corporations than she can count" (304). This is not to suggest that the theme of corporate participation in the degradation of the environment is not an important one. But it is to argue that the naturalization of corporate power about which Heise complains is in part the product of *Gain*'s residually postmodernist emphasis on consumerism, in which products—whether material or immaterial—appear as though by magic because they are dissociated from the labor that goes into them. In this way, Laura Bodey's role as epistemologically challenged consumer marks her as a residually postmodern character in a novel trying to move beyond postmodernism.

Gain does trace the devolution of agency in the workplace, although because it remains tied to the middle-class idea of the owner-proprietor it describes such lost agency most forcefully in the case not of white-collar workers but of the executives at the apices of white-collar pyramids. Thus when Clare incorporates we see Samuel Clare, one of the original founders and now its "ceremonial diplomat," learning that "a corporation president had precious little to say about the firm's development" (181). At this point in the novel we might still interpret this scene as the climax of the narrative of middle-class declension—"The invention of the corporation," Powers writes, "killed Samuel's dream of progress by completing it" (181)—but we get a similar scene near the end of the book, following Laura Bodey's death. In the book's penultimate chapter, Franklin Kennibar, Sr., Clare's current CEO, waits for a PBS camera crew, thinks about a reorganization plan that he is presenting to the company's board in two days, and muses about his vague role in the company:

> None of this is his choice. Neither the interview, nor the board meeting, nor the plan that will rock the future of these two centuries of business. It has always amused him, drawing the salary he does, how little say a CEO has about anything. The corporation's point man, the passive agent of collective bidding. (349)

To depict a CEO, as Powers does here, as a classic organization man beholden to the inhuman will of the corporation, is to deny the existence of class in general, and of a ruling class who benefits from capitalism in particular. Powers indulges in this problematic depiction not out of allegiance to the ruling class, however, but because he cannot escape the fundamentally middle-class idea that business should be, but no longer is, the realm of individual agency.

That this idea, formed in the days when the nation could lay claim to a substantial number of small-property owners, still remains potent a half-century after the transformation of the middle class into white-collar employees is brought home even more forcefully in the book's final scene. There Laura Bodey's son, Tim, grown from awkward and moody adolescence into a science prodigy, takes the settlement money Clare had paid upon Laura's death and starts a company to market the potential cancer cure that he and his colleagues have developed. Williams proposes that with this ending "Powers suggests one avenue for positive change is . . . through our corporate organization," but this is not quite right.[45] The renewed sense of agency that *Gain* posits at this moment is precisely not the product of "corporate organization," which for Powers always takes agency away.[46] Rather, it is associated here with the return of the middle-class small capitalist, now transformed (in terms Ayn Rand laid out at mid-century) into the owner and seller of intellectual property. Here the notion that "the entrepreneur lives and dies by ingenuity," voiced ironically at the moment of Samuel's death (213), returns in earnest.

Gain is thus, finally, not realism but fantasy. In this fantasy—enabled, we might note, by the tech-bubble of the late nineties—all the agency and knowledge that Laura Bodey has been denied as a postmodern consumer comes flooding back in Tim Bodey's eleventh-hour rediscovery of his middle-class inheritance. Now that the tech-bubble has burst, of course, the rest of us are back in the state of declining middle-class fortunes that was beginning to become visible in early nineties responses to phenomena like downsizing. I have tried to argue in this book that the discovery of this state is a belated one: that the middle class lost its historical agency when, at mid-century, its members became white-collar workers. With this in mind we can now return and read postmodernism dialectically, as the worldview not only of middle-class privilege but of the hollowness of this privilege: of the bitter discovery of one's lack of agency and inability to navigate the world. It would be easy enough to say that this anxiety is unreal and meaningless compared to the experience of other, even less privileged subjects of capitalism, but there is nothing to be gained from the middle-class not recognizing its downward mobility or the structural reasons behind it. The idea that the middle class remains middle class is, in fact, the chief means by which capital has controlled this class for the last fifty years. I do not propose that white-collar professionals start thinking of themselves as sweatshop workers (this would just be another fantasy) but I do propose that they stop thinking of themselves as middle class, if by this we mean occupants of a position outside the binary logic of capital.

America was founded upon the utopian dream of capital as a force that would render everyone an individual agent. Now the American middle class is finally realizing that it has returned, its sojourn over, to the real world of capitalist unfreedom. This does not mean that the dream of a world in which people are human beings, rather than parts of the system's machinery, was flawed. It just means that we have to give up our middle-class notions of how such a world can be brought about, and begin to imagine new stories of creativity, agency, and fulfillment that do not depend upon a vanished (and never really equal) world of property ownership.

Notes

INTRODUCTION: THE TWILIGHT OF THE MIDDLE CLASS

1. For an overview of criticism of cold war culture see my "Cold War Culture to Fifties Culture," *minnesota review* n.s. 55–57 (2002): 143–52.

2. Morris Dickstein, *Leopards in the Temple: The Transformation of American Fiction 1945–1970* (Cambridge: Harvard University Press, 2002), 6; hereafter cited parenthetically.

3. Thomas Hill Schaub, *American Fiction in the Cold War* (Madison: University of Wisconsin Press, 1991), 91, passim.

4. On the kitchen debate see Elaine Tyler May, *Homeward Bound: American Families in the Cold War Era* (New York: Basic, 1988), 16–20.

5. Alan Nadel, *Containment Culture: American Narratives, Postmodernism, and the Atomic Age* (Durham: Duke University Press, 1995), 91, 90–116 passim.

6. Barbara Foley, "The Rhetoric of Anticommunism in Invisible Man," *College English* 59.5 (September 1997): 530–45; hereafter cited parenthetically.

7. Barbara Foley, "From Communism to Brotherhood: The Drafts of *Invisible Man*," *Left of the Color Line: Race, Radicalism, and Twentieth-Century Literature of the United States*, ed. Bill V. Mullen and James Smethurst (Chapel Hill: University of North Carolina Press, 2003), 163–82.

8. Barbara Foley, "From Wall Street to Astor Place: Historicizing Melville's 'Bartleby,' " *American Literature* 72.1 (March 2000): 87–116.

9. An important exception to this generalization is Lary May's essay "Movie Star Politics: The Screen Actors' Guild, Cultural Conversion, and the Hollywood Red Scare," *Recasting America: Culture and Politics in the Age of Cold War*, ed. Lary May (Chicago: University of Chicago Press, 1989), 125–53. Using the movie industry as an example, May argues that postwar anticommunism was deployed by "corporate leaders" (127), against the dual backdrop of "widespread prosperity" (136) and "the greatest strike wave in the country's history" (126), to quell labor radicalism and "convert national values and popular imagery away from doctrines hostile to modern capitalism" (127).

10. Jeffrey Madrick, *The End of Affluence: The Causes and Consequences of America's Economic Dilemma* (New York: Random House, 1995), 125. See also James T. Patterson, *Grand Expectations: The United States, 1945–1974* (New York: Oxford University Press, 1996), 61–62, and Alan Brinkley, "World War II and American Liberalism," *The War in American Culture: Society and Consciousness during World War II*, ed. Lewis A. Erenberg and Susan E. Hirsch (Chicago: University of Chicago Press, 1996), 317.

11. Paul Krugman, "For Richer," *The New York Times Magazine* (20 October 2002): 62–67, 76–78, 141–42. See also Claudia Goldin and Robert A. Margo, "The Great Compression: The Wage Structure in the United States at Mid-Century," *The Quarterly Journal of Economics* 107.1 (February 1992): 1–34, whose argument Krugman mentions.

12. Michael Harrington, *The Other America: Poverty in the United States* (New York: Macmillan, 1962), 1; hereafter cited parenthetically.

13. George Lipsitz, *Rainbow at Midnight: Labor and Culture in the 1940s* (Urbana: University of Illinois Press, 1994); Alan Wald, *Writing from the Left: New Essays on Radical Culture and Politics* (New York: Verso, 1994); Joel Foreman, ed., *The Other Fifties: Interrogating Midcentury American Icons* (Urbana: University of Illinois Press, 1997). This approach is also taken by a number of the essays in May, *Recasting America*, especially part 4.

14. Robert Seguin, *Around Quitting Time: Work and Middle-Class Fantasy in American Fiction* (Durham: Duke University Press, 2001), 4, 1–5 passim; hereafter cited parenthetically.

15. Jack Beatty, "Who Speaks for the Middle Class," *Atlantic Monthly* May 1994: 65; hereafter cited parenthetically.

16. Krugman, "For Richer" 76, 62.

17. For a readable critique of the doctrine of middle-classlessness, with an emphasis on its contemporary variations but with a chapter on the history of this idea since the Revolutionary Period ("History: The Fate of Autonomy"), see Benjamin DeMott, *The Imperial Middle: Why Americans Can't Think Straight about Class* (New Haven: Yale University Press, 1990).

18. Barbara Ehrenreich, *The Hearts of Men: American Dreams and the Flight from Commitment* (Garden City: Anchor, 1983), 29; Ehrenreich's emphasis. Ehrenreich does note the sometimes devastating economic consequences for women cast outside middle-class prosperity by the converging breakdowns, since the mid-seventies, of "the family wage and the breadwinner ethic" (175, 172–80 passim).

19. Jackson Lears, "A Matter of Taste: Corporate Cultural Hegemony in a Mass-Consumption Society," in May, *Recasting America* 50; hereafter cited parenthetically.

20. Catherine Jurca, *White Diaspora: The Suburb and the Twentieth-Century American Novel* (Princeton: Princeton University Press, 2001), 140; hereafter cited parenthetically.

21. These accounts are clearly related to what Robert D. Johnston describes as the "demonization model" employed by historians of the middle class. See Johnston, *The Radical Middle Class: Populist Democracy and the Question of Capitalism in Progressive Era Portland, Oregon* (Princeton: Princeton University Press, 2003), 3–6.

22. Richard H. Pells, *The Liberal Mind in a Conservative Age: American Intellectuals in the 1940s and 1950s* (New York: Harper, 1985), 188–216.

23. William H. Whyte, *The Organization Man* (1956; Garden City: Anchor, 1957), 13; Whyte's emphasis. Hereafter cited parenthetically.

24. Ehrenreich, *Hearts* 29.

25. Richard Ohmann, "The Shaping of a Canon: U.S. Fiction, 1960–1975," *Canons*, ed. Robert von Hallberg (Chicago: University of Chicago Press, 1984), 386, 390, 377–401 passim; hereafter cited parenthetically.

26. Barbara and John Ehrenreich, "The Professional–Managerial Class," *Between Labor and Capital*, ed. Pat Walker (Boston: South End, 1979), 12, 18, 5–45 passim.

27. For a skeptical discussion of this term see Doug Henwood, *After the New Economy* (New York: New Press, 2003).

28. Robert B. Reich, *The Work of Nations: Preparing Ourselves for 21st-Century Capitalism* (New York: Knopf, 1991), 173–80.

29. Andrew Ross, "The Mental Labor Problem," *Social Text* 18.2 (2000): 1–31.

30. Karl Marx and Friedrich Engels, *The Communist Manifesto* (1848; New York: Monthly Review Press, 1998), 3.

31. Olivier Zunz, "Class," *Encyclopedia of the United States in the Twentieth Century*, ed. Stanley Kutler, Vol. I (New York: Scribner's, 1996), 195, 198.

32. Stuart Blumin argues in *The Emergence of the Middle Class: Social Experience in the American City, 1760–1900* (New York: Cambridge University Press, 1989) that a self-conscious middle class first takes shape in the Jacksonian period around the emergent distinction between manual and nonmanual labor. Taking a self-consciously culturalist approach that is as much concerned with where people live and what they consume as with how they earn their living, he conflates "entrepreneurship and salaried (as opposed to wage-earning) employment" (68). But his partly anachronistic use of the term "white-collar" suggests how the entrepreneurial ideal was already losing ground to a world in which "experienced clerks" claimed similar status with "small nonmanual businessmen" in the emergent hierarchy of head work over hand work. At the same time, his account makes clear that white-collar workers were not entirely separate from entrepreneurs, as they would later come to be. Antebellum clerks not only, like owners, "made more money than skilled workers and hardworking masters," but also "seem to have moved much more frequently into income- and wealth-enhancing business proprietorships" (121).

33. Olivier Zunz, *Making America Corporate 1870–1930* (Chicago: University of Chicago Press, 1990), 13–14, passim.

34. Ohmann's *Selling Culture: Magazines, Markets, and Class at the Turn of the Century* (New York: Verso, 1996) provides a richly researched account of the formative years of the PMC, which Ohmann credits with the birth of national mass culture. Jeffrey Sklansky's intellectual history *The Soul's Economy: Market Society and Selfhood in American Thought, 1820–1920* (Chapel Hill: University of North Carolina Press, 2002) provides a deep history of the PMC's managerial ethos as it evolves out of republican ideals of property-owning independence over the course of the nineteenth century.

35. On Populism in its classic form see Alan Trachtenberg, *The Incorporation of America: Culture & Society in the Gilded Age* (New York: Hill and Wang, 1982), 173–81. In *The Age of Reform: From Bryan to F. D. R.* (New York: Vintage, 1955), Richard Hofstadter writes that "by the turn of the century, it is possible to distinguish two chief strains of feeling in the Populist-Progressive tradition. The first, more Populist than Progressive, more rural and sectional than nationwide in its appeal, represents, in a sense, the roots of modern American isolationism" (273). Zunz describes these two strains in terms of a split within the middle class between "those who contributed to the building of corporate capitalism" and a residual but still influential group of small-property owners "who clung to proven, and presumably more fulfilling, ways of doing business" (*Making* 12–13). Johnston provides a less teleological account of this conflict. For an account of Depression-era Populism as more an outgrowth of traditional old middle-class ideals than the sort of protofascism it is sometimes depicted as, see Alan Brinkley, *Voices of Protest: Huey Long, Father Coughlin, and the Great Depression* (New York: Knopf, 1982).

36. John Blair et al., *Economic Concentration and World War II*, Report of the Smaller War Plants Corporation of the U.S. Senate Special Committee to Study Problems of American Small Business (Washington, DC: GPO, 1946), 4–20.

37. Edwin Layton, *The Revolt of the Engineers: Social Responsibility and the American Engineering Profession* (1971; Baltimore: Johns Hopkins University Press, 1986), ix. Layton describes how engineers—who had no choice but to work for corporations—prevented themselves "from becoming mere cogs in a vast industrial machine" (7) by giving their

loyalty not to employers but to a professional ethos grounded in "esoteric knowledge" and dedicated to the good of society (4–5). Cecelia Tichi covers some of the same ground in her account of the engineer as culture hero in *Shifting Gears: Technology, Literature, Culture in Modernist America* (Chapel Hill: University of North Carolina Press, 1987). For an example of the engineer's symbolic power, and the deployment of this power against fears of middle-class banality, one need only recall George Babbitt's excitement, at the conclusion of Sinclair Lewis's 1922 novel, *Babbitt*, at his son's decision to pursue an engineering career.

38. Hofstadter, *Age* 312–14, 319, 316. Hofstadter argues that "by 1933 the American public had lived with the great corporation so long that it was felt to be domesticated," with the result that the antimonopoly sentiments of the Progressives were "subordinated in the New Deal era to that restless groping for a means to bring recovery that was so characteristic of Roosevelt's efforts" (312). Thus what "Antitrust enforcement" there was "became a hunt for offenders instead of an effort to test the validity of organized power by its performance in aiding or preventing the flow of goods in commerce" (314).

39. Michael Denning, *The Cultural Front: The Laboring of American Culture in the Twentieth Century* (New York: Verso, 1996), 96–104, passim. In *New Deal Modernism: American Literature and the Invention of the Welfare State* (Durham: Duke University Press, 2000), Michael Szalay rightfully takes Denning to task for his overemphasis of the radical political dimensions of this shift (19–21). But Szalay's own account of writers worried about the transformation of their creative endeavors into routinized salaried employment within federal arts bureaucracies reinforces Denning's argument that this period saw a new stress on the "labor" in mental labor.

40. Marty Jezer, *The Dark Ages: Life in the United States 1945–1960* (Boston: South End, 1982), 25.

41. Jezer, *Dark* 25–26; Lipsitz, *Rainbow* 61.

42. Lipsitz, *Rainbow* 61.

43. Zunz, "Class" 197.

44. Brinkley, "World War II" 319–20; Robert M. Collins, *More: The Politics of Economic Growth in Postwar America* (New York: Oxford University Press, 2000).

45. Carol A. Barry, "White-Collar Employment: I—Trends and Structures," *Monthly Labor Review* (Jan. 1961): 11.

46. Zunz, "Class" 197–98.

47. Edward Bellamy, *Looking Backward, 2000–1887* (1888; Boston: Bedford, 1995); Charlotte Perkins Gilman, *Women and Economics: A Study of the Economic Relation between Men and Women as a Factor in Social Evolution* (1898; New York: Harper & Row, 1966); Thorstein Veblen, *The Engineers and the Price System* (New York: B. W. Huebsch, 1921).

48. Timothy Melley, *Empire of Conspiracy: The Culture of Paranoia in Postwar America* (Ithaca: Cornell University Press, 2000), 48, 10, passim; hereafter cited parenthetically.

49. C. Wright Mills, *White Collar: The American Middle Classes* (1951; New York: Oxford University Press, 2002); hereafter cited parenthetically. In his survey of histories of the middle class Johnston claims that *White Collar* is "still after half a century the most important book we have about the American middle classes" (4).

50. Lewis Corey, *The Crisis of the Middle Class* (New York: Covici-Friede, 1935), 146, 164; second quote italicized in the original.

51. "The change," Corey writes, "is all the more significant as salaried employees were clearly members of the middle class in 1870, while only a minority are now. Add that

minority—the 1,800,000 higher salaried employees and professionals—to the surviving independent enterprisers, and the middle class becomes 4,500,000, *or only 9% of the gainfully occupied compared with 18% in 1870, a decrease of 50%.* Include the masses of lower salaried employees and professionals, who are *not* middle class economically, and the working class becomes an overwhelming majority: 38,750,000 persons, or 75% of the gainfully occupied" (274–75; Corey's emphasis).

52. Berle makes this argument in the new preface he wrote for a reissue of the classic early thirties study of economic concentration, *The Modern Corporation and Private Property*, that he coauthored with Means. See Adolf A. Berle, "Property, Production and Revolution: A Preface to the Revised Edition" (1967), Adolf A. Berle and Gardiner C. Means, *The Modern Corporation and Private Property*, rev. ed. (1932; New York: Harcourt, 1968), ix.

53. Lipsitz, *Rainbow* 62.

54. For these terms see Sklansky, *Soul's Economy*; for the philosophical arguments underlying them, see C. B. Macpherson, *The Political Theory of Possessive Individualism: Hobbes to Locke* (Oxford: Clarendon Press, 1962).

55. For a reading that stresses this latter narrative see Melley, *Empire* 47–79.

56. David Riesman, with Nathan Glazer and Reuel Denney, *The Lonely Crowd: A Study of the Changing American Character* (1950; New Haven: Yale University Press, 1969); hereafter cited parenthetically.

57. Georg Lukács, *The Historical Novel*, trans. Hannah and Stanley Mitchell (Lincoln: University of Nebraska Press, 1983), 34, 19–88 passim; hereafter cited parenthetically.

58. Fredric Jameson, Introduction, Lukács, *Historical* 3–4.

59. Ira Wolfert, *Tucker's People* (1943; Urbana: University of Illinois Press, 1997), 3; hereafter cited parenthetically.

60. For a more complicated version of these politics see Walter Benn Michaels, *The Gold Standard and the Logic of Naturalism* (Berkeley: University of California Press, 1987).

61. Frank Norris, *The Pit* (1903; New York: Penguin, 1994), 115.

62. A prominent strand of the antiglobalization movement, for instance, criticizes giant retailers like Wal-Mart and Amazon not only for the way they treat their workers but also for "drastically undermin[ing] the traditional concepts of value and individual service that small business is known for offering." See Naomi Klein, *NO SPACE NO CHOICE NO JOBS NO LOGO: Taking Aim at the Brand Bullies* (New York: Picador, 1999), 158. Likewise, Eric Schlosser's *Fast Food Nation: The Dark Side of the All-American Meal* (2001; New York: Perennial, 2002), takes the fast food industry and agribusiness to task not only for their labor practices but also for the threat they pose to independent restaurateurs and small farmers. Schlosser's paean to In-N-Out Burger is a classic American salute to the virtues of small business. This family-owned chain, modest by the standards of McDonald's and Burger King, "has followed its own path": not only does it provide "the highest wages in the fast food industry" but "the ground beef is fresh, potatoes are peeled every day to make the fries, and the milk shakes are made from ice cream, not syrup" (259–60). Finally, Ruth Ozeki's novel *My Year of Meats* (New York: Penguin, 1998), which mounts a fascinating (and frequently very funny) attempt to revive old-middle-class values in the face of globalization (particularly global agribusiness) criticizes Wal-Mart for participating in the "demise of regional American culture" to the specific detriment of small property owners: "Main Street is dead, which is no news to the families whose families ran family businesses on Main Street" (56).

63. See chapter 1.

64. Mills, by contrast, provides a completely deromanticized description of what he calls "the lumpen-bourgeoisie," owners of marginal, failure-prone businesses and struggling farms whose reliance on family labor in particular finds Mills at his most dialectical:

> Behind the colorless census category "unpaid family worker," there lie much misery and defeat in youth. That too was and is part of the old middle-class way. Perhaps in the nineteenth century it paid off: the sons, or at least one of the sons, would take over his equipped station, and the daughter might better find a husband who would thus be set up. But the average life of these old middle-class, especially urban, units in the twentieth century is short; the coincidence of family-unit and work-situation among the old middle class is a pre-industrial fact. So even as the centralization of property contracts their "independence," it liberates the children of the old middle class's smaller entrepreneurs. (*White* 31)

65. See Brinkley's account of the communitarian as well as simply individualist aspects of Depression-Era Populism as articulated—in ways that reverberate through *Tucker's People* all the way to the current fight against Wal-Mart—around criticism of retail chains (*Voices* 144–48).

66. Elizabeth Long, *The American Dream and the Popular Novel* (Boston: Routledge & Kegan Paul, 1985), 89, 63–90 passim.

67. See also Whyte's readings of *The Man in the Gray Flannel Suit* and other popular fiction in the section of *The Organization Man* entitled "The Organization Man in Fiction" (*Organization* 267–91).

68. Cameron Hawley, *Executive Suite* (Cambridge: Riverside, 1952), 331, 333; hereafter cited parenthetically.

69. Mickey Spillane, *I, the Jury* (1947; New York: Penguin, 1975), 5–6; hereafter cited parenthetically.

70. Christopher Wilson, *Cop Knowledge: Police Power and Cultural Narrative in Twentieth-Century America* (Chicago: University of Chicago Press, 2000), 57–93.

71. Sean McCann, *Gumshoe America: Hard-Boiled Crime Fiction and the Rise and Fall of New Deal Liberalism* (Durham: Duke University Press, 2000), 212; hereafter cited parenthetically.

72. For an overview of this topic written on the eve of the 1990s see Ben Siegel, "Saul Bellow and the University as Villain," *Saul Bellow in the 1980s: A Collection of Critical Essays*, ed. Gloria L. Cronin and L. H. Goldman (East Lansing: Michigan State University Press, 1989), 137–59.

73. "Saul Bellow. The Enemy Is Academe," *Publisher's Weekly* (July 18, 1966): 35.

74. James Atlas, *Bellow: A Biography* (New York: Random House, 2000), 355.

75. Atlas, *Bellow* 449.

76. Michael T. Gilmore, *American Romanticism and the Marketplace* (Chicago: University of Chicago Press, 1985), 37, 13, 15, passim.

77. Christopher Newfield and Sklansky offer parallel arguments, for instance, that what seems like Emerson's extreme liberal individualism actually constitutes a means of accommodating the individual to a system in which small-property ownership is being replaced by bureaucratic institutions. See Christopher Newfield, *The Emerson Effect: Individualism and Submission in America* (Chicago: University of Chicago Press, 1996) and Sklansky, *Soul's Economy* 35–72.

78. John Evelev's " 'Every One to His Trade': *Mardi*, Literary Form, and Professional Ideology," *American Literature* 75.2 (2003): 305–33, offers a fine-grained account of Mel-

ville's relationship to literary professionalism, and an emergent middle-class professionalism more generally, that traces this ambiguity in the form of Melville's novel. *Mardi*, Evelev argues, formally encodes Melville's changing conceptions of professionalism insofar as its "socially engaged reformist allegory demonstrates middle-class desires to improve both professional practice and American life, while its self-referential symbolism turns away from social problems to focus exclusively on specialized concerns and discursive authority" (327–28). This latter dimension, Evelev argues, corresponds to a protomodernist sense of the market which "disassociat[es] authorship from sales" and imagines a book "inaccessible to a general contemporary readership but capable of finding a place in the pantheon at some future date" (325–26).

79. Szalay, *New Deal* 35. For more on London's relationship to the market see Jonathan Auerbach, " 'Congested Mails': Buck and Jack's 'Call,' " *Rereading Jack London*, ed. Leonard Casuto and Jeanne Campbell Reesman (Stanford: Stanford University Press, 1996), 45, 25–45 passim. On Progressive-Era literary professionalism more generally see Christopher P. Wilson, *The Labor of Words: Literary Professionalism in the Progressive Era* (Athens: University of Georgia Press, 1985).

80. Thomas Strychacz, *Modernism, Mass Culture, and Professionalism* (New York: Cambridge University Press, 1993), 22, 31, passim. See also Tichi's compelling claim that modernists like Pound and Hemingway distinguished themselves from Progressive-Era authors by adapting the engineer's professional ethos of efficiency not just as subject matter but at the level of "style or structure" (*Shifting* 74–75).

81. Lawrence Rainey, *Institutions of Modernism: Literary Elites and Public Culture* (New Haven: Yale University Press, 1999); Kevin J. H. Dettmar and Stephen Watt, eds., *Marketing Modernisms: Self-Promotion, Canonization, Rereading* (Ann Arbor: University of Michigan Press, 1996), especially part 1, "Modernist Self-Promotion."

82. Timothy Materer, "Make It Sell! Ezra Pound Advertises Modernism," in Dettmar and Watts, *Marketing*, 23.

83. Szalay, *New Deal* 75–119.

84. Mark McGurl, *The Novel Art: Elevations of American Fiction after Henry James* (Princeton: Princeton University Press, 2001), 15.

85. Harold Rosenberg, *The Tradition of the New* (1959; New York: McGraw-Hill, 1965), 266; hereafter cited parenthetically.

86. Irving Howe, "Mass Society and Post-Modern Fiction" (1959), *The American Novel Since World War II*, ed. Marcus Klein (Greenwich, Conn.: Fawcett, 1969), 124; hereafter cited parenthetically.

87. Lionel Trilling's dismayed account of the classroom transformation of modernist alienation into "received or receivable generalizations" in *Beyond Culture: Essays on Literature and Learning* (New York: Viking, 1968), 4, approaches this phenomenon from both directions. On the one hand, this transformation takes place in the university that employs Trilling and other intellectuals to teach modernism; on the other hand, the classroom provides the site for modernism's diffusion among middle-class students whose unthinking acceptance undermines its subversive claims. Gerald Graff, building on Trilling's argument in the "Babbitt at the Abyss" chapter of *Literature against Itself: Literary Ideas in Modern Society* (Chicago: University of Chicago Press, 1979), argues that contemporary fiction is decisively shaped by the middle class's "absor[ption] and commercializ[ation of] the self-consciously alienated ideologies, rhetorics, and personal styles of literary and cultural mod-

ernism" (224). Graff locates the middle-class assimilation of modernism in "the sixties and the seventies" (224), although Richard Yates's novel *Revolutionary Road* (1961; New York: Vintage, 2000) suggests that it has already happened in the fifties. Yates's unhappy suburbanites Frank and April Wheeler distinguish themselves from their fellow suburbanites in large part through their familiarity with the modernist canon. During his aimless days in college on the GI bill, Frank learned to think of himself as an "intellectual" (20) and "an intense, nicotine-stained, Jean-Paul-Sartre sort of man" (23). This pose of alienation continues to shape his self-image even now that he had a job in the same office-machine company where his father worked and a home in the novel's eponymous, ironically named subdivision. Frank accuses April during an argument of "doing a pretty good imitation of Madame Bovary" (25); he thinks of her wealthy parents as "as alien to his sympathetic understanding as anything in the novels of Evelyn Waugh" (38); when he feels guilty about an affair with one of the secretaries in his company he salves himself with the thought, "Did the swan apologize to Leda? . . . Hell, no" (101). When April suggests that the family move to Paris where she can get a job while Frank writes, he sabotages the plan out of fear that he might actually have to back up his intellectual pose. But before he does this, he fantasizes "a Henry-James sort of Venetian countess . . . on a balustrade above the Grand Canal" telling him, "You and Mrs. Wheeler are so very unlike one's preconceived idea of American business people" (208). The joke of the novel, however, is that everyone imagines themselves different in this way. When Frank tosses off one of his typically sententious remarks about "the hopeless emptiness of everything in this country," his auditor replies, "Now you've said it. The hopeless emptiness. Hell, plenty of people are on to the emptiness part; out where I used to work, on the Coast, that's all we ever talked about. We'd sit around talking about emptiness all night" (189). The modernist alienation once poised against the perceived banality of middle-class life has itself become, Yates suggests, a middle-class cliché.

88. Wallace Stevens, "To Elsie Moll," *Letters of Wallace Stevens*, ed. Holly Stevens (New York: Knopf, 1966), 121.

89. Russell Jacoby, *The Last Intellectuals: American Culture in the Age of Academe* (New York: Basic, 1987).

90. McGurl, *Novel* 12, 18, 182. In *Capitalism, the Family, and Personal Life* (New York: Harper Colophon, 1976) Eli Zaretsky argues that the modernists deployed the ideology of individual " 'genius' " as a means of resisting their own "proletarianization" vis-à-vis "the rise of mass-produced art in the twentieth century" (120–21). Following McGurl, and my own argument that with the possible exception of a brief moment in the thirties middle-class proletarianization has been visible only in massively displaced ways, I contend that Zaretsky gets the economic context right but that the conceptual framework is his own anachronistic projection.

91. Michael North, *The Dialect of Modernism: Race, Language, and Twentieth-Century Literature* (New York: Oxford University Press, 1994).

92. Tony Tanner, *City of Words: American Fiction 1950–1970* (New York: Harper & Row, 1971), 15; hereafter cited parenthetically.

93. Saul Bellow, *Dangling Man* (1944; New York: Avon, 1975), 7.

94. James E. B. Breslin, *From Modern to Contemporary: American Poetry, 1945–1965* (Chicago: University of Chicago Press, 1984), 11, 56–57.

95. See Ann Douglas, " 'Telepathic Shock and Meaning Excitement': Kerouac's Poetics of Intimacy," *College Literature* 27.1 (Winter 2000): 8–21.

96. In addition to Denning see Mills's discussion of the factors inhibiting white-collar unionism (*White* 301–23).

97. Brian Boyd, *Vladimir Nabokov: The American Years* (Princeton: Princeton University Press, 1991), 340.

98. Vladimir Nabokov, *Lolita* (1955; New York: Vintage, 1997), 3; hereafter cited parenthetically.

99. Alfred Kazin, *Bright Book of Life: American Novelists and Storytellers from Hemingway to Mailer* (1971; New York: Delta, 1974), 316.

100. Ibid., 307.

101. Frederick Whiting, " 'The Strange Particularity of the Lover's Preference': Pedophilia, Pornography, and the Anatomy of Monstrosity in *Lolita*," *American Literature* 70.4 (December 1998): 833–62.

102. Whiting, "Strange Particularity" 855; Whiting suggests that the "astonishingly scant critical attention" this fact has received might betoken a case of professional "repression."

103. Brian Boyd, *Vladimir Nabokov: The Russian Years* (Princeton: Princeton University Press, 1990), 15–160.

104. Boyd, *Russian* 3.

105. Karl Marx, *Capital: A Critique of Political Economy*, Volume One (New York: International; 1987), 151.

106. Boyd, *American* 253.

107. Whiting, "Strange Particularity" 848.

108. Zaretsky, *Capitalism* 9–10; hereafter cited parenthetically.

CHAPTER ONE: AYN RAND AND THE POLITICS OF PROPERTY

1. Sharon Stockton, "Engineering Power: Hoover, Rand, Pound, and the Heroic Architect," *American Literature* 72.4 (December 2000): 813–41; Szalay, *New Deal* 75–119.

2. Lionel Trilling, "Art and Fortune," *Partisan Review* 15.12 (December 1948): 1271; hereafter cited parenthetically.

3. *Historical Statistics of the United States, Colonial Times to 1957* (Washington, D.C.: U.S. Bureau of the Census, 1960), 139 Series F8.

4. *Historical Statistics of the United States, Colonial Times to 1957*, 167 Series G 147.

5. Schaub, *American* 47–48.

6. Leonard Peikoff, "Introduction to the 35th Anniversary Edition," Ayn Rand, *Atlas Shrugged* (1957; New York: Signet, 1992), 1.

7. Rand, *Atlas Shrugged* 630; hereafter cited parenthetically.

8. Alfred Chandler, *The Visible Hand: The Managerial Revolution in American Business* (Cambridge: Harvard University Press, 1977), 3, 79.

9. Jennifer Burns is currently writing a groundbreaking dissertation in the Berkeley history department on the complexities of Rand's reception, including her appeal among small businessmen. See Burns's essay "Godless Capitalism: Ayn Rand and the Conservative Movement," *Modern Intellectual History* 1.3 (November 2004): 1–27.

10. John F. Stover, *American Railroads* (Chicago: University of Chicago Press, 1961), 211.

11. Stover, *American* 210.

12. This is in New York City. Things are even worse in the countryside:

They drove through small towns, through obscure side roads, through the kind of places they had not seen for years. She felt uneasiness at the sight of the towns. Days passed before she realized what it was that she missed most: a glimpse of fresh paint. The houses stood like men in unpressed suits, who had lost the desire to stand straight: the cornices were like sagging shoulders, the crooked porch steps like torn hem lines, the broken windows like patches, mended with clapboard. The people in the streets stared at the new car, not as one stares at a rare sight, but as if the glittering black shape were an impossible vision from another world. There were few vehicles in the streets and too many of them were horsedrawn. She had forgotten the literal shape and usage of horse-power; she did not like to see its return. (263)

13. Stover, *American* 210.

14. Sylvia de Leon, "No Way to Run a Railroad: A Bailout Won't Solve Amtrak's Fundamental Problem," *Washington Post*, 24 June 2002, *http://web.lexis-nexis.com/universe* (accessed August 28, 2004).

15. Stover, *American* 252–53.

16. Ibid., 217.

17. Kim McQuaid, *Uneasy Partners: Big Business in American Politics, 1945–1990* (Baltimore: Johns Hopkins University Press, 1994).

18. Judith Stein, *Running Steel, Running America: Race, Economic Policy, and the Decline of Liberalism* (Chapel Hill: University of North Carolina Press, 1998), 17, 14.

19. McQuaid, *Uneasy* 48–58; David S. Painter, *Oil and the American Century: The Political Economy of U.S. Foreign Oil Policy, 1941–1945* (Baltimore: Johns Hopkins University Press, 1986).

20. McQuaid 52–54; Stein, *Running* 21.

21. Ayn Rand, *Capitalism: The Unknown Ideal* (New York: Signet, 1967), 102; hereafter cited parenthetically.

22. Krugman, "For Richer" 62.

23. See Randy Martin, *On Your Marx: Relinking Socialism and the Left* (Minneapolis: University of Minnesota Press, 2002), 159–83.

24. For a brief but useful account of Rand's critique of bureaucracy in relationship to the intellectual history of the 1940s see William Graebner, *The Age of Doubt: American Thought and Culture in the 1940s* (Boston: Twayne, 1990), 34–35.

25. Stefano Harney and Frederick Moten, "Doing Academic Work," *Chalk Lines: The Politics of Work in the Managed University*, ed. Randy Martin (Durham: Duke University Press, 1998): 157, 171.

26. Ross, "Mental Labor" 2, passim.

27. Barry, "White-Collar" I:11.

28. As Mills notes, however, what has recently happened for doctors was already happening in the late forties among the proletarianized nurses at the medical profession's feminized base. Mills describes " 'training schools' . . . owned and operated by hospitals [whose] primary purpose is not so much 'education' as simply a means for getting cheap labor, for they find it less expensive to train students than to hire graduate nurses" (*White* 117–18).

29. Szalay, *New Deal* 6, 75–119.

30. Gary S. Becker, *Human Capital: A Theoretical and Empirical Analysis with Special Reference to Education* (New York: National Bureau of Economic Research, 1964), 1.

31. Alain Touraine, *The Post-Industrial Society; Tomorrow's Social History: Classes, Conflicts and Culture in the Programmed Society*, trans. Leonard F. X. Mayhew (1969; New York: Random House, 1971); Daniel Bell, *The Coming of Post-Industrial Society: A Venture in Social Forecasting* (1973; New York: Basic, 1976); David Harvey, *The Condition of Postmodernity: An Inquiry into the Origins of Cultural Change* (Cambridge; Blackwell, 1989); Manuel Castells, *The Rise of the Network Society* (Cambridge; Blackwell, 1996); Michael Hardt and Antonio Negri, *Empire* (Cambridge: Harvard University Press, 2000). The quote is from Hardt and Negri, *Empire* 280.

32. Pierre Bourdieu, *Distinction: A Social Critique of the Judgement of Taste*, trans. Richard Nice (1979; Cambridge: Harvard University Press, 1984), 315.

33. Bell, *Post-Industrial* 410.

34. Bourdieu, *Distinction* 301–3.

35. Stephanie Armour, "Higher Pay May Be Layoff Target," *USA Today*, 23 June 2003, Money, 1B.

36. Tony Lee, "Should You Stay Energized by Changing Your Job Frequently?" CareerJournal.com, *http://www.careerjournal.com/jobhunting/strategies/19980111-reisberg.html*.

37. Harney and Moten, "Doing" 171, 154–80 passim.

38. Ross, "Mental Labor" 22.

39. Ibid., 15; Ross's emphasis.

40. Caren Irr, "Literature as Proleptic Globalization, or a Prehistory of the New Intellectual Property," *South Atlantic Quarterly* 100.3 (Summer 2001): 797–98.

41. Ibid., 795.

42. Ross, "Mental Labor" 25.

43. Brian Mansfield, "When Free Is Profitable," *USA Today*, 21 May 2004, *http://web.lexis-nexis.com/universe* (accessed August 28, 2004).

CHAPTER TWO: RACE MAN, ORGANIZATION MAN, *INVISIBLE MAN*

1. Ralph Ellison, *Invisible Man* (1952; New York: Vintage, 1995), 16; hereafter cited parenthetically.

2. See Houston A. Baker, Jr., *Blues, Ideology, and Afro-American Literature: A Vernacular Theory* (Chicago: University of Chicago Press, 1984), 172–99.

3. In stressing the novel's ambivalence about such behavior I follow Kenneth Warren, who departs from the more purely affirmative readings of Baker and others to argue that the grandfather's advice registers the novel's largely inconclusive investigation into "the nature of legitimate power and authority." See Kenneth W. Warren, "Ralph Ellison and the Problem of Cultural Authority," *boundary 2* 30.2 (Summer 2003): 166. Whereas Baker reads Bledsoe's manipulations as evidence that "the expressive 'mask' . . . is as indispensable for college blacks as it is for those beyond the school's boundaries" (195), for instance, Warren—recalling that Bledsoe threatens to "have every Negro in the country hanging on tree limbs by morning" to stay in power (*Invisible* 143)—insists upon "*Invisible Man*'s inveterate irreverence toward authority, black as well as white" (164). More recently Baker has offered a scathing critique of the novel that is not, however, entirely incompatible with his earlier account of the Trueblood episode. See Baker, *Critical Memory: Public Spheres, African American Writing, and Black Fathers and Sons in America* (Athens: University of Georgia Press, 2001), 21–40.

4. Ralph Ellison, "Working Notes for *Invisible Man*," *The Collected Essays of Ralph Ellison*, ed. John F. Callahan (New York: Modern Library, 1995), 344.

5. Baker, *Blues* 187. For similar readings see Michael G. Cooke, "Solitude," *Ralph Ellison*, ed. Harold Bloom (New York: Chelsea House, 1986), 130–31, and Robert G. O'Meally, "Checking Our Balances: Ellison on Armstrong's Humor," *boundary 2* 30.2 (Summer 2003): 124.

6. Robert Penn Warren, "The Unity of Experience," *Ralph Ellison: A Collection of Critical Essays*, ed. John Hersey (Englewood Cliffs: Prentice, 1974), 22.

7. Saul Bellow, "Man Underground," in Hersey, *Ralph Ellison* 28–29.

8. For the exchange between Howe and Ellison, and the James Baldwin essays that motivated Howe's opening salvo, see Baldwin, "Everybody's Protest Novel" (1949) and "Many Thousands Gone" (1951), *Notes of a Native Son* (New York: Bantam, 1968) 9–36; Howe, "Black Boys and Native Sons," *A World More Attractive: A View of Modern Literature and Politics* (New York: Horizon, 1963) 98–122; Howe, "A Reply to Ralph Ellison," *New Leader* 3 February 1964, 12–14; and Ellison, "The World and the Jug" (1963, 1964), *Collected Essays* 155–88. For representative critiques of Ellison on the part of those associated with the Black Arts movement, see the essays by Ernest Kaiser, Clifford Mason, and others in *Black World* 20 (December 1970).

9. Kenneth W. Warren, *So Black and Blue: Ralph Ellison and the Occasion of Criticism* (Chicago: University of Chicago Press, 2003). On Ellison's postmortem reception see pages 13–19.

10. Foley, "From Communism."

11. Schocket, "Modernism and the Aesthetics of Management, or T. S. Eliot's Labor Literature,"in Mullen and Smethurst, *Left* 14.

12. Ellison, "World and the Jug" 163.

13. Carol A. Barry, "White-Collar Employment: II—Characteristics," *Monthly Labor Review* February 1961: 140–41.

14. See George Lipsitz, *The Possessive Investment in Whiteness: How White People Profit from Identity Politics* (Philadelphia: Temple University Press, 1998). As Jacqueline Jones points out in *American Work: Four Centuries of Black and White Labor* (New York: Norton, 1998), this process was self-reinforcing:

> Employers who abandoned the inner city left behind a shrinking tax base, resulting in resource-starved schools in black neighborhoods. Although black youth were close to reaching parity with whites in terms of the number of years of formal education, employers made the connection between inner-city schools on the one hand and overcrowded classrooms, overburdened teachers, and inadequate resources on the other. As a result, a quality (i.e., suburban) high school education replaced the high school diploma as the minimal requirement for a decent job. (359)

After 1960, moreover, African Americans' exclusion from white-collar employment became an even greater liability, as the heavy industries that had provided at least some black people with better livings during the early years of the postwar boom begin to trim their labor forces (Jones, *American* 358–59).

15. Ellison, "Twentieth-Century Fiction and the Black Mask of Humanity," *Collected Essays* 87.

16. Ibid., 87.

17. Thus Invisible Man speculates about his grandfather's advice near the end of the novel: "Could he have meant—hell, he *must* have meant the principle, that we were to

affirm the principle on which the country was built and not the men, or at least not the men who did the violence. Did he mean 'yes' because he knew that the principle was greater than the men, greater than the numbers and the vicious power and all the methods used to corrupt its name?" (574; Ellison's emphasis).

18. E. Franklin Frazier, *Black Bourgeoisie: The Rise of a New Middle Class in the United States* (1957; Collier, 1962), 42; hereafter cited parenthetically.

19. Eric Arnesen, *Brotherhoods of Color: Black Railroad Workers and the Struggle for Equality* (Cambridge: Harvard University Press, 2001), 14.

20. Arnesen, *Brotherhoods* 16–17.

21. In addition to Foley, "Rhetoric" and "On Communism," see Schaub, *American* 91–115.

22. Baker, *Blues* 185; hereafter cited parenthetically.

23. Arnesen, *Brotherhoods* 18.

24. Ibid., 18.

25. *The Autobiography of Malcolm X*, as told to Alex Haley (1964; New York: Ballantine, 1999), 78.

26. Foley, "Rhetoric" 542.

27. In a similar scene from Jack Finney's 1955 novel *The Body Snatchers* (New York: Gregg Press, 1976), the protagonist, Dr. Miles Bennell, and his old flame, Becky Driscoll, realize that the residents of Santa Mira are being taken over by pod-sprung alien duplicates. The pair has gone to Driscoll's house to see if her family has fallen victim as well, and, crouching on the front porch, they hear Driscoll's father, cousin, aunt, and uncle having an apparently normal conversation. But something alerts Bennell that all is not as it seems. In particular, something in the Driscolls' voices reminds Bennell of Billy, a middle-aged black shoeshine man he had known in his college days. "Billy professed a genuine love for shoes" (119) and appeared to enjoy the service he provided his patronizing white customers. But one morning, following "a student escapade" (119) Bennell awoke to find himself in his car "in the run-down section of town" (119) and overheard Billy engaging in a "quietly hysterical parody" (120) of his own servility for another black man. "[N]ever before in my life," Bennell tells us, "had I heard such ugly, bitter, and vicious contempt in a voice, contempt for the people taken in by his daily antics, but even more for himself, the man who supplied the servility they bought from him" (120). The narrative then flashes back to Driscoll's family, now obviously pod people, engaging in a similar parody of conversations they have had with Bennell. The shoeshine-man Billy, *The Body Snatchers* presciently suggests, represents the white-collar middle class's literally alien-ated future.

28. The literature on this tendency is by now too large to cite in full. The classic formulations remain W.E.B. DuBois, *Black Reconstruction in America: An Essay Toward a History of the Part Which Black Folk Played in the Attempt to Reconstruct Democracy in America, 1860–1880*, Studies in American Negro Life, August Meier, General Editor (1935; New York: Atheneum, 1970), 596, passim, and David Roediger, *The Wages of Whiteness: Race and the American Working Class* (New York: Verso, 1991).

29. Sloan Wilson, *The Man in the Gray Flannel Suit* (New York: Simon & Schuster, 1955), 153.

30. Randal Doane, "Ralph Ellison's Sociological Imagination," *The Sociological Quarterly* 45.1 (Winter 2004): 168.

31. For Ellison's full reading of Twain's novel see "Twentieth-Century," 86–90.

32. At the same time—and in contradiction to the passage's own parenthetical expression of exclusion—the narrator's identification is probably overdetermined by the different kind of frontier nostalgia Ellison expresses when he writes about his home state. In "Going to the Territory" (1979), for instance, he notes that "Oklahoma had attracted many of the descendants of the freed slaves, who considered it a territory of hope, and a place where they could create their own opportunities" (*Collected Essays* 601).

33. In the passage that gives the novel its title Tom Rath says, "I really don't know what I was looking for when I got back from the war, but it seemed as though all I could see was a lot of bright young men in gray flannel suits rushing around New York in a frantic parade to nowhere. They seemed to me to be pursuing neither ideals nor happiness—they were pursuing a routine. . . . [I]t was quite a shock to glance down and see that I too was wearing a gray flannel suit" (300).

34. Ellison, "*An American Dilemma*: A Review" (w. 1944; unpublished), *Collected Essays* 330.

35. In Washington's *Up from Slavery* (reprinted in *Three Negro Classics* New York: Avon, 1965), such management revolves around explicit invocations of the now outmoded yeoman ideal. Washington continually cites farming and the typically old-middle-class combination of "property, intelligence, and high character" (156) as his ideal for the African American masses. In what is perhaps the most unintentionally damning moment in the book, however, he implies a very different (and more historically accurate) trajectory for black labor. Describing a trip to England, Washington notes that "the English servant expects, as a rule, to be nothing but a servant, and so he perfects himself in the art to a degree that no class of servants in America has yet reached. In our country, the servant expects to become, in a few years, a 'master' himself. Which system is preferable? I will not venture an answer" (184–85). If one were to venture an answer for Washington, one might begin by noting that he elsewhere criticizes African Americans who abandon the agricultural South and "yield to the temptation to become hotel waiters and Pullman-car porters as their life-work" (76). But the resonance between his praise for British servants and his doctrine "that any man, regardless of colour, will be recognized and rewarded just in proportion as he learns to do something well . . . however humble the thing may be" (181) suggests that he objects not to service employment per se, but to the unreasonable desires for upward mobility it incites. The thing that separates Washington from the rest of the PMC here is that whereas they face the collapse of such upward mobility for white workers, he represents a constituency that by and large never enjoyed it.

36. Ellison, "World" 170–71.

37. Ellison, "*American Dilemma*" 339.

38. Ellison, "World" 159; italicized in original.

39. Schaub, *American* 112; first bracket is Schaub, second is mine.

40. Ellison, *Shadow and Act* (1953; New York: Vintage, 1972), 10–11.

41. Alice Echols, " 'We Gotta Get Out of this Place': Notes Toward a Remapping of the Sixties," *Socialist Review* 22 (1992): 9–31; Eric Lott, "White Like Me: Racial Cross-Dressing and the Construction of American Whiteness," *Cultures of United States Imperialism,* ed. Amy Kaplan and Donald E. Pease (Durham: Duke University Press, 1993), 474–95.

42. Norman Mailer, "The White Negro: Superficial Reflections on the Hipster," *The Portable Beat Reader,* ed. Ann Charters (New York: Penguin, 1992), 585.

43. Barry "White-Collar" I:13, table 2.

44. Ibid., II:142, table 2.

45. Jones, *American* 364.

46. Jack Kerouac, *On the Road* (1957; New York; Penguin, 1991), 180; hereafter cited parenthetically. For a related reading of *On the Road's* racial politics, see Mark Richardson, "Peasant Dreams: Reading *On the Road*," *Texas Studies in Literature and Language* 43.2 (Summer 2001): 218–42.

CHAPTER THREE: "THE SO-CALLED JEWISH NOVEL"

1. Elizabeth Freeman, *The Wedding Complex: Forms of Belonging in Modern American Culture* (Durham: Duke University Press, 2002), 202–3.

2. This dynamic is central to the form of modern identity that, Walter Benn Michaels argues in *Our America: Nativism, Modernism, and Pluralism* (Durham: Duke University Press, 1995), makes identity "into an object of cathexis" by making it "something that might be lost or found, defended or surrendered" (141). *Our America* locates the birth of this form of identity in the 1920s; Michaels deals more directly with recent texts in *The Shape of the Signifier: 1967 to the End of History* (Princeton: Princeton University Press, 2004).

3. Freeman, *Wedding* 203.

4. In thinking about identity in this chapter and the subsequent one, I have been inspired by Lee Medovoi's very different approach to historicizing this topic in his forthcoming book about the significance of youth in postwar culture.

5. Karen Brodkin, *How Jews Became White Folks and What That Says about Race in America* (New Brunswick: Rutgers University Press, 1998); hereafter cited parenthetically. For another account of the rightward shift in Jewish politics during this period that associates it with the rise of cold war anticommunism, see Andrew Ross, *No Respect: Intellectuals & Popular Culture* (New York: Routledge, 1989), 15–41.

6. Patterson, *Grand Expectations* 17, 326.

7. Jeffrey S. Gurocks, "A Synthesis for the New American Jewish Historiography," *Reviews in American History* 26.2 (1998): 385–86.

8. Brodkin, *How Jews*; Lipsitz, *Possessive Investment*.

9. Melvin I. Urofsky, *We Are One! American Jewry and Israel* (Garden City: Doubleday, 1978), 210.

10. Urofsky, *We Are One!* 324.

11. Eugene Goodheart, "Jew d'Esprit," *Shofar: An Interdisciplinary Journal of Jewish Studies* 21.3 (2003): 15.

12. Edward S. Shapiro, *A Time for Healing: American Jewry since World War II*, The Jewish People in America, Vol. 5 (Baltimore: Johns Hopkins University Press, 1992), 254. Shapiro discusses the debates between transformationists (sociologists who argue for the persistence of Jewish identity in spite of or through its adaptation to the larger culture) and assimilationists (those who fear its decline and eventual disappearance) on pages 250–54, although the title of his final chapter ("The Question of Survival") telegraphs his own agreement with the latter group.

13. The quote is from Patterson, *Grand Expectations* 74. Patterson briefly outlines the postwar critique of suburban conformity on pp. 337–42; see also Lears, "Matter," and Jurca, *White* 133–59, especially 134–35.

14. Will Herberg, *Protestant-Catholic-Jew: An Essay in American Religious Sociology* (1955; Garden City: Doubleday, 1956), 205; hereafter cited parenthetically.

15. Nathan Glazer, "What Sociology Knows about American Jews: Many Problems, Some Studies, Few Conclusions," *Commentary* 9.3 (March 1950): 280.

16. Leslie Fiedler, Preface, *Fiedler on the Roof: Essays on Literature and Jewish Identity* (Boston: David R. Godine, 1991), xii.

17. Ross Posnock, "Purity and Danger: On Philip Roth," *Raritan* 21 (Fall 2001): 85–101; Michael T. Gilmore, *Surface and Depth: The Quest for Legibility in American Culture* (New York: Oxford University Press, 2003), 174–77.

18. Kazin, *Bright* 130; hereafter cited parenthetically.

19. Similarly, Jules Chametsky argues in *Our Decentralized Literature: Cultural Mediations in Selected Jewish and Southern Writers* (Amherst: University of Massachusetts Press, 1986) that the newly "secure position" of writers of Bellow's generation frees them for a "fresh exploration of self" in "reaction to a certain bland, characterless image of American society from which so many intellectuals recoiled in the gray-flannel-suited Eisenhower years" (57).

20. Atlas, *Bellow* 59, 129; hereafter cited parenthetically

21. Saul Bellow, *The Adventures of Augie March*, (1953; New York: Penguin, 1984), 529; hereafter cited parenthetically.

22. Allen Ginsberg, "Howl," *Howl and Other Poems* (1956; San Francisco: City Lights, 1998), 9.

23. Riesman writes in *The Lonely Crowd* that

biography as well as fiction allows children, in a society dependent on inner-direction, to move in imagination away from home and into a rationalized world—cooperating in this way with the parental installation of internal, self-piloting processes. In the George Washington myth, for instance, little boys learn that they may grow up to be president and are given scales by which to measure and discipline themselves for the job during boyhood: if they do not tell lies, if they work hard, and so on—if, that is, they act in their boyhoods as the legendary Washington acted in his—then they may succeed to his adult role. The role, moreover, by its very nature, is a continuing one; somebody is always president; thus its heroes do not have the once-for-all quality of those in the myths and legends of the earlier era. In fantasy the little boy not only identifies with young Washington in the French and Indian wars but also with the adult role of president—either role will take him far from home, socially and geographically. (94)

24. The title of the chapter in which Tanner discusses *Augie March* and *Catch-22* is "A Mode of Motion."

25. Saul Bellow, "Distractions of a Fiction Writer," *The Living Novel: A Symposium*, ed. Granville Hicks (1957; New York: Collier, 1962), 21.

26. Saul Bellow, "The University as Villain," *The Nation* 185.16 (November 16, 1957): 362–63; Bellow's emphasis.

27. "Saul Bellow: The Enemy Is Academe," *Publisher's Weekly* (July 18, 1966): 34–35.

28. Of course we might here note that Bellow exhibits what Jurca describes as the classic middle-class behavior of loudly proclaiming his own exceptional status as the one university writer who transcended the institutional constraints on his individuality. Atlas notes that in the mid-sixties Bellow was touring the college circuit with a talk declaring professors

" 'manufacturers of intellectual opinion,' 'agents, managers or impresarios of Henry James or the French Symbolists' " (*Bellow* 354)—a position that, interestingly, would probably have found a sympathetic audience among precisely the members of the new left and counterculture that also began drawing his fire around this time. This conjunction is no doubt uncoincidental: if, as Atlas suggests, Bellow's animus against the sixties left stemmed in part from the fact that its critiques of mainstream culture and its promotion of sexual freedom "made his own conduct less singular" (*Bellow* 387–88)—an argument born out largely by the difference between *Sammler* and the novel that had preceded it, *Herzog* (1965)—then it must have been just as galling to see student radicals take up their own version of his critique of the university.

29. Morris Dickstein, "For Art's Sake," *Partisan Review* 33.4 (Fall 1966): 618.

30. Atlas, *Bellow* 181; "Achievement and Ambivalence, 1945–1973," *Jewish American Literature: An Anthology,* ed. Jules Chametzky, John Felstiner, Hilene Flanzbaum, and Kathryn Hellerstein (New York: Norton, 2001), 576.

31. Herberg, *Protestant-Catholic-Jew* 197.

32. Lausch's selectiveness on the subject of observance arguably only identifies her all the more firmly with the Eastern European version of Jewishness that, according to Herberg, organizes itself not around the religious self-conception of German Jews but rather the "religio-cultural complex" of *Yiddishkait.* Jewish "secularists," in Herberg's account, "merely replaced the element of traditional religion in this complex with their particular radical gospel." See Herberg, *Protestant-Catholic-Jew* 196–97.

33. Saul Bellows [*sic*], "The Einhorns," *Partisan Review* 18.6 (November–December 1951): 619–45.

34. Norman Podhoretz, "The Adventures of Saul Bellow" (1959), *Doings and Undoings: The Fifties and After in American Writing* (New York: Noonday, 1964), 206; hereafter cited parenthetically.

35. Bellow's friend R.W.B. Lewis describes Augie in *The American Adam: Innocence Tragedy and Tradition in the Nineteenth Century* (Chicago: University of Chicago Press, 1955) as a postwar Huckleberry Finn "willing, with marvelously inadequate equipment, to take on as much of the world as is available to him, without ever fully submitting to any of the world's determining categories" (198). Podhoretz also compares Augie to Huck Finn ("Adventures" 216–17).

36. Deidre Shauna Lynch, *The Economy of Character: Novels, Market Culture, and the Business of Inner Meaning* (Chicago: University of Chicago Press, 1998), 87.

37. Cf. Atlas, *Bellow* 189.

38. Philip Roth, *Goodbye, Columbus and Five Short Stories* (1959; New York: Vintage, 1987), 4; hereafter cited parenthetically.

CHAPTER FOUR: FLANNERY O'CONNOR AND THE SOUTHERN
ORIGINS OF IDENTITY POLITICS

1. Flannery O'Connor, *Wise Blood, Collected Works* (New York: Library of America, 1988), 13; hereafter cited parenthetically.

2. O'Connor, "To Carl Hartman," *Collected Works* 919, 920.

3. Jon Lance Bacon, *Flannery O'Connor and Cold War Culture* (New York: Cambridge University Press, 1993), 138.

4. O'Connor, "To Sister Mariella Gable," *Collected Works* 1183.

5. O'Connor, "The Catholic Novelist in the Protestant South," *Collected Works* 859.

6. "When the poor hold sacred history in common," O'Connor writes in "The Catholic Novelist in the Protestant South," "they have concrete ties to the universal and the holy which allow the meaning of their every action to be heightened and seen under the aspect of eternity" (*Collected Works* 858). O'Connor here anticipates, and suggests some of the Catholic intellectual roots of, what Walter Benn Michaels has recently described as Michael Hardt and Antonio Negri's transformation of poverty into an identity category around the figure of St. Francis of Assisi. See Michaels, *Shape* 177–82.

7. See Scott Lindlaw, "Bush Lays Claim to Championing Values of Heartland," *St. Louis Post-Dispatch*, 14 July 2004, A4.

8. Wendy Brown departs from other critics of identity politics in her minute albeit largely unhistoricized attention, via Nietzsche, to such middle-class *ressentiment*. See Brown, *States of Injury: Power and Freedom in Late Modernity* (Princeton: Princeton University Press, 1995) (esp. chap. 3, "Wounded Attachments") and *Politics Out of History* (Princeton: Princeton University Press, 2001). For a fascinating and ethnographically informed account of contemporary middle-class *ressentiment*, see Thomas Frank, *What's the Matter with Kansas? How Conservatives Won the Heart of America* (New York: Metropolitan, 2004).

9. Dewey W. Grantham, *The South in Modern America: A Region at Odds* (New York: HarperPerennial, 1994), 194–95. See also Numan V. Bartley, *The New South: 1945–1980*, A History of the South, Vol. XI (Baton Rouge: Louisiana State University Press, 1995), 1–37.

10. C. Vann Woodward, *The Burden of Southern History* (Baton Rouge: Louisiana State University Press, 1960), 6; hereafter cited parenthetically.

11. O'Connor, "The Regional Writer," *Collected Works* 846.

12. Bartley, *New South* 111; 261–77 passim. Bartley, who cites O'Connor frequently in his account of social and religious issues in the postwar South, refers to the passage from "The Regional Writer" above after noting that "in the midfifties three out of four immigrants from the North held white-collar status" (*New South* 277).

13. Ibid., 262–63.

14. Ibid., 276–77.

15. Ibid., 110.

16. Ibid., 263.

17. This information is from Sally Fitzgerald's chronology of O'Connor's life in the *Collected Works* (1237–1239).

18. See Richard N. Current, *Northernizing the South* (Athens: University of Georgia Press, 1983).

19. Bartley, *New South* 69. Bartley here alludes to Franklin Roosevelt's description of the South as "the Nation's No. 1 economic problem" in the letter commissioning the 1938 *Report on Economic Conditions in the South*. See National Emergency Council, *Report on Economic Conditions of the South* (Washington, D.C.: GPO, 1938), 1.

20. Current, *Northernizing* 13, passim.

21. Bartley, *The Rise of Massive Resistance: Race and Politics in the South During the 1950's* (Baton Rouge: Louisiana State University Press, 1969), 17.

22. Twelve Southerners, *I'll Take My Stand* (1930; New York: Harper & Row, 1962). The Agrarians' elaboration of the "genuine humanism . . . rooted in the agrarian life of the

older South and of other parts of the country that shared in such a tradition" (xxvi) in large part reproduces, of course, traditional celebrations of the antebellum planter aristocracy. But Andrew Nelson Lytle's contribution "The Hind Tit" also finds virtue in "the yeoman South" (208) of small farmers reduced to tenantry by the collapse of the plantation system. And John Crowe Ransom describes "Unregenerate Southerners . . . trying to live the good life on a shabby equipment," arguing that while "they were grotesque in their effort to make an art out of living when they were not decently making the living" they nonetheless evinced "something heroic . . . in their extreme attachment to a certain theory of life" (16). Lytle comes close to glorifying hardscrabble subsistence farming, while Ransom describes poor Southerners as misguided but nonetheless vaguely noble participants in a freely chosen lifestyle.

Here it is no doubt crucial that, as Paul Bové has persuasively argued in *Mastering Discourse: The Politics of Intellectual Culture* (Durham: Duke University Press, 1992), the Agrarians participate for regionally specific reasons (the rise of agribusiness and the consolidation of small holdings into factory farms) in an early version of intellectual debate over middle-class proletarianization that pits them as "traditional: clerical, humanistic, petite bourgeois" intellectuals against the "technical: bureaucratic, scientific, professional" (126) intellectuals represented by "county agents and [teachers in] agricultural schools" (122). As described by Bové the Agrarians anticipate postwar white-collar intellectuals in their distrust of the late-PMC managerial aspirations of their opponents, in their (partially occluded) conflict with large capital, and in their idealization of "small-held property" as a basis for a secure "sense of self" (137). From this perspective Lytle's account of the yeomanry's fall sounds like a veritable parable of middle-class proletarianization. Incorporated following the Civil War into a "money economy" that sometimes "paid [the yeoman] well for his labors" but "offered no assurance that this would continue," the yeomen were transformed into tenant farmers (214). Once independent but now forced to labor for others, Lytle's yeomen are organization men *avant la lettre*.

23. See Kenneth C. Davis, *Two-Bit Culture: The Paperbacking of America* (Boston: Houghton Mifflin, 1984), 118–23 and Thomas L. Bonn, *Heavy Traffic and High Culture: New American Library as Literary Gatekeeper in the Paperback Revolution* (Carbondale: Southern Illinois University Press, 1989), 22, 26. The quotes are from Alfred Kazin, *On Native Grounds: An Interpretation of Modern American Prose Literature* (New York: Harcourt, 1942), 379, 372. Kazin's account mediates between the two versions of Caldwell both temporally and thematically: he ranks Caldwell with the left-wing naturalists but suggests that "his delight in cruelty and outrage [and] the sexual antics of his poor whites" also fit him for "a purveyor of Gothic tidbits for the delectation of urban sophisticates who thought Jeeter Lester [the protagonist of Caldwell's first novel] a representative Southern citizen, but amusing" (380). Caldwell's transformation into a postwar paperback phenomenon—the reprint of *God's Little Acre* alone sells 4.5 million copies between 1946 and 1949 (Davis 121)—clearly extends this appeal beyond the limited audience of urban sophisticates.

24. Will's life with his father parallels that of the "squatter" in an antebellum traveler's story enthusiastically recounted by Lytle. This squatter "worked a little truck patch on somebody else's land; hunted at night for pelts; fished in Stone's River; and ra'red around when he was a mind to," and—the point of the anecdote—meets Martin Van Buren on a level of perfect equality that the planter who introduces them cannot match (212–13). This story embodies the transitional nature of Lytle's essay: if at times he describes the

yeoman as a typical Jeffersonian freeholder (see 216–34), this squatter's middle-class virtues of self-worth and indifference to social hierarchy derive not from owning property but from *not* owning property.

25. Mac Hyman, *No Time for Sergeants* (1954; New York: Signet, 1956), 61; hereafter cited parenthetically.

26. David Farber, *The Age of Great Dreams: America in the 1960s* (New York: Hill and Wang, 1994), 52.

27. Bacon, *Flannery O'Connor* 36–40; Farber, *Age* 52–55.

28. Bacon, *Flannery O'Connor* 40.

29. Farber, *Age* 55. Farber also suggests that these characters served as pedagogical examples for Americans themselves new to the middle class and the suburbs (53–54).

30. See Lears, "Matter" 53. Melley's reading of *Catch-22* (*Empire* 63–79) suggests that its politics were already more progressive than other postwar polemics against bureaucracy even before it was taken up as an anti-Vietnam novel.

31. See John Egerton, *The Americanization of Dixie: The Southernization of America* (New York: Harper's Magazine Press, 1974), 127–31.

32. On the (in retrospect unfortunately prophetic) political dimensions of Robert Zemeckis's 1994 film see Lauren Berlant, *The Queen of America Goes to Washington City: Essays on Sex and Citizenship* (Durham: Duke University Press, 1997), 180–86. As the subtitle of Garry Wills's *Nixon Agonistes: The Crisis of the Self-Made Man* (1971; New York: NAL, 1979) makes clear, Wills understands Nixon as central to this phantasmatic revival of "America's pre-Depression classical liberalism" (527). Wills argues that "commentators" are mistaken to cast Nixon as an organization man—or, in more recent terms, a flip-flopper—whose "policy [is] a matter of zigs and zags, a welter of compromises, a muddling through the moment under prods of hope or fear" (528). The authentic Nixon, he rather suggests, is the petit bourgeois victim-opponent of the Establishment, the "sweaty moral self-doubting self-made bustling brooding type" (531). If we take Nixon in the late sixties and early seventies as struggling to replace the former figure with the latter one, then his use of Merle Haggard's 1969 song "Okie from Muskogee" in the 1972 election (Egerton, *Americanization* 138) suggests the class dimensions of the Southern (now red state) strategy. Just as Bush's Texan persona masks his aristocratic background, Haggard lends to his fellow Californian Nixon the working-class, Southern migrant (Haggard's family moved from Oklahoma during the Depression) aura that George Wallace taught Nixon to cultivate.

33. Bacon, *Flannery O'Connor* 130; O'Connor, "To Sally and Robert Fitzgerald," *Collected Works* 1009, and "To A.," *Collected Works* 1016.

34. Grantham, *South* 172.

35. Whyte's understanding of the relationship between these two phenomena is quite concrete, insofar as he suggests that corporate policies of "periodic transfer" designed to make organization men "interchangeable" are in large measure responsible for the rise of "a culture increasingly national" (*Organization* 305).

36. See also Susan Edmunds, "Through a Glass Darkly: Visions of Integrated Community in Flannery O'Connor's *Wise Blood*," *Contemporary Literature* 37.4 (Winter 1996): 559–85, especially 564–73.

37. Bartley, *Rise* 17.

38. Edmunds, "Through" 570.

39. O'Connor, "To Maryat Lee," *Collected Works* 1094–95.

40. Edmunds, "Through" 560.

41. Walter Benn Michaels, "Empires of the Senseless: (The Response to) Terror and (the End of) History," *Radical History Review* 85 (Winter 2003): 106.

42. Egerton, *Americanization* 20–21; hereafter cited parenthetically.

43. Current, *Northernizing* 114. For other examples of this multicultural version of Southern identity see 113–16.

44. O'Connor, "To John Hawkes," *Collected Works* 1108.

45. O'Connor, "To Ben Griffith," *Collected Works* 931.

46. Bartley, *New South* 280–85.

47. Ibid., 268.

48. O'Connor, "Catholic Novelist" 861.

49. Flannery O'Connor, *The Habit of Being*, ed. Sally Fitzgerald (1979; New York: Vintage, 1980), 151. Fitzgerald identifies the countries in question as Poland and Czechoslovakia in *Collected Works*'s chronology (1249).

50. Bacon, *Flannery O'Connor* 3.

51. Ibid., 49.

52. Flannery O'Connor, "A Good Man Is Hard to Find," *Collected Works* 137; hereafter cited parenthetically.

53. Schaub, *American* 128.

54. Bacon, *Flannery O'Connor* 49.

55. Bartley, *New South* 124.

56. Stephanie Coontz, *The Way We Never Were: American Families and the Nostalgia Trap* (New York: Basic, 1992), 1–22.

57. Schaub, *American* 129,130.

58. Schaub, *American* 130.

59. Nabokov, *Lolita* 155, 154–59 passim.

60. Don DeLillo, *White Noise* (1985; New York: Penguin, 1986), 12.

61. I take this phrase from John Aldridge who in the mid-fifties argues—somewhat anachronistically from the perspective of O'Connor's fiction—that in contrast to the "gray new world" described by Riesman the South still provides "a living tradition and a . . . myth" of use to fiction writers. See Aldridge, *In Search of Heresy: American Literature in an Age of Conformity* (New York: McGraw-Hill, 1956), 110–25, 143.

62. Ibid., 117.

63. Thomas Pynchon, *The Crying of Lot 49* (1965; New York: Harper & Row, 1990), 14.

64. DeLillo, *White Noise* 119.

65. Kent Blaser, " 'Pictures from Life's Other Side': Hank Williams, Country Music, and Popular Culture in America," *South Atlantic Quarterly* 84 (1985): 19.

66. Bacon, *Flannery O'Connor* 131.

67. O'Connor, "Regional Writer" 846.

68. McGurl, *Novel* 135–57.

69. O'Connor, "To Robie Macauley," *Collected Works* 885.

70. O'Connor, "Regional Writer" 846.

71. O'Connor, "Some Aspects of the Grotesque in Southern Fiction," *Collected Works* 818.

72. Harold Bloom, *The Anxiety of Influence: A Theory of Poetry* (New York: Oxford University Press, 1973).

73. O'Connor, "To John Hawkes" 1119; "To John Hawkes" 1125–26; "To Mr. ——" 1148–49; "To John Hawkes" 1150.

74. O'Connor, "To John Hawkes" 1119.

75. Frederick Asals, *Flannery O'Connor: The Imagination of Extremity* (Athens: University of Georgia Press, 1982) 144–45.

76. Miles Orvell, *Invisible Parade: The Fiction of Flannery O'Connor* (Philadelphia: Temple University Press, 1972), 134–35.

77. Cf. Schaub, *American* 128. Despite my disagreements with Schaub, readers familiar with his book will recognize this paragraph's indebtedness to his claim that O'Connor's efforts to move the story outside history via The Misfit's introduction—"convert[ing] a world of reason without ground to an irrational world grounded in Christ" (133)—in fact take shape within the historical framework of cold war liberalism.

78. Asals, *Flannery O'Connor* 149–50.

79. O'Connor, "Regional Writer" 846–47.

80. Woodward, *Burden* 5.

81. O'Connor, "Catholic Novelist" 862; "To John Hawkes," *Collected Works* 1160.

82. O'Connor, "Some Aspects" 815.

83. John Burt, "What You Can't Talk About," *Flannery O'Connor*, ed. Harold Bloom (New York: Chelsea House, 1986), 136.

84. O'Connor, "To Carl Hartman," *Collected Works* 921; O'Connor, "To Ben Griffith," *Collected Works* 923.

85. O'Connor, "To John Hawkes," *Collected Works* 1107.

86. Burt, "What" 130.

87. Richard Giannone, *Flannery O'Connor: Hermit Novelist* (Urbana: University of Illinois Press, 2000), 63.

EPILOGUE: THE POSTMODERN FALLACY

1. Don DeLillo, *The Names* (1982; New York: Vintage, 1989), 94; hereafter cited parenthetically.

2. Gilmore, *Surface and Depth*.

3. See Douglas Keesey, *Don DeLillo* (New York: Twayne, 1993), 116–32, especially 117–18.

4. Ibid., 116.

5. David Bosworth, "The Fiction of Don DeLillo," *Critical Essays on Don DeLillo*, ed. Hugh Ruppersburg and Tim Engles (New York: G. K. Hall, 2000), 48; originally published in the *Boston Review* (April 1983): 29–30.

6. See Edward Comentale, "Ian Fleming, Corporate England, and the Ruins of Modernism," the abstract of a paper delivered at "The Cultural Politics of Ian Fleming and 007" conference at Indiana University, 30 May 2003. *http://www.indiana.edu/~engweb/jamesbond/papers.html*.

7. Leslie Fiedler, "Cross the Border—Close the Gap" (1969), *A Fiedler Reader* (New York: Stein and Day, 1977), 270–94; Ihab Hassan, "POSTmodernISM: A Paracritical Bibliography" (1971), *The Postmodern Turn: Essays in Postmodern Theory and Culture* (Columbus: Ohio State University Press, 1987), 25–45, especially 41, 45; Fredric Jameson, *Post-*

modernism, or, The Cultural Logic of Late Capitalism (Durham: Duke University Press, 1991), 2–3 passim. Jameson hereafter cited parenthetically.

8. Ellen H. Johnson, "The Image Duplicators—Lichtenstein, Rauschenberg and Warhol," *The Critical Response to Andy Warhol*, ed. Alan R. Pratt (Wesport: Greenwood, 1997), 21; originally published in *Canadian Art* 23 (January–February 1966): 12–19.

9. Paul Bergin, "Andy Warhol: The Artist as Machine," Pratt 29, 28–34 passim; originally published *Art Journal* 26.4 (Summer 1967): 359–63.

10. Gerard Malanga, "Andy Warhol on Automation: An Interview," Pratt 37; originally published in *Chelsea* 18 (1968): 83–86. For an excellent, detailed study of Warhol's work habits that makes clear that "The Factory" was more than just a clever name, see Steven Watson, *Factory Made: Warhol and the Sixties* (New York: Pantheon, 2003).

11. Johnson, "Image Duplicators" 16.

12. Ibid., 23.

13. Ibid., 23.

14. On this move see Mike Featherstone, *Consumer Culture and Postmodernism* (London: SAGE, 1991).

15. Bergin, "Andy Warhol" 30.

16. Fredric Jameson, "Notes on Globalization as a Philosophical Issue," *The Cultures of Globalization*, ed. Fredric Jameson and Masao Miyoshi (Durham: Duke University Press, 1998), 56.

17. For a related, powerful critique of Jameson's writings on postmodernism see Barbara Foley's review of Jameson's *The Seeds of Time*, *Modern Philology* 94.3 (February 1997): 422–26.

18. Featherstone, *Consumer Culture* 44, 45.

19. Ibid., 45.

20. Hardt and Negri, *Empire* 290, 280–303 passim; Hardt and Negri's emphasis.

21. Ibid., 285.

22. Featherstone, *Consumer Culture* 44.

23. Pynchon, *Crying* 83; hereafter cited parenthetically.

24. J. Peter Euben, *The Tragedy of Political Theory: The Road Not Taken* (Princeton: Princeton University Press, 1990), 303.

25. Robert J. Hansen, "Law, History, and the Subversion of Postwar America in Thomas Pynchon's *The Crying of Lot 49*," *Oklahoma City University Law Review* 24.3 (1999): 606.

26. Ibid., 604.

27. Euben, *Tragedy* 303. See also Hansen, "Law" 600–605.

28. Betty Friedan, *The Feminine Mystique* (1963; New York: Dell, 1983). On the postwar narrowing of women's employment opportunities (despite the fact that the number of working women actually went up following the war), see May, *Homeward Bound* 75–91. As Mills already noted in 1951, white-collar pyramids tended to be "youthful and feminine" at their bases (*White* 76).

29. Friedan, *Feminine* 344–45.

30. Ibid., 345.

31. Euben puts this distinction in terms of Pynchon's favored trope of entropy:

In thermodynamics, as in information theory, the danger is redundancy or sameness *and* cacophony or utter difference, a rage to order that is part of escalating disorder and a reactive disorder that leaves the order it would overturn more firmly entrenched. The challenge is to have unprogrammed messages that are intelligible, systems that are not incestuous, narcissistic projections of meaning oblivious to contrary meaning." (*Tragedy* 289–90; Euben's emphasis)

32. Ibid., 298, 298–308 passim.

33. Hansen, "Law" 590.

34. Stefan Mattessich, *Lines of Flight: Discursive Time and Countercultural Desire in the Work of Thomas Pynchon* (Durham: Duke University Press, 2002), 69, 43–69 passim; hereafter cited parenthetically.

35. DeLillo, *White Noise* 155, 326; DeLillo's emphasis; hereafter cited parenthetically.

36. For an extended reading of the novel in this vein see Mark Osteen, *American Magic and Dread: Don DeLillo's Dialogue with Culture* (Philadelphia: University of Pennsylvania Press, 2000), 165–91.

37. The 1984 *Newsweek* article that helped give the word "yuppie" widespread currency is surprisingly forthcoming about the ideological work that the term does, noting that "the glamour of this group obscures a more significant trend toward *downward* mobility among their peers. The Research Institute of America has found that median income for families in the 25-to-34 age bracket fell 14 percent (in constant dollars) from 1979 to 1983." See "The Year of the Yuppie," *Newsweek*, 31 December 1984: 16; *Newsweek*'s emphasis.

38. On the Bush adminstration's effort to overhaul overtime laws see David Moberg, "Blood from a Turnip: Proposed Overtime Rules Would Squeeze Workers," *In These Times*, 1 September 2003, *http://web.lexis-nexis.com/universe* (accessed 28 August 2004). This paragraph, and my critique of the postmodern emphasis on consumption more generally, has been influenced by Rosemary's Hennessy's related argument about the troubled recent confluence between queer politics and the commodification of gay identities in *Profit and Pleasure: Sexual Identities in Late Capitalism* (New York: Routledge, 2000), especially 74–142.

39. Ursula K. Heise, "Toxins, Drugs, and Global Systems: Risk and Narrative in the Contemporary Novel," *American Literature* 74.4 (December 2002): 772–73.

40. Jeffrey Williams, "The Issue of Corporations: Richard Powers' *Gain*," *Cultural Logic* 2.2 (Spring 1999): *http://eserver.org/clogic/2–2/Williamsrev.html*, offers the best account to date of the novel's narrative strategies. As Williams notes, the novel incorporates a third, "retro-modernist" strand in the form of its Dos Passos-like "collage of ads and other material" from Clare's history. Powers discusses the intentionally ambiguous relationship between Bodey's illness and Clare's products with Williams in "The Last Generalist: An Interview with Richard Powers," *Cultural Logic* 2.2 (Spring 1999): *http://eserver.org/clogic/2–2/williams.html*.

41. Williams, "Issue."

42. Richard Powers, *Gain* (New York: Picador, 1998), 213; hereafter cited parenthetically.

43. Heise, "Toxins" 773.

44. Williams, "Issue."

45. Ibid.

46. Williams intuits this, immediately noting that "the problem with incorporation, noted at the moment Clare becomes a corporation, is the concerted disavowal of responsibility." But lacking the notion of small capital's ongoing resonance in a world that has been materially transformed by big capital, he can only understand Tim Bodey's agency as "corporate."

Index